Archaeotecture: Second Floor

Papers from the Archaeology of Architecture sessions held at the EAA Meetings in St Petersburg (2003) and Lyon (2004)

Edited by

Xurxo Ayán
Patricia Mañana
Rebeca Blanco

BAR International Series 1971
2009

Published in 2019 by
BAR Publishing, Oxford

BAR International Series 1971

Archaeotecture: Second Floor

© The editors and contributors severally and the Publisher 2009

The authors' moral rights under the 1988 UK Copyright,
Designs and Patents Act are hereby expressly asserted.

All rights reserved. No part of this work may be copied, reproduced, stored,
sold, distributed, scanned, saved in any form of digital format or transmitted
in any form digitally, without the written permission of the Publisher.

ISBN 9781407305042 paperback
ISBN 9781407334899 e-book
DOI https://doi.org/10.30861/9781407305042

A catalogue record for this book is available in the British Library.

BAR Publishing is the trading name of British Archaeological Reports (Oxford) Ltd.
British Archaeological Reports was first incorporated in 1974 to publish the BAR
Series, International and British. In 1992 Hadrian Books Ltd became part of the BAR
group. This volume was originally published by Archaeopress in conjunction with
British Archaeological Reports (Oxford) Ltd / Hadrian Books Ltd, the Series principal
publisher, in 2009. This present volume is published by BAR Publishing, 2016.

PUBLISHING

BAR titles are available from:

BAR Publishing
122 Banbury Rd, Oxford, OX2 7BP, UK
EMAIL info@barpublishing.com
PHONE +44 (0)1865 310431
FAX +44 (0)1865 316916
www.barpublishing.com

Contents

Preface iii
Xurxo M. Ayán Vila, Patricia Mañana Borrazás and Rebeca Blanco Rotea

1 The Lower Danube Chalcolithic Megaron House with Internal Column: the Technology
of Building interpreted through experiments 1
Dragos Gheorghiu

2 Liminality and the management of space on Late Bronze Age settlements in central
and Eastern Slovenia 11
Phil Mason

3 Architectural analysis of monumental motives Towards a methodological investigation
into Iron Age drystone roundhouses in Scotland: an interim's statement from an
architectural perspective 21
Tanja Romankiewicz

4 Landscape, Material Culture and Social Process along Galician Iron Age:
the Architecture of Castros of Neixón (Galicia, Spain) 33
Xurxo M. Ayán Vila

5 The ordinary medieval house: the use of wall stratification in French preventive
archaeology of built space 41
Astrid Huser

6 Concepts dominants en construction ancienne de maisons d'habitation de la zone
forestière de la région de l'Oural ouest 49
Elisaveta Tchernykh

7 The fortress of Rocha Forte and European military building trends
A concentric castle (14th century) 53
Xosé M. Sánchez Sánchez

8 The Archaeological impact of the Lisbon earthquake (1755): the Archaeology of Built
Space applied to the monastery of Santa María de Melón (Galice, Spain) 67
Rebeca Blanco Rotea and Begoña Fernández González

9 Deep-mapping the Gumuz house 79
Alfredo González Ruibal, Xurxo M. Ayán Vila and Álvaro Falquina Aparicio

Preface

This volume represents a significant step forward in promoting the dissemination work done by the Archaeology of Built Space Research Team from the Landscape Archaeology Laboratory, Padre Sarmiento Institute of Galician Studies (CSIC-Xunta de Galicia) in Santiago de Compostela (www-gtarpa.usc.es). This work focused attention on the design of a renewed theoretical-methodological device on which a comprehensive Archaeology of Architecture could be based[1] (Mañana et al. 2002). It also revolved around the organization during the Annual Meetings of European Association of Archaeologists of consecutive sessions related to this subject. The previous volume in BAR International Series[2] collects the contributions presented in Lisbon 2000 and Esslingen am Neckar 2001. Afterwards, two sessions were again organized in San Petersburg 2003 and Lyon 2004. The interest in this line of work became evident in both sessions, with outstanding contributions from several European specialists, who at the same time, focused attention on chronological-cultural matters spanning the period from the Neolithic to the Modern Age.

This research is the main body of this, second architectonical instalment. It again proves the potential of interdisciplinary studies which maximize the study of architecture as a tool to build the social reality in the past as well as a necessary means for an Integral Management of the Cultural Heritage nowadays.

This synergy between basic research and applied research becomes evident in several articles in the book. For example the experimental Archaeological Project developed in Romania by Professor Dragos Gheorghiu's team (chapter 1), or Phil Mason's work (chapter 2). Here, the new knowledge of the space organization in Slovene settlements during the Late Bronze period in the framework of a project of Evaluation and Correction of Archaeological Impact is emphasized.

Also, the interdisciplinary perspective defended by the *Archaeotecture* Project is highlighted in studies that combine theoretical-methodological tools from the Architecture itself; for example the interesting approach made by Tanja Romankiewicz to the domestic architecture during the Scottish Iron Age (chapter 3). In this respect, we also echo the Ethnoarchaeology of built space, halfway between the Landscape Archaeology, Anthropology, and Cultural Heritage, including studies like the ethnoarchaeologist analysis of the housing area in the old communities from the region of Kama, in western Urals (chapter 6) or the Gumuz houses in western Ethiopia (chapter 9). This last study was developed during these last few years in the framework of the Spanish Archaeological Mission in the Blue Nile.

On the other hand, this volume sets out the recent development of the Archaeology of Architecture as a fundamental study tool for the management and interpretation of historical buildings. The contribution of Astrid Huser (chapter 5) is within this line. It is a good example of the research developed from the French I.N.R.A.P. in the field of Urban Archaeology and Preventive Archaeology; also the complete analysis of the Melon monastery (Galicia, Spain) carried out by Rebeca Blanco and Begoña Fernández from Santiago de Compostela University (chapter 8) as well as the historical study of the medieval fortress of A Rocha Forte by Xoxé Manoel Sánchez (chapter 7) are worth mentioning.

All in all, this book is a catalogue of tendencies and topics which have centralized the European archaeological agenda during the last few years, such us the Experimental Archaeology, the Landscape Archaeology, the Ethnoarchaeology, the Archaeology of Architecture, the Medieval Archaeology or the Evaluation and Control of the Archaeological Impact. All these points of view enrich the archaeological discipline and have an open approach to the archaeological methodology of the built area and to the historic and pre-historic architecture. This is why we, in our Laboratory, will keep working along this research line, opening new spaces for debates and exchanging projects and experiences on a European scale. In fact, the next step is the organization of a session during the next EAA Annual Meeting that will take place in Riva del Garda, Italy, in September 2009 dealing with *Fortified Landscapes*. See you there!

Xurxo M. Ayán Vila

Patricia Mañana Borrazás

Rebeca Blanco Rotea

---

[1] Mañana Borrazás, P., Blanco Rotea, R. and Ayán Vila, X. M. 2002. *Arqueotectura 1: Bases Teórico-Metodológicas para una Arqueología de la Arquitectura*. TAPA (*Traballos en Arqueoloxía da Paisaxe*) 25. Santiago de Compostela: Laboratorio de Arqueoloxía (CSIC-XuGa). [http://www-gtarpa.usc.es/descarga/CapaTapa/Tapa/TAPA25.pdf]

[2] Ayán Vila, X. M., Blanco Rotea, R. and Mañana Borrazás, P. 2003. *Archaeotecture: Archaeology of Architecture. BAR International Series*, 1175. Oxford: Archaeopress.

The Lower Danube Chalcolithic Megaron House with Internal Column: the Technology of Building interpreted through experiments

Dragos Gheorghiu

Department of MA studies, National University of Arts, Bucharest

Abstract

This work shows an experimental Archaeological Project focused on the production of a replica of the *megaron houses* from Gumelnita-Karanovo VI, a calcolithic house typical from the Low Danube and the Balkans. This project is an integral part of the design plan for the creation of an archaeological park in the calcolithic site of Vadastra, in south Romania. Our work applies ethnological patterns, architectonical techniques and contributions of iconographic studies about the artistic/cultural expression of the era. Regarding this, the article shows the different building stages and tries to rebuild the technical-operative chain followed by the calcolithic communities when building this type of domestic architecture. Also, this experience allows the set out of a number of hypotheses and interpretations of the social organization and the process of organization into a hierarchy experienced by these communities.

Introduction

In spite of the recent virtual reality, the physical reconstruction of the prehistoric architectural objects using the old method of experimentation, seems to be (despite the high costs in money and time) a functional instrument that allows archaeologists to understand structural problems, material behavior, constructive details, as well as to correct false hypotheses. To real experiment prehistoric architecture means to reconstruct at a full scale the architectural structure that should be studied in order to have a valid understanding of the subject analyzed.

Another approach to prehistoric architecture is the ethnological analogy, which could help the archaeologist to become familiar with the diversity of contextual designs.

Both approaches seem to be limitative and to direct to a MRT in the Archaeology of Architecture. But the reality is not so simple. Beside the right study of material behavior one should not ignore the importance of embodiment resulted from the experimentation of the own production or from experimentation of the ethnological examples, as a direct result of the contact of the human body with the architectural elements. The real sensorial experience of the built space conducts to a more complex understanding of the relationships between technique and society, and could offer remarkable results.

The Lower Danube Chalcolithic Megaron House

A subject never present in experiments that still produces disagreement between archaeologists is the Lower Danube Chalcolithic megaron house; some believe that only few houses were two-storied, there is no convincing explanation for foundation trenches, or the architectural structure above the ground, for instance the method of fixing the wooden structure into the soil, the shape of the roof was never put into question, and the functioning of the heating system inside houses was not at all imagined.

This is the reason why I chose as subject of study, and therefore experimentation, the megaron houses of Gumelnita-Karanovo VI, a Chalcolithic tradition from the Lower Danube-Balkans (Gheorghiu 2001 a), whose domestic architecture seemed to offer to experimentalists lots of subjects of reflection.

How could experimentalists work on such a subject?

I believe that a synthesizing approach between the physical reconstructions of architectural features, starting from the archaeological remains, combined with a hermeneutical approach of the cultural representations from the same context would be an appropriate method to approach prehistoric architecture. In this perspective I combined the work of the archaeologist, ethnologist and architect with that of the artist, to simultaneously represent and evoke the architectural space and stimulate the archaeological imagination when there were insufficient data, as was the case for facades and the decoration of the inner space of the house.

The experimental method employed is original due to its synthesizing approach, which combines the MRT of experimental archaeology with ethnological models and iconographic studies. Let's explain myself. The study of architecture, that begins with the study of archaeological remains, focuses on the structural/mechanical logic dictated by the dimension of materials (here analogies from contemporary studies or from ethological models are used). When data from these sources is absent, complementary information could be taken out from iconography, i.e. artistic representations of the period studied.

The experiments on Chalcolithic architecture were carried out in the village of Vadastra, Olt County, south of Romania, due to financial support from the Slatina Department of the Romanian Ministry of Culture and the Department of Archaeology of the University of Missouri-Columbia. Vadastra is a Chalcolithic site where I set up an international centre of pyro-experiments (see Gheorghiu 2002a; Gheorghiu 2003 a) and, starting with 2003, an archaeo-parc.

The experiments consisted of building a megaron-house of 6 X 3.5 meters, with a wooden platform, an internal pillar sustaining the main longitudinal cross-beam, a clay bench, an oven and a grinding place, using as main model the plan of a house from Radovanu tell (building E, level II, Comsa 1990: 89) (south of Romania, near the river Arges, a tributary of the Danube), dated early Gumelnita (Pandrea 2000).

A first stage in the process of reconstruction was the collection of all data on the architecture of the Gumelnita-Karanovo VI tradition from Romania and Bulgaria that included beside the features that will be mentioned below, the art representations of architectural objects under the shape of ceramic models (see Comsa 1990: 85; Dumitrescu 1970; Todorova 1982: 41, ills. 1-3).

The archaeological architectural remains accessible in Gumelnita- Karanovo VI tradition that were used for the house reconstruction were the following:

1. rectangular plans of houses of megaron type, with wood platforms, (Todorova 1982; Marinescu-Bilcu et al. 1997);
2. foundation trenches with post holes (Todorova 1982: 81, fig. 41; Marinescu-Bilcu et al. 1997: 68);
3. post holes of variable dimension; as evidence for main and secondary posts (Todorova 1982: 23-32, figs. 13-22); these features are present always in foundation trenches;
4. evidence for pointed posts (Todorova 1982: 81, fig. 42), inferring the thrusting into the soil by pressure or rotation;
5. wattle and daub fragments of walls and ceilings as evidence for a building technique with the wood structure hidden in the wall material;
6. various techniques of construction in the same building (Pandrea et al. 1999: 147);
7. wooden platforms made of split wood (Comsa 1990: 88, fig. 47; Todorova 1982: 153, figs. 96 and 97);
8. post holes at a certain distance from the walls (see Comsa 1990: 87, fig. 46; Todorova 1982: 23-32, figs.13-22), as evidence for a wattle and daub building technique with visible plastered and painted wood structure in the form of interior columns, (as the "columns" from Cascioarele island, Dumitrescu 1986);
9. imprints of vegetal cords for bonding wooden structures (Comsa 1990: 84, figs. 44a and b);
10. interior architectural features as fixed pyroinstruments (ovens or fireplaces), concave spaces for grinding, clay benches (Comsa 1990: 86; Todorova 1982: 118, fig. 70);
11. volumetric decoration on interior walls (Comsa 1990: 81);
12. uncolored or colored overlapped layers of fine finishing on walls or ovens
13. paintings on exterior and interior walls with red pigment (Comsa 1990: 81);
14. architectural clay models representing houses and houses forming settlements.

Although the reconstructed house employed all the features mentioned, the present paper will discuss the experiments of replicating of only part of the features mentioned.

All the architectural traces (as post holes, foundation - trenches, clay imprints of wattle and cords, etc.) were translated into possible architectural structures (established by the limits of the materials used and the principle of efficiency), then modeled after the proportions of the prehistoric art representations (i.e. the architectural clay models) and finally transferred in a full scale architectural model.

A secondary source that helped to visualize the architectural structure and the spatial order of the built space was the ethnographic model; in this perspective several architectural details used were designed using study cases from the Danube area and elsewhere.

The first stage in the process of replicating the Chalcolithic house was the digging of "U" shaped foundation trenches (0.40m deep and 0.40 m wide) (Fig. 1), architectural features whose role seems to have been primarily symbolical: to separate the interior space from the exterior, in an analogous way as the perimeter ditch separated the tell settlement from the neighboring environment.

Figure 1. Foundation trenches and the space left for the entrance.

I believe that houses with perimeter foundation were an adaptation to the weak riverine and lacustrine subside soils, as well as to the weak compressed soils of the tells resulted from many overlapped demolished buildings, in order to build massive buildings with a seasonal upper floor.

One functional role of the foundation trenches discovered through experimentation could have been the following: the walls of the channel could act as a sort of mould/shutter to fix with wet pressed soil the base of the posts and twigs already thrust in the foundation, as well as to fasten the foundation with the walls. Another role would be to collect water and in this way to make easy the thrust of the post into the soil; a trench filled with water by the builders or by rain facilitates the easy rotational thrust of the posts into the soil, as experiments and ethnographic evidence from Lower Danube region demonstrate.

To replace the oak posts identified in several Gumelnita settlements, I employed complete and split trunks of local acacia wood (Fig. 2), since oak trees are now absent in the Danube area. The basic architectural structure to sustain the roof, made of trunks of 15 - 20 cm diameter, was positioned at a distance of 1.5 m along the foundation trench perimeter; and a second one, made of trunks of 7 - 10 cm was added in the intervals left, to support the wattle plaiting (Fig. 3).

Both kinds of posts, sharpened at one end, were thrust approx. 40 cm into the wet soil using a rhythmical movement of rotation (Fig.4). In my opinion, the rotational thrust into the wet soil would have been a technique at hand, with no additional effort as the beaten of the posts using a scaffold.

Figure 2. Barking the tree trunks with an adze.

At the house E, level II at Radovanu the excavator suggests the use of a foundation wooden beam with the vertical posts fixed in it, since he did not discover any trace of post holes at the base of the walls (Comsa 1990: 81), a current technique in the Carpathian area in historic times.

Figure 3. Two types of posts and wattle.

Because the door was positioned on the centre of the façade, as shown on ceramic clay models, the structural posts were positioned on each side of the entrance, which created a slight technical difficulty for fixing the attic's façade post on the door's beam (Fig. 5).

A post of 20 diameter and 5 m long was thrust on the central axis of the house, at 1.5 m distance from the wall facing the entrance (Fig. 6). Looking at the plans of the Bulgarian tells dug exhaustively, one can conclude that a great number of medium and large houses had an internal wooden structure made of posts positioned on the central axis of the dwellings with the role to offer a larger aperture of the interior space (see Todorova 1982:13-22, figs. 23-32).

Moreover such a structure which suggests an emergence of the complexity of the spatial organization allowed a flexible design of the dwelt space by means of the partition of the room according two axes of composition.

An inner post of large dimensions (as at Radovanu building E, level II) positioned on the central axis could sustain two transversal beams of large size, expanding the width of the room, as well as two master beams, expanding the length of the same room. Moreover a large post, positioned on the centre of the inner space could sustain a solid and heavy ceiling and attic made of large pieces of wood, allowing a secondary level of (temporary) dwelling.

Figure 4. Rotating the post into the foundation trench; see the vase with water for moistening the soil.

An independent wooden structure, positioned near the oven could have been protected against fire by a thick clay coating; in archaeological remains this is to be found as a hollow clay structure, as the ones found inside a building dated Gumelnita phase A from Cascioarele island (Dumitrescu 1970).

Figure 5. The two posts flanking the entrance.

Ethnological examples (see Coiffier 1992: 53, fig.7), infer that one of the roles of a central or interior post arc could be symbolic and in relationship with social organization (Kus and Raharijaona 2000). It is possible that an analogous symbolism could have been applied in the Gumelnita tradition, in the perspective of Chalcolithic emergent social stratification (see Gheorghiu 2001a: 374 ff.).

Figure 6. The interior post with the base coated with clay.

I believe that one of the symbolic roles of the interior column was a cosmic one. The perceptive experience we had of the post during night time, when the house still had no roof was that the post was in a relationship with the celestial vault; moreover, when the house was finished the sunset shed light on the red painted column, creating a dramatic visual effect. Consequently, one could infer that house orientation generated a connection between sunlight, column and architectural openings.

The plastered and decorated clay columns found at Cascioarele could have had a meaning of social differentiation as well as of orientation of the living space towards Kosmos, in such a way creating a relationship between social and celestial worlds.

Figure 7. Throwing clay balls on the wattle structure.

Next step was the construction of the wattle and daub walls, a technique predominant in wooded environments (Perles 2001: 198), and according to Treuil (1983) specific for the European Neolithic, but mentioned also at an earlier subphase at Çayönü (Perles 2001: 197).

Wattle plaited structure confers to walls an inner resistant core and allows the adherence of daub made of wet clay mixed with straws and chaff. This method required the throw with force of clay balls of 1.5 – 2 kilograms on the wattle plaiting and wooden posts to fix the clay on the wood structure (Fig. 7). By plaiting the twigs around the posts thrust in the foundation trenches and by covering this structure with pressed clay the wall functioned as a monolith mechanical structure (Fig. 8).

Figure 8. The wattle structure fixed with clay; see the wooden platform made of split trunks in the foreground.

As experiments demonstrate, daub preparation was a laborious water consuming process involving a large group of individuals (Fig.9). For building and plastering a house of 6 x 3.5 x 2.50 m a quantity of 5000 liters of water was used to mix 120 cube meters of clay with 600 kg of straws, such a large quantity of water creating transport difficulties, since the source of water was not near the settlement. The excavated soil used for building the house created a large hole in the ground of 2.5 x 6 x 0.80 m (Fig. 10), such a large volume requiring the use of clay not from the settlement but from the deep perimeter trench that surrounded the tell settlement for the first level of settling, as well as the reuse of the clay from the demolished walls for the next levels of settling (Gheorghiu 2001b).

Because the archaeological record shows variations in the technique of building (for example the Gumelnita settlements on the Calmatui river, west of the Romanian Plain, used wattle and daub for exterior walls and *pisé* technique for the interior walls, Pandrea 2002: 56, and the buildings from Bucsani settlement, south of Romanian Plain, used only the *pisé* technology, Marinescu-Bilcu et al. 1997: 65), I utilized the *pisé* technology for constructing parts of the interior architectural clay pieces as the bench and the separating wall.

Wattle and daub technique demands a high compression of the walls, since the clay balls are thrown with force on the wooden structure for adherence, and the resulted wall surface is beat to produce a homogeneous material like in the *pisé* technique.

Figure 9. Moistening the clay for the walls construction.

The main advantages of the composite material resulted from the mix of clay with straws and chaff is a good thermal isolation and a high thermal inertia, due to the empty spaces left in the material fabric by the vegetal fibers.

The role of the protruding wattle and daub walls flanking the entrance (Fig. 11) was complex. They increase the mechanical resistance of the lateral walls by the addition of at least one structural post fixed by the wattle plaiting to the rest of the construction; they protect the entrance, and subsequently the façade from the destructive action of weathering, creating a protected space for the veranda.

Figure 10. Mixing clay with straws and water.

After the vertical structure of the walls was set up, a wood platform made of split trunks (Fig. 12) was fixed within the perimeter delimited by the posts, and then plastered with clay, creating a waterproofed and a fire protected structure. A further role of the platform would be the creation of a firm surface for dwelling, especially at the upper levels of the tell, to cover the numerous perforations produced by the posts of the lower levels of dwelling (for example the Ovcarovo house no. 6 at level 3, which overlaps the foundation trenches of levels 1 and 2 had a wood platform to cover the perforated, and therefore weakened soil surface; see Todorova 1982: 194, figs. 135, 137 and 196, fig. 139).

Figure 11. One of the protruding walls flanking the entrance.

After finishing the platform the next operation was the positioning of the beams forming the attic. All this architectural structure, as well as the cross-beam, is represented as perforations on a clay model of a house from Ovcarovo, Bulgaria (see Todorova 1982: 41, fig. 25/1).

The wooden structure of the roof consisted of a main crossbeam made of two joined trunks which supported 11 rafters on each side of the roof, this number representing a minimum to cover the length of the megaron (Fig. 13).

Making the cross-beam from two joined pieces was the merely architectural structural solution inferred by the presence of the inner large post and also by the length of the megaron.

To fix a structure made of a large number of wood pieces, the carpenter joints were fastened with 80 wooden nails (Fig. 14), the later being hit in holes made with the help of a bow drill. Unless absent in the archeological record, the wooden nails, as shown by historical examples from the Carpathian-Danube area (displayed at the Village Museum in Bucharest), were used as the simplest efficient technique to fix separate wood pieces.

An extra method of fastening the roof's structure was to bind the carpenter joints with the help of 150 m of hemp cords (Fig. 15) (for the use of vegetal cords in ethnological examples see Coudart 1998: 62 ff).

To protect the wood and cords against weathering, the parts which were not covered by the roof or not incorporated into the wall clay were coated with sheep grease. In the end, the complete wooden structure, fastened by wood joints, wood nails and rope bonds worked as a very flexible structure at the same time very robust. When covered with clay, this flexible structure became rigid, and after the shrinking process the tensions in clay and ligneous material produced cracks along the main posts and beams, without weakening the robustness of the building (Fig. 16).

Figure 12. A part of the wood platform forming the threshold.

A difficult task was the reconstruction of the facades of the house. As one could see from the archaeological evidence mentioned before, solid archaeological data come from the plan and little from elevation. So we were compelled to make use of art representation from the same context and to put in relationship shape and proportion with the logic of wooden architecture.

The main source was the clay model (Fig. 17) from Cascioarele island (Dumitrescu 1968) interpreted by me as representing a row of megarons (Gheorghiu 2003 b: 41, fig 5.), followed by several architectural clay models from Sultana, Gumelnita eponymous site, Spantov, and Vladiceasca (see Done 1997: 248-251, figs. 1-4). Less difficult to interpret architecturally was the X-like joint (Fig. 18), made by the crossing of rafters supported by the crossbeam, having a symbolic role, probably of protection, and a functional one to fix or to support the central plaited reed bunches.(Fig. 19).

Figure 13. Fixing a rafter (photo Corina Sarbu).

This horn-like shape of the roof as shown by the clay models could be reproduced as an architectural structure by joining the first two rafters of the roof, a carpenter joining that needs to be fixed by means of wooden nails and cords. Another architectural solution with similar visual effects could have been the crossed positioning of two rods to fix the thatched material of the roof, as shown by examples from the Carpathian area (to be seen at the Museum Village in Bucharest).

Figure 14. Two longitudinal beams fixed with nails and ropes.

One seemingly non-structural detail, present on the Cascioarele model, was the horn-like protuberance at the junction of the facade's rafters and the façade's wall post, which I interpreted as being a simple method to fix the rafter with the vertical main post by means of a diagonal wood piece, this wooden nail having the secondary role to better fix the bunch of reed on the façade rafter (Fig. 20). Beside the functional roles the horn-like nail could have been an apotropaic role, continuing the symbol of horns.

Figure 15. The wooden structure fastened with hemp ropes and wooden nails.

The protruding walls of the megaron's façade could have been the subsequent functional roles: to protect the entrance from the dominant winds and to create a thermal mass illuminated by winter sun, that would warmed the building. In the warm season the two protruding walls cast a shadow that cooled the façade during the morning and afternoon. Seen from the same perspective of passive solar design, in the warm season the roof cast a shadow only on the lower part of the lateral façade, and in winter it warmed all the surface of one lateral façade. This is the reason why I positioned the round window in such a manner to allow low winter sun to penetrate into the house.

Figure 16. Cracks produced along a beam due to rapid shrinkage.

The ceiling of the house was made of plastered middle size trunks (as clay imprints from Bulgarian settlements demonstrate, A. Chokadziev personal communication) positioned on three transversal beams and therefore forming a solid structure that could support heavy loads, allowing the attic to be inhabited during the warm season (Fig. 21). In this perspective the few special "two-storey buildings" discovered in Gumelnita tradition could be in fact normal houses. If the small trunks could have been plastered completely, the cross-beams were visible, and probably were plastered with a thin layer of clay too, to prevent ignition.

Figure 17. A replica of the clay model from Cascioarele (made by Andreea Oprita).

Experiments demonstrated that a second role for the attic, after that of temporal residence, could have been that of food smoking during cold season, since the thatched roof's permeability would produce an air draught which would evacuate the oven's smoke through the ceiling aperture/opening, but not allowing the rain to go through the bunches of reeds. The smoking of the wooden structure produces in time a fire-proofed material with similar properties with the clay coated one.

In the backside of the dwelt space some houses, including the Radovanu example (Comsa 1990: 87, fig. 46) there was a long and narrow clay platform, designed most probably as vase stand (Fig. 22) since numerous fragments and whole vessels were found in its proximity (Todorova 1982: 118, fig. 70). An out of sight positioning of this vase support and its relationships with the grinding place, the central post and oven confers to this structure a possible cultic role. (Fig. 23).

Figure 18. Crossed rafters protected with sheep grease against weathering

Architectural structures needed periodical coatings because they were made up of two materials with different degrees of shrinkage, a ritual action that was performed probably within renewal ceremonies. (Fig. 24)

At the end of summer, after the walls of the building dried, one could notice a series of deep cracks along the main wooden structure and a series of superficial cracks evenly disposed; to annul these effects of shrinkage the cracks should be coated with layers of clay mixed with dung that produced a very elastic protecting coating for the clay and straw mixture of the daub. Finally the overlapped coatings were covered with a thin red slip layer.

Figure 19. Fixing the thatched roof on the crossed rafters.

Similar to the walls, ovens and floors suffered repeated operations of coating, since they too suffered from erosion.

The system of heating consisted of a fixed oven and of a multitude of movable pyro-objects, as braziers and amber-protectors.

Generally the oven's shape copies that of the building's, being built in the form of a small house (see the model from Izvoarele, Gumelnita A2, Done 1997: 250, fig. 3/6), whose lateral window aperture serves for up-draught and smoke evacuation (Fig. 25). There is a functional relationship between the oven and the ceiling aperture for visiting the attic, the later having the role of aspiring the hot air and smoke produced by the oven, when the window is closed.

Figure 20. Wooden nail fixing the first rafter on a pole

As archaeological evidence and clay models illustrate (see Todorova 1982: 40, ill. 24), customary the oven was situated on the Eastern wall, when the house was positioned on a North-South axis, therefore the oven (and the round window for smoke evacuation) being in a symbolic relationship with sun's light and heat, similar to the house.

The architectural experiments were supported by an ethnoarchaeological approach when I tried to imagine the door and the shutter of the window. One frequent metaphor in Chalcolithic ceramics was "the vase - house" (Gheorghiu 2002b), consequently I approached the living space as being the metaphor of a vase and imagined the door and shutter as lids that closed the architectural space.

The same solution was employed to close up the oven's opening with a ceramic plaque with fingers impressions to facilitate prehension, an object frequent into Chalcolithic households whose functional role was until present not understood by archaeologists.

For the shape and positioning of household objects that, together with architecture generated the house's space, the source of inspiration was the traditional household from the Lower Danube area.

Figure 21. A view from the attic during the thatching process

Conclusion: The embodied experience from experiments

It is only at the end of experiment that I realized the power of the embodied experience in helping me to understand the relationship between technology and social behavior.

One main conclusion was to validate the social changes occurring in the Lower Danube Chalcolithic societies through the study of the energy consumed to build the house. The large dimensions of the Chalcolithic surface houses, compared with the Middle Neolithic semi-subterranean ones (cf. Neagu 1997: 13), the strength of the walls due to the foundation trenches, the thick posts and the plaited core of the walls made of twigs and poles, the waterproof wood platforms characteristic for surface buildings, the central pole that allowed a large opening of the interior space, were not possible without the joined effort of a relatively large group of people, that could be interpreted as an emergent social control, and represent possible data in favor of the emergent social stratification (see Webster 1990) and the competitive spirit that characterizes the Danube-Balkan Chalcolithic.

Figure 22. The platform with vases (photo Corina Sarbu).

The house resulted from the experiments is a very robust structure (Fig. 26) which, without the occurrence of an external dramatic event as earthquake or flooding could have had a long lifespan without major repairs, which contradict the archaeological reality, since the small number of re-plastering of floors, walls or ovens infer a relatively short utilization of the architectural objects. An explanation for this contradiction could have a social source. A short time utilization of a robust building could be explained by means of a social control, the surface Chalcolithic house being in this perspective not the result of a collective work of an egalitarian society, but of a controlled one, with emergent social stratification. Furthermore, in this perspective one can perceive the controlled destruction of buildings as a type of social competition (potlatch-like?), that included the intentional firing of houses (see Tringham 1999; Stefanovic 2002), followed by reconstruction on the same surface (with a rotation in time of the positioning of some buildings to have a solid soil for foundation, Gheorghiu 2002).

Figure 23. The platform in relationship with the column and oven

I agree that a large majority of Gumelnita fired houses were the result of a deliberate action of sacrificing the architectural objects.

Experiments infer the idea that destruction by fire was an anthropic controlled phenomenon, since the architectural object was fire protected by layers of fireproof clay. A recent catastrophe (May 2002) in Bucharest at the Village Museum offers additional arguments in favor of the abovementioned hypothesis: during the fire of the museum, the traditional wooden houses coated with clay were very well preserved, loosing only the roof structure. To conclude, to fire a wattle and daub macro-object a large quantity of fuel is needed, the wood furniture and the textile objects that formed the interior design being insufficient for such a process.

A second main conclusion of the experiment was the strong determinism of the inner space towards the Kosmos, i.e. towards sun, stars, fire, water, and wind. Apparently simple in visual representations, the structure of the space is very strong when experienced through the body, and "orientates" the inhabitant to the phenomenon mentioned.

The position of the openings was in a similar relationship: the lower winter sun could enter through the lower window and light the interior of the house, a phenomenon which is not possible in summer when the roof casts a shadow on the window's opening.

Figure 24. Coating a wall with clay mixed with dung and red pigment

Figure 25. The oven with the ceramic plaque acting a shutter and a vase closing the lateral opening

Figure 26. The house before finishing the closing of the attic (the façade and interior decoration by Corina Sarbu)

Acknowledgements

The author is indebted to Professors Dorin Theodorescu (Slatina, Romania) and Ralph M.Rowlett (Missouri-Columbia) for the financial support to build the Chalcolithic house. Many thanks too Alexander Chodzaiev (Bulgaria) who helped with data on ceilings and walls from Bulgarian Chalcolithic houses, and to the Major of the Vadastra village as well to the Mr. Liiceanu and other people from the village who helped to build the house. Thanks also to the students who participated in the project and to my assistant Costel Chitea who made a very precise and helpful model of the house.

Last, but not least my gratitude goes to my assistant Corina Sarbu whose continuous support during the process of construction was decisive to achieve the task, and whose art intervention transformed a scientific reconstruction into a work of art.

References

Coiffier, C. 1992. From Exploitation of the forest to urban dependence in Papua New Guinea. *Traditional Dwellings and Settlements Review*: 49-58.

Coudart, A. 1998. *Architecture et societe neolithique. L'unite et la variance de la maison danubienne*. Paris: Edition de la Maison des sciences de l'homme.

Done, S. 1997. Modele de locuire si sanctuare eneolitice. *Cultura si civilizatie la Dunarea de Jos*, XV: 232-9.

Dumitrescu, Vl. 1986. A doua coloana de lut ars din sanctuarul fazei Boian-Spantov de la Cascioarele (Jud.calarasi). *Cultura si civilizatie la Dunarea de Jos*, 2: 69-72.

Dumitrescu, Vl. 1970. Edifice destine au culte decouvert dans la couche Boian-Spantov de la satation de Cascioarele. *Dacia*, 14: 5-24.

Dumitrescu, H. 1968. Un modele de sanctuaire decouvert dans la station eneolithique de Cascioarele. *Dacia NS*, XII : 381-94.

Todorova, H. 1982. *Kupferzeitliche Siedlungen in Nordostbulgarien*. Muenchen: C. H. Beck.

Gheorghiu, D. 2001a. Southeastern European Late Chalcolithic. In Peregrine, P. (ed.): *Encyclopedia of Prehistory*, vol. 4: 367-80. New York, Boston, Dordrecht, London, Moscow: Kluwer Academic/Plenum Publishers.

Gheorghiu, D. 2001b. Tropes in material Culture. In Gheorghiu, D. (ed.): *Material, Virtual and Temporal Compositions. On the Relationships between Objects*. BAR International Series 953. Oxford: Archaeopress.

Gheorghiu, D.. 2002a. Le projet Vadastra. *Prehistorie Europeenne*,16-17. Liège.

Gheorghiu, D. 2002b. On Palisades, Houses, Vases and Miniatures: the Formative Processes and Metaphors of Chalcolithic Tells. In Gibson, A. (ed.), *Behind Wooden Walls: Neolithic Palisaded Enclosures in Europe*, BAR International Series 1013: 93-117. Oxford: Archaeopress.

Gheorghiu, D. 2003a. Archaeology and Society: News from Vadastra Project. *Old Potter's Almanach*.

Gheorghiu, D. 2003b. Water, tells and textures: A Multiscalar approach to Gumelnita hydrostrategies. In Gheorghiu, D. (ed.): *Chalcolithic and Early Bronze Age Hydrostrategies*. BAR International Series 1123. Oxford: Archaeopress.

Marinescu Bilcu, S., D.Popovici, G.Trohani and R.Andreescu. 1997. Archaeological researches at Bordusani-Popina (1993-1994). In *Cercetari Arheologice*, 10: 65-9.

Kus, S. and Raharijaona, V. 2000. Houses to palace, village to state: Scaling up architecture and ideology. *American Anthropologist*, 102: 98-113.

Neagu, M., 1997. Comunitatile Boian in Campia Dunarii. *Istros*, VIII: 9-25.

Pandrea, S., 2002. Culturile Boian si Gumelnita in nord-estul Campeiei Romane. *Phd. Dissertation*.

Pandrea, S. 2000. Cateva observatii referitoare la periodizarea culturii Boian. *Istros*, X: 35-70.

Pandrea, S., V. Sarbu and M. Neagu. 1999. Cercetari arheologice in asezarea gumelniteana de la Insuratei-Popina I, Jud. Braila. Campaniile 1995-1999. *Istros*, IX: 145-70.

Perles, C. 2001. *The Early Neolithic in Greece.The First farming communities of Europe*. Cambridge: Cambridge University Press.

Treuil, R., 1983. *Le Neolithique et le Bronze Ancien Egeens. Les problemes stratigraphiques et chronologiques, les techniques et les hommes*. Ecole Française d'Athenes, diffusion de Brocard, Paris, Bibliotheque des Ecoles françaises d'Athenes et de Rome.

Tringham, R. 1992. Households with faces: The Chalange of Gender in Prehistoric Architectural remains. In Gero, J. and M.Conkey (eds.): *Engendering archaeology. Women in Prehistory*: 93-131. Blackwell, Oxford and Cambridge.

Stefanovic, M. 2002. Burned Houses in the Neolithic of Southeastern Europe. In Gheorghiu, D. (ed.): *Fire in Archaeology*. BAR International Series 1098: 55-62. Oxford: Archaeopress.

Webster, S. G. 1990. Labor control and emergent stratification in prehistoric Europe. *Current Anthropology*, 31 (4): 337-66.

2

Liminality and the management of space on Late Bronze Age settlements in central and Eastern Slovenia

Phil Mason

Zavod za varstvo kulturne dediščine Slovenije, OE Novo Mesto

Abstract

This article studies the types of settlement and the occupational models in the Late Bronze communities in central and eastern Slovenia from the new knowledge arisen from recent projects of Evaluation and Control of Archaeological Impact of the construction of highways in this part of the country. Excavations at site allowed the increase of our knowledge about the housing areas during that period, dealing not only with the inner spatial organization, but also with their location and position within the region. Also, these works help us to understand the spatial relationship between the domestic area and the funerary complex, mainly the cremation necropolis and ritual areas, which are sited on the outskirts of the settlements.

Introduction

Recent large scale field survey and excavations in advance of motorway construction in eastern and central Slovenia have provided a wealth of new data about lowland settlement in the Late Bronze Age in Central and Eastern Slovenia. This has resulted in a revolution in our understanding of the management of space in lowland settlements and organisation of the landscape in the Late Bronze Age. It provides a different picture to that provided by the previously known Late Bronze Age enclosed upland settlements, rare lowland settlements, flat cremation cemeteries and hoards.

The Late Bronze Age of Central and Eastern Slovenia: the data prior to the motorway excavations

The enclosed upland settlements were usually located on prominent highly visible features in the landscape, especially prominent hills overlooking river valleys or extensive lowland basins (Figure 1). They began at the end of the Ha A period, but their main floruit is in the Ha B period, that is the first part of the 1st millennium BC (Dular 1993: 104-7; Teržan 1999: 103-5, 107-8). The sites in the Dolenjska and Bela krajina regions rarely exceed 1hectare in area and were often enclosed by simple palisades, as at Golšaj in the Krka valley. However the settlements in the Štajerska region are frequently larger. Larger sites also occur in the Krka valley, such as Cvinger near Dolenjske Toplice. This site is distinguished by an elaborate timber revetted earth rampart, which encloses an area of 3.40 hectares (Dular and Križ 2004: 207-50).

Limited excavation on the above sites has revealed that dwellings were of a post framed type, often located on terraces within the settlement. Unfortunately the limited nature of excavation means that little is actually known about the internal organisation of these settlements. There is no available data on intra-site communications or storage/activity zones, data which is available in abundance for the lowland sites.

The few known lowland settlements were confined to the north-eastern part of the country. The sites of Rabelčja vas, Šiman near Gotovlje and Dolnji Lakoš are located on river terraces and date to the end of the Middle Bronze Age (BA B/C) and the beginning of the Late Bronze Age (BA D). The former two sites were open settlements, but it is possible that the settlement at Dolnji Lakoš was enclosed by a ditch and palisade. However, it has also been suggested that this feature was a modified stream channel (Teržan 1999: 102).

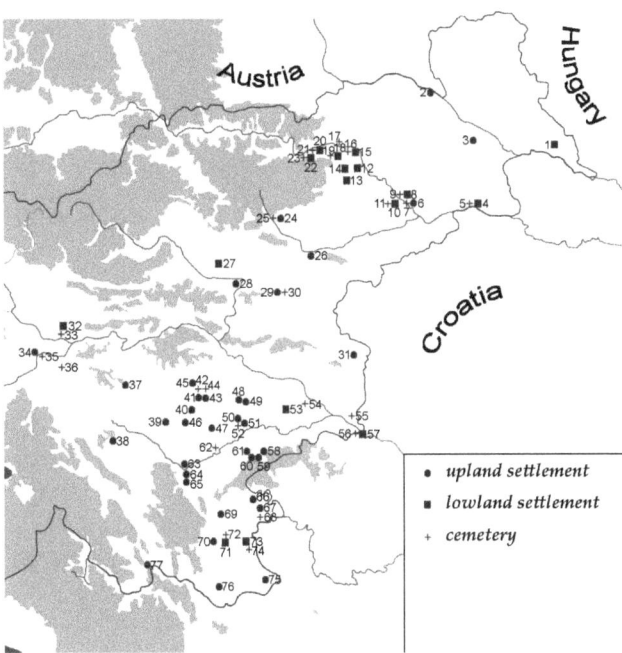

Figure 1. Distribution of upland settlements, extensive lowland settlements and flat cremation cemeteries in the Late Bronze Age in Central and Eastern Slovenia (After Teržan 1999: 103, figure 1; Dular 1993: 103, figure 1, with additions from Dular et al. 1995: 90, figure 1; Dular et al. 2000: 120, figure 1; Dular et al. 2003: 160, figure 1).

The enclosed lowland site of Ormož in the Drava valley began at the end of the Ha A period, but flourished in the Ha B period. It thus has a similar chronological span to that of the upland settlements mentioned above. It was a large settle-

11

ment with a low earthen rampart or bank, enclosing an area of 1.5 hectares (Teržan 1999: 105). A total of 0.5 hectares has been excavated on this site, but the precise date of the earthen rampart has been obscured by the Late Iron Age refortification of the site. Here the post framed aisled dwellings varied in size and were arranged according to a deliberate plan in blocks with a regular alignment along cobbled paths. Storage/economic activity areas are found in direct association with the domestic units (Teržan 1999: 106, figure 5). Thus, they are interpreted as belonging to the individual domestic units, not placed in a central position to the domestic units, or externalised in a peripheral position, as they are on the open settlements (Strmčnik Gulič 2001: 124-5; Teržan 1999: 105-7). However, this apparent absence of a peripheral or central storage/activity zone may be a result of limited excavation.

The locations of the upland settlements are similar to those of the upland Br D and Ha A hoards in Eastern and Central Slovenia, which tend to be in inaccessible upland locations and on potential lines of communication. It should also be noted that there are very few examples of hoards from wet/marshy locations, which are so familiar from other parts of Europe (Čerče and Turk 1996: 11; Turk 1996: 89-124). A further problem lies in the nature of hoard discovery. Few hoards are complete and the great majority were accidental finds. This means that in practice there is little precise information on find location and hoard structure for the earlier finds. Single finds of metalwork (axes, spears, swords, sickles, knives, awls, jewellery and bronze vessels) are found in both upland and wet/marshy/fluvial locations, spanning the entire Late Bronze Age. They are also known from Neolithic/Eneolithic settlement sites and prominent isolated features in the landscape, which later became Early Iron Age settlements (Šinkovec 1996: 125, 129-161).

The flat cremation cemeteries, associated with the settlement sites, are also often located on hilltops or hill slopes (Križ 1995: 10-11; 1997), but some continue to occupy terrace slope and river valley locations, as at Ljubljana (Puš 1971; 1982). Hollow ways and pottery spreads have also been found on some of these sites, e.g. Kapiteljska njiva in the Krka valley (Križ pers. comm.). The beginning of burial in the flat cemeteries shows a similar pattern to that of settlement of the upland sites, beginning in the Ha A1 period, but intensifying in the Ha B period (Teržan 1999: 111-9). It is also interesting that the upland cemetery locations, unlike the upland settlement locations, are often only visible from the immediate vicinity.

The Late Bronze Age lowland settlement evidence: the impact of open area excavation

The new data provided by the motorway excavations has essentially supplied much settlement evidence for the period preceding that of the main floruit of the enclosed upland settlements and the cremation cemeteries, but contemporary with the majority of the known hoards. It is this evidence that will be considered below.

The Late Bronze Age lowland settlement complexes are known to date to the Ha A period, but were still occupied in the Ha B period, that is from 1250 BC to 800 BC (Teržan 1999: 102-4, 107). They were extensive in nature and were located on river terraces beside tributary streams of the major rivers (Figure 1). Excavation has of necessity been linear in nature, providing a 25m to 50m wide excavated transect through sites such as Velike njive in the Sava river valley (2.04 hectares), Rogoza (3.00 hectares) and Slivnica 2 (0.5 hectares) in the Drava valley and Dragomelj (1.25 hectares) in the Ljubljana basin (Djurić 2003b: 273; Strmčnik Gulič 1999: 117, 122; 2003 a: 49; 2003b: 239; Turk 2000: 110; 2003, 126-8). The full extent of these settlement complexes has not been fully defined, but they are known to have extended well outside the excavated area within the motorway route. At best, the excavations have revealed the limits of the settlements in two directions, as is the case at Rogoza and Velike njive. The true extent of such settlements can only be understood by examining field survey data. Thus, surface survey at Dragomelj revealed settlement activity over an area of 4 to 5 hectares (Turk 2000: 110). Intensive surface collection at Griblje in the Kolpa valley indicated that Late Bronze Age settlement activity extends for a distance of at least 750m along the edge of the river terrace and some 800m into the hinterland behind it (Mason 2001: 7-27) (Figure 2). They are thus considerably larger than Late Bronze Age upland sites. It has also led to the use of the term extensive settlement to contrast them with the contemporary and slightly later enclosed upland settlements, which may also have a more formal plan (see Ormož above), suggesting strict rules on the management of space within them.

Intra-settlement spatial organisation: the case of Velike njive

The recently excavated site of Velike njive will be used to illuminate the lay out of these extensive unenclosed lowland settlements. The excavated part of the site covers an area of 2.04 hectares and extends for almost a kilometre in length on the Pleistocene Sava gravels to the west of the Velikovaški potok stream (Djurić 2003b: 273) (Figure 3). The now regulated stream occupied at least three palaeochannels in the western part of the excavated area during the LBA, although it is not clear as to whether the channels functioned at the same time. The western part of the eastern part of the site was subject to fluvial activity in the early Holocene, showing evidence of a further three paleochannels that predate Late Bronze Age occupation. There is also some evidence of post- Late Bronze Age alluvial deposits in this area. The area to the west of the present regulated course was also excavated and showed only sporadic evidence of Late Bronze Age activity – it seems to have been a relatively marshy floodplain with further palaeochannels (Verbič 2003: 3). The western part of the site exhibits a low density Late Bronze Age occupation, which gradually increases towards the main area of intensive occupation in the eastern part of the site. This intensive occupation extends for a distance of 370m, gradually decreasing in intensity towards the eastern margins of the settlement (Figure 3).

The area of intense occupation or central zone seems to be dominated by domestic dwelling units based around large rectangular post framed buildings (Plate 1) (Figure 2: 6). It is frequently difficult to define individual dwelling units due to the lack of surviving floor levels and hearths within the potential domestic structures. Some pit ovens were recovered,

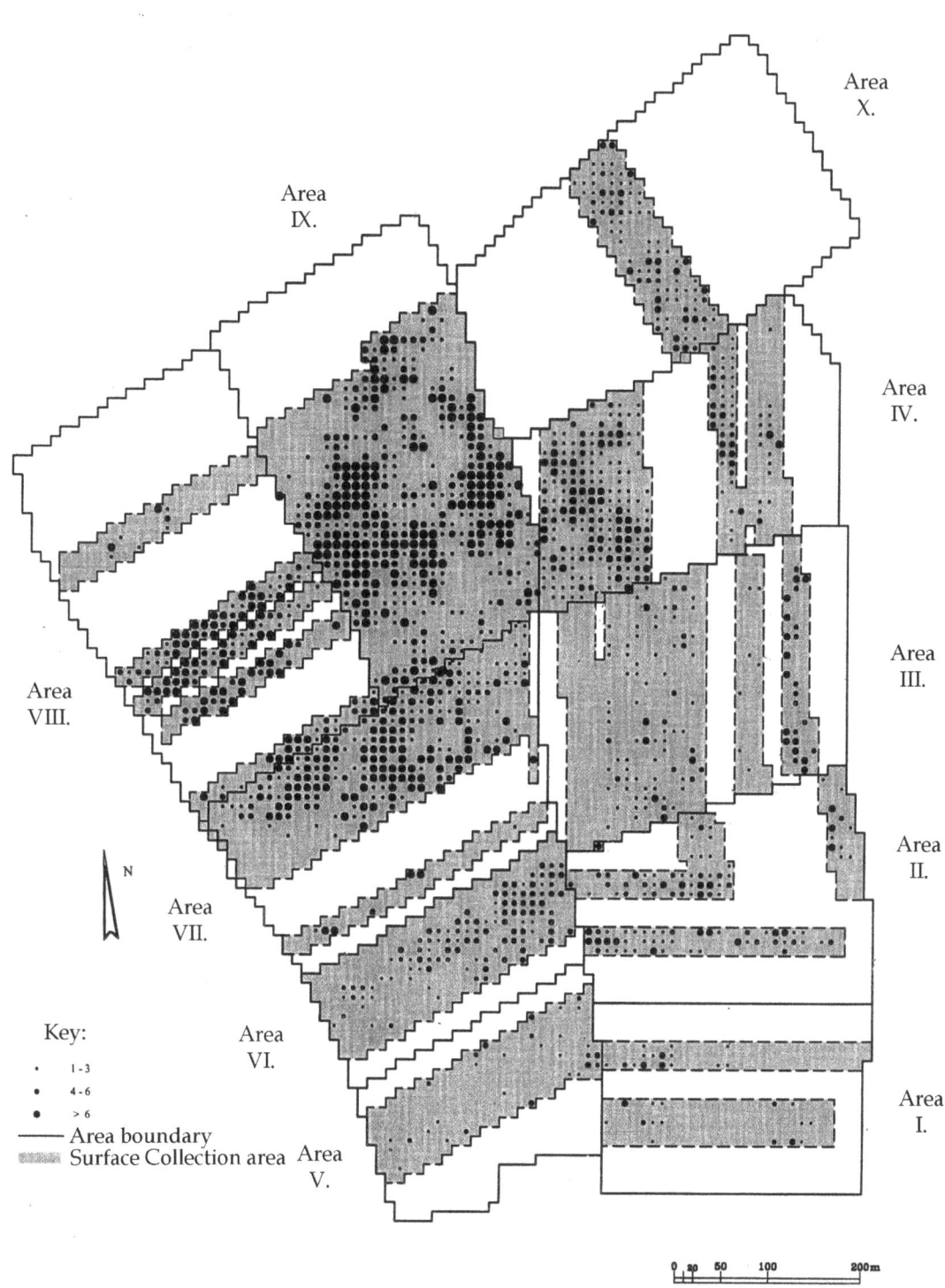

Figure 2. Prehistoric potsherd distribution from the 1999 surface survey on the Late Bronze Age settlement at Griblje - Kohane.

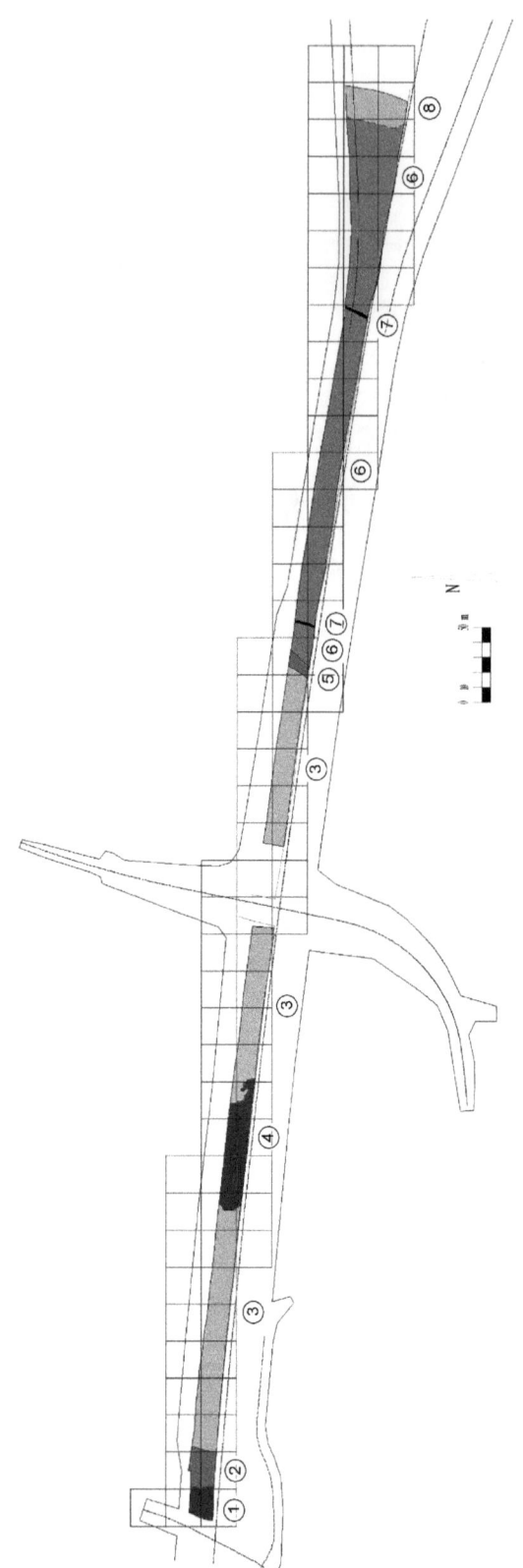

reinforced by the presence of borrow pits and occasional storage pits around the individual dwelling units. A similar situation can be seen at Dragomelj, where the excavator posits the presence of a low density of not necessarily contemporary homesteads dispersed over the settlement area and separated from each other by relatively empty areas. It is one of these areas between two dwelling units that two ingot hoards were discovered (Turk 2000: 111-3).

In contrast to this, the outer zone is characterised by a lower density of structures, comprising isolated postholes and large storage pits, which often exhibit evidence of extensive re-cutting. Some of the large pits contain large storage jars, but the majority contain few finds of any type. There is one example of a special deposit, a dump of large potsherds from several different vessels, which were carefully placed in a final re-cut in the upper fill. This can be interpreted as an abandonment or sealing deposit. The isolated postholes show some indications of forming small discrete structures, which may have been used for grain storage. It is posited that this is relatively low density of occupation was a zone of economic activity or possibly of storage (Figure 3: 3, 8).

Plate 1. Part of the domestic zone in the Late Bronze Age settlement at Velike njive during excavations in 2003 (Photo Ildikó Pintér).

Liminality at the intra settlement level

However it should be noted that this division into a central domestic dwelling zone and a zone of economic/storage activity is not merely a functional spatial division on the settlement as perceived by the excavator, but that they were perceived as such in the Late Bronze Age. The boundaries between these zones were emphasised at Velike njive by paths and especially burnt stone mounds/midden areas. This is especially clear, where the western edge of the central domestic dwelling zone was defined by a path or hollow way, which was later utilised as a burnt stone mound or rubbish deposit (Figure 3: 5) (Plate 2). The burnt stone mound was 7 m wide and ran for a length of 25m within the excavated area. However it was visible in the ploughed field surface for a distance of 25m to the north, and was also visible in the fields to the south of the existing 25 m wide main road, which bounded the excavation to the south. It thus extended for a distance of at least 75m.

Figure 3. Schematic division of the excavated Late Bronze Age settlement at Velike njive

but these are located outside such structures. The large number of postholes and the lack of a clear ground plan further complicate the definition of buildings, but this would tend to suggest repeated repair, rebuilding and/or reoccupation of the same locations within the central zone. This is further

Plate 2. Detail of the Late Bronze Age burnt stone mound on the western edge of the domestic zone at Velike njive (Photo plan Ildikó Pintér)

A similar sequence was also found on the edge of the Late Bronze Age channel of the Velikovaški potok stream at the extreme western edge of the excavated area (Figure 3: 2). The primary Late Bronze Age activity in this area was characterised by a 26m wide cobbled surface on the edge of the stream. The surface showed signs of lateral flood damage and was covered by 20cm layer of alluvial deposits. A Late Bronze Age deposit of large potsherds and cracked or burnt river cobbles of similar dimensions was deposited on top of the alluvium, respecting position of the former cobbled surface. The material from both the burnt stone mound and the potsherd deposit was dominated by river cobbles, many of which showed signs of fracture or burning, but there was also a large amount of pottery present. The pottery in the deposit on the extreme western edge of the site is dominated by large sherds of small and medium sized jars or storage vessels, whilst the pottery from the burnt stone mound at the western edge of the domestic zone also contained bowls and handled vessels, possibly associated with food serving or drinking. The finds from the latter context, thus, suggest a connection with communal food preparation or feasting.

The eastern edge of the settlement was also marked by a cobbled path and two large pits or water holes, but there is no evidence of a burnt stone mound or pottery deposit in this area. However, it should be noted that this eastern boundary was respected in the Early Iron Age, when two barrows were erected to the east of the path some time after the settlement was abandoned (Tica per.comm.).

A similar situation has been detected on other settlements. At Rogoza, a limited area of midden or rubbish deposition was found on the edge of the palaeochannel that marked the southern edge of the settlement. The channel edge was also the location of a deposit of a bronze ingot in a complete vessel (Strmčnik Gulič 2001: 122; 2003a: 52) (Figure 4). The northern edge of the settlement was defined by a cobbled path, which also formed the boundary between the Late Bronze Age settlement and four Late Bronze Age /Early Iron Age barrows (Strmčnik Gulič 2001: 122-4). These barrows are also probably later than the settlement. A slightly earlier example can be seen at Obrežje in the Sava valley, where a deposit of large potsherds and burnt stone occurs in a palaeochannel on the edge of a settlement from the end of the Middle Bronze Age (Djurić 2003a: 204). A slightly different situation can be seen on the recently excavated Middle Bronze Age site at Pince in Prekmurje, where a central zone, containing linear features, is surrounded by a zone of dwelling structures. This is surrounded by a zone of storage/rubbish pits, which are separated from a stream channel or marshy depression by a zone of pottery spreads and individual finds of metalwork (Kerman, B. pers. comm.). The Late Bronze Age complex at Griblje also provides putative evidence of similar activity at the edge of the river Kolpa floodplain and around seasonal pools. Here surface collection has recovered large quantities of cracked or fire damaged sandstone river cobbles, which suggests that burnt stone mounds similar to that at Velike njive are also present on this site (Mason 2001: 16-7, 24) (Figure 5).

There is important evidence for the presence of burnt stone mounds as liminal features in the Late Bronze Age in Britain. A large burnt stone mound was found along the edge of a palaeochannel at the Reading Business Park site (Brossler 2001: 133). The excavator has also posited that this unenclosed site was divided into a primary domestic zone, encircled by a secondary economic activity/storage zone and a tertiary exterior zone. However, the settlement boundary was further defined by the presence the burnt stone mound on the edge of the stream channel (op.cit. 135-7). One should be noted that the burnt stone mound on this site and the majority of the other known burnt stone mound sites in Britain and Ireland contrast sharply with the Velike njive site, in that they do not contain large quantities of pottery (op.cit. 133).

Figure 4. The Late Bronze Age settlement at Rogoza (After Stmčnik Gulič 1999, 123, figure 9)

Liminality and the management of space on Late Bronze Age settlements in central and Eastern Slovenia

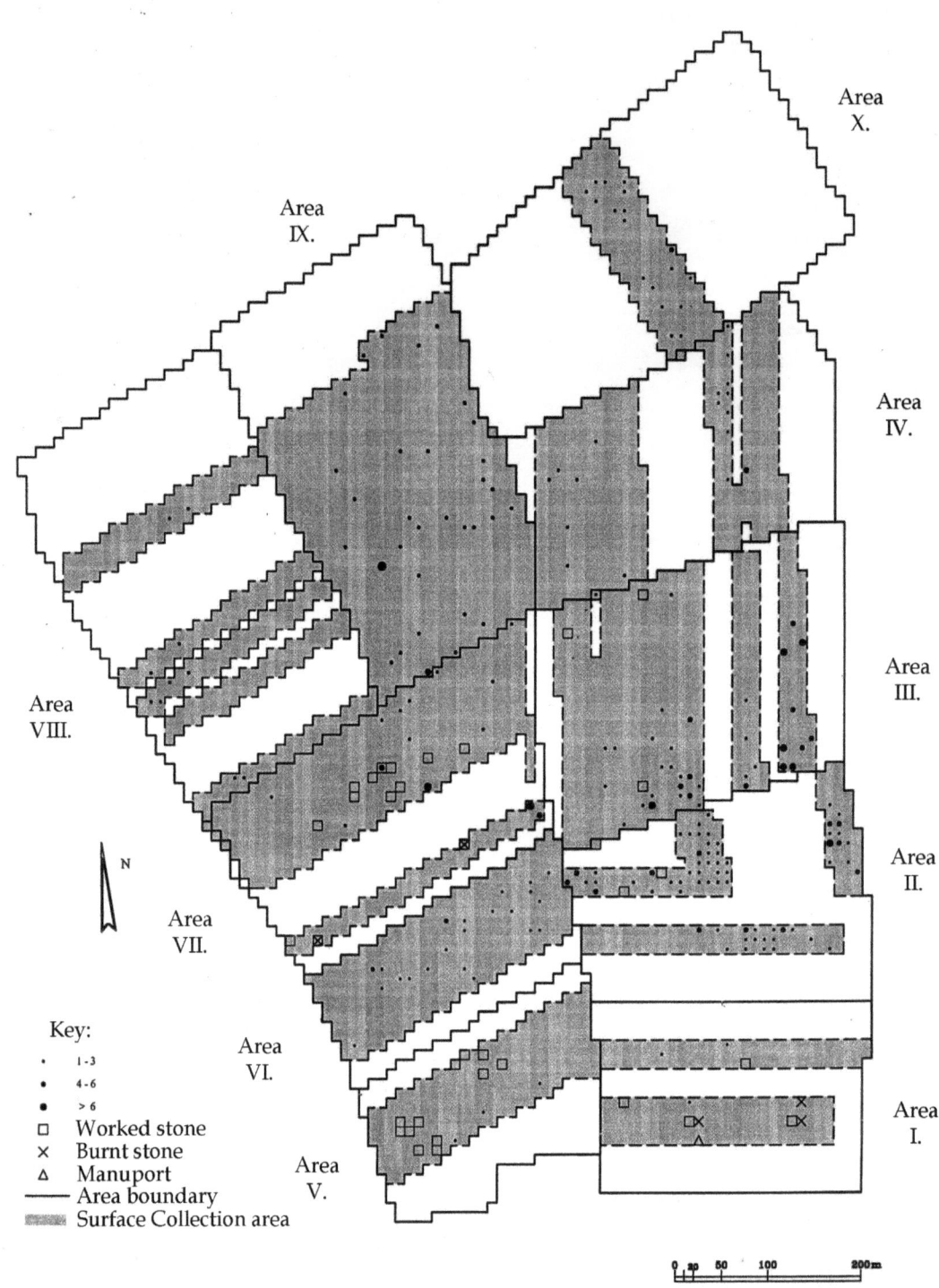

Figure 5. Worked flint distribution from the 1999 surface survey on the Late Bronze Age settlement at Griblje - Kohane.

It may thus be posited that special attention was paid to liminal areas associated with watercourses and marshy areas close to settlement areas and that further emphasis was placed on the transition zone between domestic zones and zones of economic/storage activity on Late Bronze Age settlements in Eastern and Central Slovenia. The margins of settlements were marked by paths, which in themselves are characteristic of transition, but only paths associated with the transition to zones of economic activity in marshy areas warranted reinforcement through the deposition of material associated with communal consumption, feasting or the deposition of domestic debris. Metalwork might also be found in these contexts, but might also occur in the boundaries between individual dwelling units within the domestic zone (Turk 2000: 112, 113-4).

The deposition of grain and artefacts associated with grain processing also defines the boundaries of zones of economic activity with watercourses and marshy areas, subject to seasonal flooding directly adjacent to the Late Bronze Age settlement in the river meander at Črnomelj. Deposits of burnt grain and pits containing broken querns were located on the very edge of the contemporary channel (Mason 1999a: 34) (Plate 3). These deposits occur in an area where grain could neither be stored, nor grown. It would thus seem that such seasonally flooded areas were seen as liminal and were connected with fertility. This may also be an explanation for the presence of grain, grain processing equipment and equally for material associated with communal consumption. However, a single interpretation of the symbolism attached to these areas should not be attempted. This is borne out by the use or treatment of these marginal zones within the wider Late Bronze Age lowland landscape, apart from their use on rare occasions for the deposition of metalwork as is the case in many parts of Europe (Čerče and Turk 1996: 11).

The Late Bronze Age phase of the multiperiod site at Dolge njive is an example of such use of these marginal wet areas. The site was located beside a palaeochannel on the edge of the first terrace of the river Krka floodplain and was subject to seasonally flooding in the Late Bronze Age. It produced evidence of three stone platforms connected by a cobbled path or hollow way, the margins of which were further defined by boulders (Plate 4). Charcoal and burnt human bone was associated the path and two of the platforms, which were subject to repeated resurfacing. These structures are interpreted as a mortuary complex, possibly linked to an as yet undiscovered cremation cemetery, or to deposition of mortuary remains in the river. The nearest known Late Bronze Age settlements in the area are of the enclosed upland type (Mason 2003b: 120). A group of three stone mortuary platforms was on the edge of a palaeochannel also found at Podgorica, 360 m south of the major settlement at Dragomelj. However, the associated cremation graves suggest a date in the 6th century BC, although there is evidence of earlier, Late Bronze Age metallurgical and settlement activity on the site (Novšak 2003: 216-8).

Late Bronze Age cremation cemeteries might also occur close to such marginal locations as is the case at Obrežje. The large Late Bronze Age cremation cemetery on this site comprised 366 graves, which were located on Pleistocene gravel point bars on the slope and within the marshy valley

Plate 3. The Late Bronze Age pit complex on the edge of the palaeochannel of the river Lahinja, Črnomelj (Photo Phil Mason)

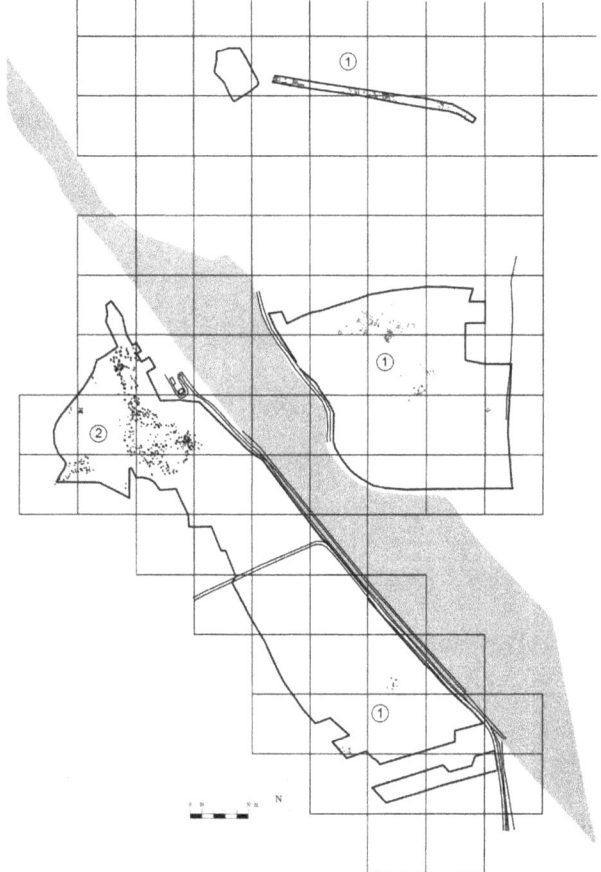

Figure 6. The Late Bronze Age cemetery and Middle Bronze Age settlement complex at Obrežje.

of the Struga stream, a now defunct tributary of the river Sava (Mason 2003a: 67-8) (Figure 6). The marshy areas between the point bars contained discrete spreads of pottery fragments, which are dominated by jar fragments. These deposits are probably connected with feasting as part of the mortuary ritual, although once again storage jars are relatively common in the assemblage, as they were in the westernmost deposit at Velike njive. The cemetery complex was associated with a potential extensive Late Bronze Age settlement, which was defined through field survey on the adjacent Pleistocene terrace of the river Sava (Djurič 2003a: 204).

Plate 4. The Late Bronze Age hollow way and eastern mortuary platforms under excavation at Dolge njive in 2002 (Photo Goran Skelac)

Marshy areas, associated with river/stream flood plain environments close to settlements and in the wider landscape, were also associated with mortuary complexes and areas of ritual activity, in which the connection between fertility and death was emphasised. They were often separated from settlements by paths and watercourses and lay within bounded areas, which were only visible from the immediate vicinity, from the settlement itself. The connection between fertility and life is emphasised in the flood plain, river edge or marshy areas, although some of this apparent storage activity was evidently symbolic in nature, as was the case at Črnomelj. The boundaries of the domestic zone and storage zone, as well as between the storage zone and flood plain edge were suitable points for the deposition of material derived from communal consumption, hence the locations of the burnt stone mounds/pottery deposits at Velike njive, Obrežje, Pince and Rogoza. These serve to mark boundaries between the community and "dangerous" transitional areas, boundaries, which had to be reinforced communal feasting.

This is a sharp contrast with the upland locations of hoards in the BR D and Ha A periods and the highly visible upland settlements of the end of the Ha A period and the Ha B period. The extensive settlements would have been highly visible from a distance, but the reinforcement of their boundaries with special deposits was only detectable in the immediate vicinity. These boundaries were no less real than the enclosures of the Late Bronze Age upland settlements, some of which developed into hillforts in the Early Iron Age (Mason 1996a: 121-5; 1996b: 273-82; 1999b: 145-6). Indeed it is clear that the lowland settlement sites continued to have symbolic meaning in the Early Iron Age, when barrows might be placed on them, or even directly respecting the earlier boundaries of these settlements (Mason 2001: 24; Strmčnik Gulič 2001: 122; Tica pers. comm.). This transformed them into places of the ancestors for the hillfort communities.

Acknowledgments

This article is based on a paper presented in at the 11th Annual meeting of the EAA in Cork. I would like to thank Xurxo M. Ayán Vila for the opportunity to contribute to this volume. I would like to thank Janez Dular (SAZU) and Jana Horvat (SAZU) for permission to use cartographic data. Peter Turk (Narodni muzej Slovenije) kindly supplied with information on the Dragomelj site. Mira Strmčnik Gulič (Zavod za varstvo kulturne dediščine Slovenije, OE Maribor) kindly gave me permission use the site plan from Rogoza. Finally, I would like to thank Ildikó Pintér, who produced the drawings and put up with me, while I finished the article.

References

Brossler, A. 2001. Reading Business Park: the results of phases 1 and 2. In Brück, J. (ed.) *Bronze Age Landscapes: Traditions and Transformations.* 129-138, Oxford

Čerce, P. and Turk, P. 1996. Depoji pozne bronaste dobe – najdiščne okoliščine in struktura najdb (Hoards of the Late Bronze Age – The Circumstances of their discovery and the Structure of the Finds). In Teržan, B. (ed.): *Depojske in posamezne najdbe kovinske najdbe bakrene in bronaste dobe na Slovenskem (Hoards and individual metal finds from the Eneolithic and Bronze Ages in Slovenia).* Katalogi in Monografiji, 30: 7-30. Ljubljana

Djurić, B. 2003a Obrežje – Draga-Goričko. In Djurić, B. (ed.): *Zemlja pod vašimi nogami: arheologija na avtocestah Slovenije: vodnik po najdiščih,* 204. Ljubljana

Djurić, B. 2003b Velike njive pri Veliki vasi. In Djurić, B. (ed.) *Zemlja pod vašimi nogami: arheologija na avtocestah Slovenije: vodnik po najdiščih,* 273. Ljubljana

Dular, J. 1985. *Topografsko področje XI (Bela krajina)*. Arheološka topografija Slovenije. Ljubljana

Dular., J. 1993. Začetki železnodobne poselitve v osrednji Sloveniji (Der Beginn der eisenzeilichen Besiedlung in Zentralslowenien). *Arheološki vestnik*, 44: 101-2. Ljubljana.

Dular, J. and Križ, B. 2004. Železnodobno naselje na Cvingerju pri Dolenjskih Toplicah (Die eisenzeitliche Siedlung auf dem Cvinger bei Dolenjske Toplice). *Arheološki vestnik 55*, 207-50. Ljubljana.

Dular., J., Križ, B., Svoljšak, D. and Tecco Hvala, S. 1995. Prazgodovinska višinska naselja v Suhi krajini (Vorgeschichtliche Höhensiedlungen in der Suhectares krajina). *Arheološki vestnik 46*, 89-168. Ljubljana

Dular., J., Križ, B., Pavlin, P., Svoljšak, D. and Tecco Hvala, S. 2000. Prazgodovinska višinska naselja v dolini Krke (Vorgeschichtliche Höhensiedlungen im Krkatal). *Arheološki vestnik*, 51: 119-70. Ljubljana

Dular, J., Križ, B., Pavlin, P., Svoljšak, D. and Tecco Hvala, S. 2003. Prazgodovinska višinska naselja v okolici Dol pri Litiji (Vorgeschichtliche Höhensiedlungen in der Umbegung von Dole pri Litiji). *Arheološki vestnik*, 54: 159-224, Ljubljana.

Križ, B. 1995. *Novo mesto pred Iliri*. Novo mesto.

Križ, B. 1997. *Kapiteljska njiva, Novo mesto*. Novo mesto.

Mason, P. 1992 Iron, Land and Power: The Social Landscape of the Southeastern Alps and the Karst in the Iron Age. *Arheo*, 15: 32-8. Ljubljana.

Mason P. 1996a. *The Early Iron Age of Slovenia*. British Archaeological Report International Series 643. Oxford.

Mason P. 1996b. Iron, Land and Power: The Social Landscape in the Southeastern Alps in the Late Bronze Age and the Early Iron Age. In Jerem, E. and Lippert, A.: *Internationales Symposium, Die Osthectaresllstattkultur*. Archaeolingua: 274-282, Budapest .

Mason, P. 1999a. Črnomelj – Arheološko najdišče. In Batič, J.: *Kulturne poti 1999: vodnik po spomenikih*: 33-41, Ljubljana

Mason, P. 1999b. The Road to the South: the role of Bela krajina in the long-distance exchange networks between the Adriatic and the Eastern Alps in the early 1st millennium BC in the light of recent settlement excavation. In: Jerem, E. and Poroszlai, I.: *Archaeology of the Bronze and Iron Age, Environmental Archaeology, Experimental Archaeology and Archaeological Parks. Proceedings of the International Archaeological Conference, Százhalombatta, 3-7 October 1996*, Archaeolingua 7: 143-55. Budapest.

Mason, P. 2001. Griblje in problem nižinskih arheoloških kompleksov v Sloveniji. *Varstvo spomenikov* 39: 7-27. Ljubljana.

Mason, P. 2003[a]. Rimska vojaška utrdba. In Djurić, B. (ed.): *Zemlja pod vašimi nogami: arheologija na avtocestah Slovenije: vodnik po najdiščih*: 66-71. Ljubljana

Mason, P. 2003b Dolge njive pri Beli Cerkvi. In Djurić, B. (ed): *Zemlja pod vašimi nogami: arheologija na avtocestah Slovenije: vodnik po najdiščih*: 119-21. Ljubljana

Novšak, M. 2003. Podgorica. In Djurić, B. (ed) *Zemlja pod vašimi nogami: arheologija na avtocestah Slovenije: vodnik po najdiščih*: 216-8, Ljubljana

Puš, I. 1971. *Žarnogrobiščna nekropola na dvorišču SAZU v Ljubljani* Razprave 1.razreda SAZU 7/1, Ljubljana

Puš, I. 1982. *Prazgodovinsko žarno grobišče v Ljubljani* Razprave 1.razreda SAZU 13/2, Ljubljana

Strmčnik Gulič, M. 1999. Nova podoba prazgodovinske poselitve na zahodnem obrobju Dravskega polja (Das neue Bild der prähistorischen Besiedlung am östlichen Rand des Draufeldes). *Arheološki vestnik*, 52: 115-130, Ljubljana.

Strmčnik Gulic, M. 2003a Bronastodobna naselbina pod Pohorjem. In Djurić, B. (ed.): *Zemlja pod vašimi nogami: arheologija na avtocestah Slovenije: vodnik po najdiščih*, 49-53. Ljubljana

Strmčnik Gulic, M. 2003b. Slivnica pri Mariboru 2. In Djurić, B. (ed) *Zemlja pod vašimi nogami: arheologija na avtocestah Slovenije: vodnik po najdiščih*: 239. Ljubljana

Šinkovec, I. 1996. Posamezne kovinske najdbe bakrene in bronaste dobe (Individual metal finds from the Eneolithic and Bronze Ages). In Teržan, B. (ed): *Depojske in posamezne najdbe kovinske najdbe bakrene in bronaste dobe na Slovenskem (Hoards and individual metal finds from the Eneolithic and Bronze Ages in Slovenia)*. Katalogi in Monografiji 30: 125-63. Ljubljana

Teržan, B. 1999. An Outline of the Urnfield Culture Period in Slovenia. *Arheološki vestnik*, 50: 97-143. Ljubljana.

Turk, P. 1996 Datacija poznobronastodobnih depojev (The dating of Late Bronze Age Hoards). In Teržan, B. (ed): *Depojske in posamezne najdbe kovinske najdbe bakrene in bronaste dobe na Slovenskem (Hoards and individual metal finds from the Eneolithic and Bronze Ages in Slovenia)*. Katalogi in Monografiji, 30: 89-124. Ljubljana

Turk, P. 2000. Late Bronze Age Lowland Settlements in Central Slovenia - Hamlets, Villages or Proto-urban Centres. In Thrane, H. (ed.): *Diachronic Settlement Studies in the Metal Ages: Report on the EFS workshop at Moesgård, Denmark, 14-18 October 2000*: 109-19. Århus

Turk, P 2003. Dragomelj. In Djurić, B. (ed.): *Zemlja pod vašimi nogami: arheologija na avtocestah Slovenije: vodnik po najdiščih*: 126-8. Ljubljana.

Verbič, T. 2003. *Poročilu o geološkem pregledu arheoloških izkopavanj na odseku AC Smednik - Krška vas*, unpublished report. Ljubljana.

3

Architectural analysis of monumental motives
Towards a methodological investigation into Iron Age drystone roundhouses in Scotland: an interim's statement from an architectural perspective

Tanja Romankiewicz

Technical University of Berlin, Germany

Abstract

This paper intends to outline the development of a methodology of architectural analysis currently worked on in the author's PhD-thesis (Romankiewicz in prep.). Monumental Iron Age roundhouses in Scotland are analysed from an architectural perspective, designed to identify and evaluate their construction and aesthetical aspects. This is achieved by studying ground plans, elevations, structural systems and building materials and reconstructing the construction process and lost building parts.

This architectural approach hopes to provide a new perspective for the study of Iron Age roundhouses in Scotland and intends to prove interrelations of design and structure to reveal their complexities and the architectural sophistication of Iron Age roundhouses. The results are verified according to architectural and engineering principles to support archaeological discussions on wider interpretations of Iron Age societies.

Starting with a general definition of architecture, the different Iron Age stone roundhouse types found in Scotland are introduced, concluding that all achieve monumentality by different means. An analysis of internal space, expounding its role in the overall design of the houses is followed by a discussion of the possible motives behind the designs that created different ground plan patterns in relation to external elevation. These motives not only help to explain the development of monumental design, but also allow conclusion about the organisation of the societies that built them.

Introduction to Architecture

Architecture is the art and science of designing and constructing buildings through a conscious act of forming building parts to produce a unifying and coherent structure (Ching 1995: 9). Architecture is therefore the language composed of form and function, expressing the relations between primary functions, such as providing sufficient accommodation and adequate structural soundness.

Built environments can be seen as human markers within the landscape; they provide space for sleeping, working, storing, hiding, for all kinds of human activity, and offer real or imagined shelter from natural and supernatural forces. Buildings support life with physical substance, they constitute a safe environment and demonstrate the relations of humans to a defined but previously undistinguished space. However, a shelter built against the storm does not equal architecture if it is only a random collection of materials. Only when the building parts are essential for its function, does it receive a meaning beyond practicality. This implies that nothing in the design is unsuitable or redundant, nothing is accidental.

The location of the site broadly determines its architecture; climate, technology, material and economy shape the design. Social identity and status constitute the situation of the builder and set the limit of the design of the building.

Architecture is hence the interplay of all these aspects, creating an organism in which the different organs (building parts) support each other to fulfil practical, structural and aesthetical tasks. Behind architecture there is a designing mind that combines these aspects for a purpose. This deliberate architectural design process is characteristic of and specific to, people, place and time. If these processes are repeated at a given time and place, an architectural style is created.

Architectural analysis

The design of a house is the interaction between aesthetical preferences, structural demands and functional needs. Architecture has to be an idea first before it can become built reality. The abstract process of planning is always concerned with ordering time, activity, status, roles and behaviour.

To analyse architecture is to investigate the thoughts behind the structure, to detect these patterns of order, and to understand the design purpose. "Inner relations" of form and function that are the essence of architectural design are revealed (Binding 1999: 1); and the first step is to find out if these interrelations were created deliberately or accidentally. This is to judge the level of elaboration the architecture.

For the process of analysis, three different aspects of design have to be handled separately resulting in an analysis of space, structure and aesthetical composition. By considering these aspects individually, the analyst can detect how far requirements for one aspect influence and limit the extent of others. A 'perfect' design would acknowledge the needs of all aspects and would allow them to mutually benefit rather than to hinder each other's function. The level and sophistication of this interaction form essentially the scale by which architecture and the motives behind it are measured and valuated.

Architectural function and the function of architecture

Function as considered in architectural terms, does not conflict with ritual and the former term is therefore not used in the same sense as in archaeological debates. Ritual factors in building designs were clearly practical from a ritual perspective of the builders and therefore every design that caters for rites or expresses beliefs is purely functional in an architectural sense.

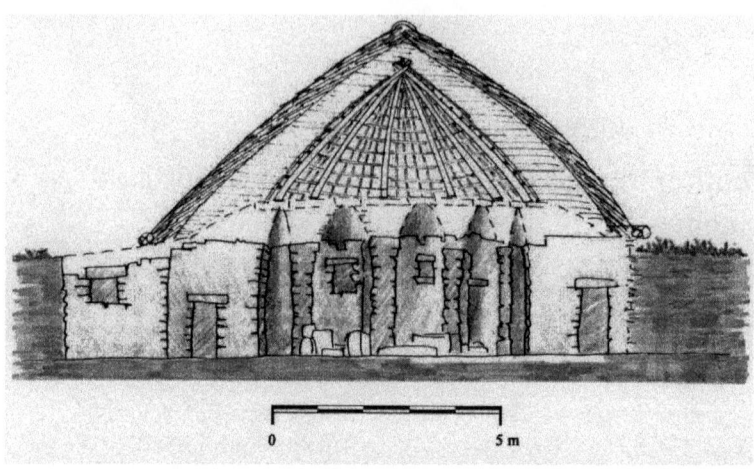

Illustration 1. Sketch reconstruction of Kilpheder wheelhouse, Western Isles, to show the semi-subterranean construction.

ings on a monumental scale. Monumentality is an architectural statement that expresses magnitude and solidity, whether a given structure is build in solid substance or only creates the image of immensity and enduring materials (Glendinning et al. 1996: 505). It is also intended to impress either humans directly or, more abstractly, nature or natural forces, spirits or gods.

Monumentality is often related to massiveness and therefore the use of stone as building material. This view, though, is influenced by the grand edifices of Greek and Roman architects who apparently knew how to employ materials to create immaterial impressions (Rakob 1985: 89). In fact, the development of building techniques such as the Greek *emplekton* or the Roman *opus caementicium* was fuelled by the need to efficiently create monumental buildings (Romankiewicz 2002: 13-5).

More strictly, the term 'function' explicitly relates to the practical use of a building and explains the form of its ground plan. In order not to confuse the different meanings of 'function,' it is important to distinguish 'practical' or 'technical' aspects of the building design from 'functional' as the latter is applied to the use of the building for its primary purpose, which is assumed to be for dwelling in the case of this study.

Practical requirements of buildings are more than obvious; they have to provide a safe shelter from the elements and from fauna, offer accommodation and storage and retain heat and allow light for comfort and commodity. Design motives are harder to grasp because they are closely related to cultural traditions. Although these aspects are not directly evident, it is through architecture as well as artworks, burial practices and spatial organisation and that they were indirectly manifested. The motives behind their creation can be of emotional (e.g. feeling of security), ritual (e.g. symbolic interpretation) or social influence (e.g. hierarchical order), which can be transmitted not only by the outward appearance of a building, but also by its structure e.g. thick walls built to protect (emotional), building parts imitating or evoking nature or spiritual beliefs (ritual), or monumental dimensions as a symbol of power and status (social) (Trigger 1978: 170-6).

Additionally, there is the influence of the environment in which architecture is interpreted as a response that meets "the challenge of an environment with the building materials that same environment offers" (ibid, 171). This reflects a regional character of architecture and a very local background to developments. Beside these traceable and logically explicable reasons, there is and has always been "secular tastes and fashions" (ibid, 176), which could result in the adaptation of design and construction methods that are completely unsuitable in both ecological and economical terms with choice purely guided by individual taste.

Functional monumentality

Design aesthetics often expand beyond pure practicality and are intended to convey and transmit abstract concepts of social or religious order, human potential and individual taste. One of these means of communication is the creation of build-

This premise that monumentality is uniquely a feature of stone architecture is disproved by the impressive posthole sizes and floor dimensions of certain timber roundhouses recorded for Iron Age Britain and Scotland in particular (e.g. Scotstarvit, Fife and Bersu 1950). The evidence suggests the construction of monumental houses purely in timber (Hingley 1992: 27). It is also deceiving to relate monumentality only to the external appearance of buildings and their external impression. Subterranean wheelhouses of the Scottish Later Iron Age did not appear monumental externally, but provided an elegant and spacious interior that was probably even more effective as a means to impress, because it was so unexpected from outside (Illus. 1; Armit 1997a: 43). The well-known broch towers such as Mousa on Shetland (Illus. 2) however, reflect the 'classic' concept of enduring masonry built to externalise monumental dimensions (Armit 2003).

Introduction to archaeological evidence

Domestic architecture in Iron Age Scotland is dominated by roundhouses, either in stone or in timber. This difference, it has been argued, is due in part to the availability of materials (Armit/Ralston 2003: 191) and has been used by archaeological typologists to differentiate the houses in general into stone and timber structures according to the material of their main structural elements. Obviously, the properties of the building material influences style and construction, but within these two material classes, different house types were developed, making individual use of the materials, and the building conditions. The resulting variability perhaps reflects not only regionally diverse social organisation and group status but also individual preference and choice.

Monumental houses

At the beginning of the Scottish Iron Age around 700BC, Scotland, and the North and West in particular, could look back on a long tradition of monumental stone constructions. The ability to erect regularly-layered corbelling for chambered cairns (Barber 1992: 18f) or to raise huge monoliths as standing stones or in stone circles proves that structural engineering in stone was already well developed in the Neolithic. The early efforts concentrated on architecture for rites

Illustration 2. The broch of Mousa, Shetland, in 2004.

and burial practices, and it was not until the end of the second millennium BC that the general focus shifted towards domestic buildings (Parker Pearson/Sharples 1999: 1). Domestic architecture was therefore recognised as a medium deliberately to display social identity, and this led to the design of buildings that created a dominant presence within the landscape. Previously, settlement sites such as the semi-subterranean Neolithic settlement at Skara Brae, Orkney, had not so imposed on the landscape. This, and the way they created relations of domestic space and social identity, probably evolved over time out of practical organisation of space rather than being the result of a planned and executed design process. In contrast to this, the new type of monumental Iron Age roundhouses became identifiable within the topography and could in turn be identified with a certain ambition in design. The increasing importance of domestic buildings hints at a new conception of architecture. The deliberate design of an edifice not only to meet the functional needs of accommodation but also to render visible the possession of a place in the landscape probably for the first time allows the general application of the term 'monumental architecture' to domestic buildings in Scotland.

The heavy structures: stone roundhouses

Architecturally-elaborate stone roundhouses in Scotland are characterised by a very structured wall construction. The best-known structures are the *brochs*; these conical structures were tower-like in appearance although their original height did probably not exceed their base diameter. The term 'broch' was established in archaeological usage in the late 19th century (Anderson 1883: 201; summarised in RCAHMS 1946: 28), deriving from the Norse word *borg* for castle or stronghold (Grant 1941: 275).

For classification and comparative studies certain traits have been identified as the definition of a true broch; most of all, the circular ground plan, the double-wall construction creating intramural space (which is described as 'galleried wall construction') and a variety of architectural details concerning the entrance passage and door fittings (MacKie 2002: 1f). Beyond the similarity of basic architectural traits of design and construction, structural comparisons reveal the diversity of brochs rather than a unified blueprint to which all structures conformed (Hedges 1987 contra MacKie 1965, 1977). Added to this, the state of preservation often prevents classification within a strict taxonomy; nevertheless, oval or odd-shaped structures that lack one or more of the key traits were excluded from the broch category and had been classified as galleried duns (Harding 2000: 5). The term 'dun' causes even more confusion, as it encompasses various types of enclosure, single or double-walled which could have been used as individual houses or envisaged as forts (Nieke 1990: 131; overview in Jones/Mattingly 1990: 61-3).

Illustration 3. Voids within inner wall face, Dun Telve.

The 'broch'-terminology has been debated as the initial associations of the term imply a defensive function for these structures. Although the architectural design emphasises strength and durability, and offers shelter and protection within apparently thick walls, this impression is conveyed only by the outer appearance, which lacks any openings bar a small single entrance. From the inside however, the hollowed character of the allegedly massive walls can be experienced, as walkways and stairs lead to intramural space and upper floor levels. The massiveness of the walls is further reduced by the insertion of voids; vertical bands of small scale openings, interrupted by lintels and allowing communication of light, air and sound between the different floor levels and the intramural spaces (Illus. 3 and 4). It is the design of the interior that reveals the real character of the buildings and it is clear that this is neither massive nor defensive against siege or artillery warfare but airy, elegant and fragile. The delicate intramural structure which creates floor areas peripheral to the central space not only reveals the sophisticated engineering of masonry with minimal dimensions but also hints at the domestic character of the buildings which is suggested by the archaeological evidence (Armit 1997b: 250). The elegant aspects of broch design can not be judged from the outside at all but are apparent once inside.

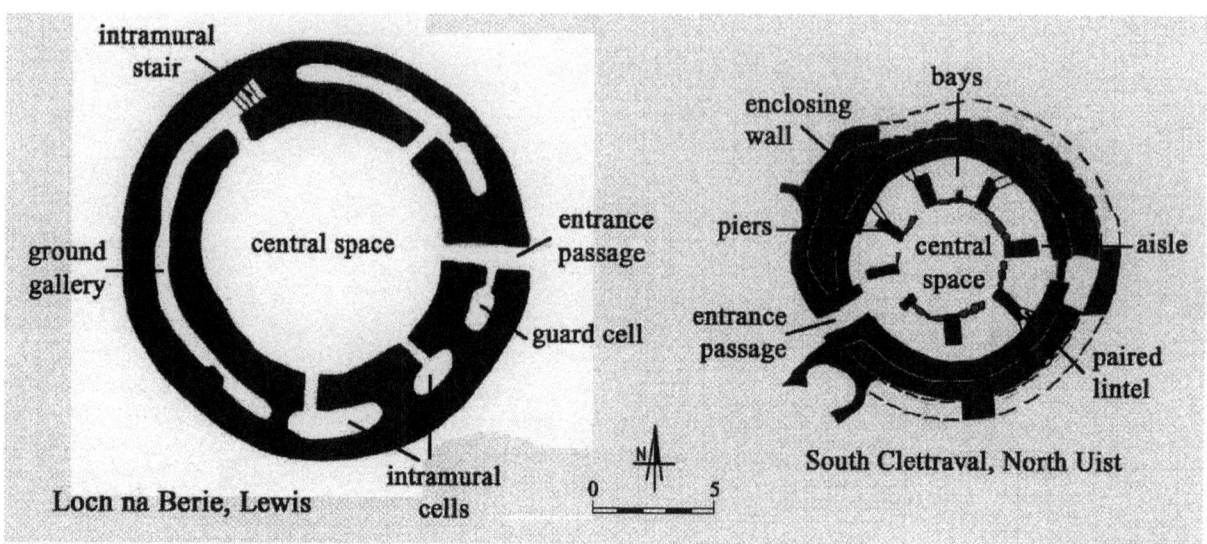

Illustration 4: Ground plans of Iron Age stone roundhouses: a) left: Complex Atlantic roundhouse Loch na Berie, Western Isles; b) right: Wheelhouse South Clettraval, Western Isles.

The prominent structural feature of wheelhouses, the radial piers, appears to indicate a completely different architectural tradition to double-walled brochs. This structural system divides the interior into a circular central area to be used as a central floor space; the peripheral floor space is separates into several bays (Armit 1996: 135). Where these are preserved, the thickness of the piers increased with height, rising into a corbelled construction, so that each pair of adjacent piers gradually created a corbelled roof over the bay between them. This arrangement left only the central space to be roofed over by other means.

The terminology of the 1990s

To emphasise similarities between sites in archaeological terms, a new terminology was developed in the 1990s (Armit 1990a: 438; 1990b: 59f; 1992: 19). This distinguished simple from more complex structures rather than considering the presence or absence of individual architectural traits, sometimes including original features such as height, that could not be verified from the surviving remains. This new terminology was intended to bring together roundhouses with comparable architectural traits and to overcome the artificial division between brochs and duns. The links between simple and more complex structures argued for a long and strong tradition in architecture, based on the continuous organisation of domestic space (Armit, 1990c: 196-7). In this new terminology, complex roundhouses encompass some elaborate architectural details, but the lack of one of these details does not immediately disqualify a structure as 'non-complex'. The high, tower-like brochs are classified within this complex class as a subgroup of 'broch towers' (Armit, 1996: 114). As a result, this (now well-established) terminology includes all brochs and galleried duns in one category: 'complex Atlantic roundhouse'.

Highlands

Criticism of this terminology has arisen particularly because of the exclusion of wheelhouses from the category (Sharples & Parker Pearson 1997: 255). Wheelhouses are strictly limited to some parts of Piggott's Atlantic province(1966: 3).

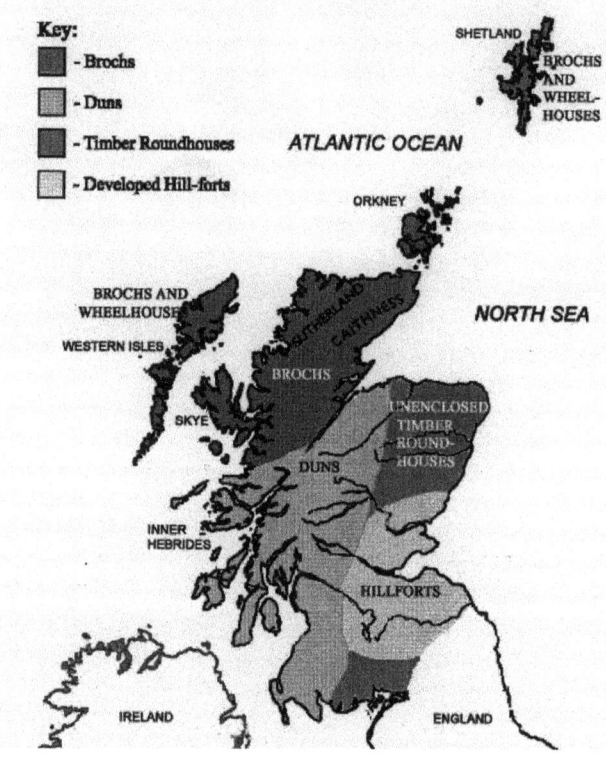

Illustration 5. Map of Scotland with provinces and dominant regional settlement types.

It is argued that, with their series of piers, they display an equally elaborate masonry construction. Therefore, they could be described as complex Atlantic roundhouses, though it makes sense to distinguish wheelhouses, with their pier construction and lack of external monumentality, as a different architectural type from brochs and galleried duns.

Although the old terminology of brochs and duns still provides a convenient shorthand, Armit's version is preferred here for various reasons (contra Sharples/Parker Pearson 1997: 255; Baines 2002: 8). Armit's classification is more orientated towards structural aspects, such as the complexity of the wall construction rather than less significant elements such as circular ground plan layout or door details; it does not create artificial differences between similar construction types. Furthermore, it reduces the biased picture created by surface-recording of insufficiently-preserved structures, which traditionally have been assumed to be brochs in the North but are assigned as galleried duns in Argyll and the West, although essentially all the structures under consideration belong to the same architectural type (Illus. 5). Wheelhouses are considered as a different type of buildings and termed as such.

Architectural analysis

Architecture orders space by bounding it. In architectural context, settlement space is confined to the area occupied by architecture and the spatial organisation within the building itself (Fletcher 1978: 229). The spatial order that is evident could result from a planned design manifesting a pattern of access, relation and communication, or it could be the accidental accumulation of architectural units. However, even an unplanned arrangement could demonstrate underlying patterns that convey the relations and functions between units, simply developed out of practicality. This means that even when the development of spatial order is apparently accidental, the spatial organisation can still reflect practical needs, convenience or certain taboos.

Spatial order is not manifested only in ground plans and in dimensions, but is also reflected in the third dimension. The organisation of elevations can use the topography to distinguish structures of similar heights in elevated and less elevated positions to separate tall from modest structures. Spatial order tends to show hierarchies, defining central and peripheral areas, public and private spaces or distinction and equality.

The analysis of space has to acknowledge that the emergence of spatial order can be achieved by chance (Hillier et al. 1978: 349) and that there are different levels of organisation, which have different change rates that relate to a particular space, scale and time (Fletcher 1978: 226). However, by analysing the particular spatial order and by comparing different spatial organisations, patterns can be detected that provide information about the intentions behind the ground plan layout. The analyst might even be able to recognize systematic design, whether conscious or accidental. The important aspect for the interpretation of spatial order is to detect hierarchies in the use of space within the ground plan and to identify different characters of space.

To analyse the use of space and to read spatial relations, a morphic language was identified and employed to infer social relations from spatial patterns (Hillier et al. 1978). This *space syntax* has been recognised in the organisation of broch sites such as Gurness/Orkney, with its maze of low, small-scale outbuildings ad was used to illustrate differential access and by extension site hierarchy (Foster 1989). Whether the main and peripheral structures had been contemporary is only important if this analysis is intended to investigate the motives behind the design of the central broch tower. Since the outbuildings encircle the broch but the design of the broch does not react to the outbuildings, the motives behind the design of the broch can only be approached by ground plan analysis of the broch itself.

The approach to architectural analysis suggested in the present paper is different from an archaeological study. Only those roundhouses which have evidence of sufficient architectural details are included. For stone roundhouses this means they need to display a degree of structural complexity, beyond possessing massive drystone masonry. Since the roundhouses are to be interpreted in terms of their architecture, the selection of sites probably represents the most complete structures of Iron Age roundhouse architecture in Scotland rather than including prototypes or failures. However, it is the atypical structure, the structural collapses and extraordinary design traits that can reveal structural weaknesses and the impact of individual choice. Well-excavated and archaeologically important sites like the broch at Jarlshof/Shetland have to be excluded due to the incompleteness of the structure.

Ground plan analysis

Two primary functions of space can be identified: to provide access within the building to individual rooms (access space) and to create room for the dwelling function itself (dwelling space). Therefore the first step of ground plan analysis is to identify the two different characters of space. Since the main function of access space is to allow circulation between rooms, its character is dynamic and therefore the term *dynamic space* was developed to characterise access space best (see Romankiewicz in prep). Dwelling space, in comparison to access space, is usually used for less mobile activities such as preparing food or sleeping as well as working, storing or keeping animals. To encapsulate the different functions represented by dwelling space and to distinguish it from access space, the term *static space* was introduced (ibid).

The analysis of ground plans is designed to identify dynamic and static areas or zones within the ground plans of individual houses. The main differentiation between rooms is their level of accessibility and privacy. The extent of accessibility, together with the size and position of a room in relation to the overall ground plan determines its quality for a public or more discrete function. The degree of privacy is reflected by the terms *public space*, *semi-public space* and *private space*. With this system, the spatial arrangements of a house can be deduced, but not, however, the function of individual rooms. This is an important limit to ground plan analysis, because the sense and meaning of privacy has almost certainly changed through time. Activities that are today seen as clearly private, such as begetting children or relieving oneself, may have been regarded as more public in the Iron Age. Hence the function of rooms can only be inferred from archaeological evidence; spatial analysis of privacy levels can offer help in relatating these archaeological finds to the character of the space. When artefactual evidence is combined with the analysis of privacy levels, interpretations regarding the spatial function of the ground plan can be postulated, explaining how the house functioned as an organism for the inhabitants and what pursuits were undertaken at what kind of level of privacy.

Character of space: dynamic and static

For the basis of this theoretical analysis it is postulated that dynamic space can never be absolutely private, since it connects zones and is therefore not peripheral to the overall circulation. The deeper rooms become within the overall ground plan sytem, the more accessibility is reduced and the character of the dynamic space changes to become semi-public. Private space however is assumed as static as privacy does not allow for further dynamic spaces beyond the limits of the private space. Public and semi-public space can contain dynamic and static zones, depending on the position (or depth) of the room in relation to the general pattern of access.

It is further postulated that the dimensions of a room also define its level of privacy. Large, spacious and high rooms are less private than small, low chambers, even though they have the same level of access. In general, larger rooms can combine dynamic and static, public and private zones, depending on their shape and layout, whereas the usage of smaller rooms is much more defined as they can only be dynamic or static. To analyse ground plans it is important to distinguish these dynamic and static zones. The pattern becomes apparent in the amount of dynamic space that connects the different entrances of the rooms with each other (Illus. 6).

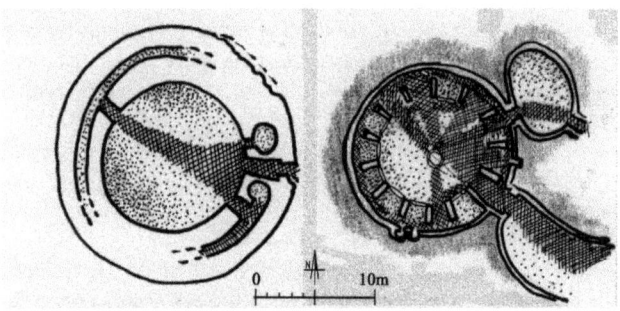

Illustration 6: Interpretation of dynamic and static space within ground plans; the hatched area marks dynamic space, the dotted area marks static space.

The problem with the roundhouse evidence in Scotland

Internal partitioning can guide or alter the distribution of dynamic space, but the evidence for internal partitioning for Iron Age roundhouses in Scotland is probably incomplete since organic material must have been used but evidence for it is mostly lost. Wattle-work, framed screens spanned with cloth, leather or hides as partitioning rarely leave traces in the ground and any modification within ground plans will probably be equally incomprehensible. Even if stonework was used for partitioning, its stratigraphic relationship to the primary phase of the building is often unclear. All this renders the organisation of space almost unrecognisable archaeologically (Hedges 1975: 66; Watkins 1980: 183).

For these reasons it has to be admitted that the spatial analysis of Iron Age ground plans for Scotland can only be a theoretical exercise, particularly because of the weak control of stratgraphical evidence of early excavations. Therefore, even such important figures as central hearths or cooking pits are ignored although it has to be acknowledged that they would have altered the theoretical access pattern that is suggested here. The reason for this theoretical approach is that a general evaluation of space could be achieved, identifying the dynamic and static qualities of rooms and room zones and quantifying its distribution.

If it is intended to interpret building use patterns, artefactual finds have to be considered as well, and by allocating functions to certain areas of the house referred from pit-contents and floor deposits speculations about the use of the room can be made. Attempts to analyse how these deposits were orientated towards cardinal directions (Marshall et al. 2004: 70f) seem plausible, but it has to be considered that those finds could represent a single event rather than habitual use. Although there is clearly scope for future work in this subject, this architectural approach concentrates on a theoretical analysis derived from architectural theory. Therefore the whole analysis can only provide a framework to interpret different levels of activity and privacy within the roundhouse. Those levels would then have to be related to the artefactual evidence, but it would still be difficult to conclude the function of the space concerned. Only when patterns of several similar sites can be detected, hypothesis could be constructed.

Hierarchy of space: additive and agglomerative

Two major types of space hierarchies can be discerned. The *additive* ground plan type adds room upon room, either successively or concentrically (Illus. 7a). This organisation of space displays a consecutive access pattern from public to private, depending on the distance of the individual room from the first main entrance. For the *agglomerative* type, rooms are designed around a centre, generating central and peripheral spaces (Illus. 7b). Since rooms at similar levels of access share the same degree of privacy, this type is less hierarchical.

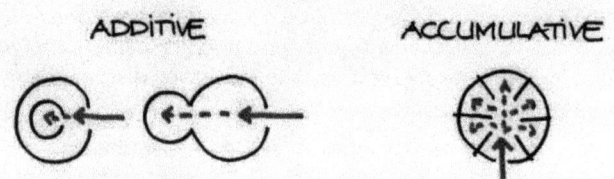

Illustration 7.: Theoretical ground plan patterns of Iron Age roundhouses in Scotland: a) additive, b) accumulative.

In the additivel type a clear hierarchy is created: this achieves more privacy with increasing depth. Starting from the main entrance area, the roundhouse space is differentiated into zones that become more and more private, whilst allowance for movements diminishes sequentially with every room. The use of dynamic space within an additive ground plan pattern is linear and sequential and by adding room upon room, zones of privacy are that increase the static zones. Static space is considered as more valuable for a dwelling function because its use can be assumed to be repetitive and uninterrupted, whereas the dynamic nature of access space makes it impossible to provide room for recurring activities or for permanent storage.

In the agglomerative pattern, the area of dynamic space is much more concentrated, resulting in a disproportional amount of dynamic space. Every room in the ground plan is accessible from the central access area, which in turn has no private character. The low proportion of static space dramatically reduces the levels of privacy and the space for static activities. The advantage of agglomerative patterns is that the levels of accessibility are not as strict and selective as in the additive pattern, with fewer possibilities to restrict access and create exclusiveness; it is generally more communal. The qualities of intermediate rooms that provide semi-public spaces and the subtleties of successive room organisation can not be created. However, dichotomous boundaries between absolutely public and absolutely private achieve an egalitarian and unrestricted ground plan pattern that offers a larger amount of communication between rooms. The only option to distinguish the character of individual peripheral zones in agglomerative ground plans lies in the design of their entrance: whether broad and inviting, or as narrow and difficult to traverse.

Ground plans thus provide data for the analyst about the character of space, of communication between rooms and their level of privacy. Beside this qualitative evaluation, it can also allow the quantification of space available for dynamic and static activities.

Levels of privacy	Character of space		Ground plan pattern	
	Dynamic space	Static space	Additive	Agglomerative
Public space	access space	zones within public rooms	successive or concentric addition of rooms from public to private	central space
Semi-public space	access space	zones within semi-public rooms		-
Private space	-	peripheral rooms		peripheral space

The analysis of ground plans gives information about the theoretical character of the house plan and allows speculations about its public and private zones as well as estimating the general hierarchical layout of the ground plan. Repetition in layouts would not only suggest similar degrees of privacy and hence comparable functions, but also hint at a deliberate design of similar ground plans. The deliberate creation of hierarchy levels in the ground plans could reflect the social function of individual rooms and of the whole building ground plan. It is hence from the level of hierarchies of the ground plan pattern that architectural assumptions regarding the social order of the community can be inferred.

Ground plan evaluation of Iron Age round houses in Scotland

A preliminarily ground plan analysis is being undertaken of selected Iron Age stone roundhouses. A first evaluation demonstrated that both ground plan patterns, additive and agglomerative patterns, occur with the roundhouses. Even within wheelhouses with a layout highly restricted by the piers, additive and agglomerative layouts were recognised, although the construction would suggest an over-proportional occurrence of agglomerative patterns (see Illus. 6). However, trends are visible, with the complex Atlantic roundhouses preferentially employing additive patterns, whereas wheelhouses generally create a more agglomerative space pattern.

This raises several questions. First of all it is interesting to see how far the construction of the different types of roundhouse influences and limits the possibilities of the ground plan. The construction of a double wall within complex Atlantic roundhouses creates a considerable amount of privacy and dynamic space at the same time by providing cells for privacy and stretches of galleries and stairs to access upper level. Furthermore, the distribution of this intramural space influences structural as well as functional characteristics. A 'classic' additive plan pattern within a complex Atlantic roundhouse (such as Dun Beag/Skye; see Illus. 6a) distributes the wall-perforating intramural space opposite the main entrance. The weak points in the overall stability of the massive ring-wall, the main entrance and the intramural cell, are placed opposite each other creating a well-balanced structure. An unbalanced structure with the intramural space organised close to the main entrance passage concentrates all interruptions of the massive masonry at one point, which reduces the structural stability dramatically (eg. Clumlie/Shetland; see Illus. 8a). However, this latter type of additive ground plan pattern is very beneficial in the creation of private and static space by leaving large parts of the central area without the need for passage to further intramural space (dynamic space). It could be argued that the requirements for the soundness of the structure were compromised in favour of a hierarchical access pattern and a large area of dwelling space.

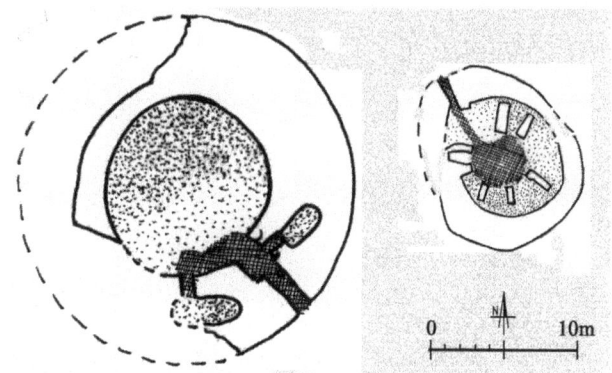

Illustration 8: Ground plans layouts: a) unbalanced distribution of intramural space creating a minimum of dynamic space, but compromising structural stability, Clumlie, Shetland; b) typical accumulative ground plan pattern of wheelhouses, Eilean Maleit, Western Isles.

The piers of wheelhouses apparently already create an agglomerative partitioning, suggesting that this is the classic layout for this stone roundhouse type (Illus. 8b). By blocking off access from the central area to individual bays or diverting access to the peripheral space along the outer wall, different levels of access and privacy were created that can be interpreted as additive patterns (see Illus. 6b). It is apparent that even the pier construction allowed for ground plan variation and outplay for individual needs of public, semi-public and private space.

The similarities in ground plan patterns of roundhouses with different structural systems, such as an agglomerative broch plan and an agglomerative wheelhouse plan, raise several interesting questions.

- Could the different hierarchy levels in ground plan layouts imply different use of space?
- Could different use of internal space imply different functions for the whole building?
- Why do roundhouses with the same architectural details have divergent ground plan layouts?
- Are roundhouses with the same general architectural details and method of construction but with different ground plan layouts still to be categorised within the same terminology?

These questions cast doubt on whether architecturally categorised structures such as complex Atlantic roundhouses or wheelhouses with different ground plan layouts can be compared and discussed as buildings with similar function.

Space and structure

The relationships between structure and ground plan use are an indicator of the elaboration and adequateness of the design. The quality of their interaction can be one point to judge the sophistication of the architecture. The fact that apparently similar ground plan patterns were combined with different structural systems seems to undermine any assumption of a strict design master plan for Scottish Iron Age roundhouses. Instead this could suggest that similar architectural ideas such as those found in a complex Atlantic roundhouse or a wheelhouse were generally adopted whereas individual structural details and ground plan layouts were rooted in earlier traditions of the community, transferred into the new architectural style. This needs to be tested if patterns relate to specific regions, size of the roundhouse or possible height (see Romankiewicz in prep.).

Monumental motives?

The analysis of ground plans and the evaluation of design quality could help in understanding the societies that build such structures; assumptions may be made about their motives for such designs.

The key question regarding domestic Iron Age architecture in Atlantic Scotland remains why such complexity developed and the reason for building monumentally has always been a stimulus for wider social interpretations.

From a purely functionalistic perspective it could be argued that the use of the building material and the design of wheelhouses and brochs were essentially topographically determined, due to climatic conditions and the availability of building material. Furthermore, massive masonry construction concerned with the adoption of stone as the main material for formal or permanent architecture was related to the fact that timber resources began to diminish in certain regions. The subterranean structure of wheelhouses is for instance regarded as the reaction to worsening climatic conditions and the need for shelter (Armit 1997a: 42).

A closer look at the design of Iron Age stone roundhouses in Scotland reveals that the deliberate design of heavy walls and external wall-faces with minimal openings utilised the scarce resources in a very conspicuous manner. If the stone buildings were just compromised structures resulting from a lack of building timber, then it seems more logical that the design would have tried to imitate timber architecture and tried to disguise the weighty and inorganic properties of the stones. The actually built stone roundhouses not only acknowledged the potential of the constructional material, but employed it to create a massive, powerful and enduring architecture from the outside and a flimsy but elegant masonry interior. The design of the massive tall and tapering outer walls of complex Atlantic roundhouses clearly respond to all architectural qualities that stone has to offer and the interior of them as well as of wheelhouses played with the limits of the material; an ability that could only have developed from long experience and tradition in building with stone. In repetition of this architectural theme of masonry, stone architecture was transformed into aesthetics as a matter of cultural preference. This theme became a recurring architectural characteristic for Scotland throughout the castle architecture of the Middle Ages and into post-medieval times (Glendinning et al., 1996: 503).

The impression of complex Atlantic roundhouses from the outside is highly cold, rejecting and easily interpreted as defensive; the artefactual evidence and the elegant interior reveal that this was only intended to convey a strong and impermeable impression for the outside. Hence the defensive character was only an impression; an aesthetic but not a practical aspect of the design. This has been realised in recent debate, although not architecturally tested, and led to an interpretation of the monumentality of complex Atlantic roundhouses, the thickness of their walls, the possible height of up to 15m and the most impressive interior as being designed to express potency, permanence and essentially power (Sharples 1984: 119-21). The similarity of the structural appearance across the area was seen as a result of competition with the houses as symbols of status (Barrett 1981: 215). Barrett concluded that not only the finished structure, but also the process of construction, was set out to impress, and as an acknowledgement of the authority that was able to commission such building projects. It seems that the environment for such an undertaking requires stability to allow expending material and human resources on architecture. This perspective would deny that the architecture was born in times of threat. Monumental architecture would need time and security to develop, but the reasons for building monumental structures most likely arose in times of social stress or insecurity, where reassurance of power and status had to be visualised by means of built statements.

The fact that wheelhouses create an exclusively internal monumentality was read as a different way of conveying status and power, probably in a different social environment as these structures impress once inside and not externally. This requires the person to be impressed by the elegance of the pier masonry and the sophistication of the whole construction of the internal space to be allowed into the house (Armit 1997: 43). While the impression of monumental complex Atlantic roundhouses is rather abstract and general, the monumentality of wheelhouses is designed for more specific and individual aims.

Beside this interpretation as symbols of power, Hingley proposed two further meanings of monumental houses (1995:

187). He suggested that the design of the building was a symbol of deliberate isolation and division, and interpreted this in a social meaning of isolation of a single domestic group against others, and in an environmental sense as a division between cultural space and the outside world. Thinking his reading of the house design further would mean that it is based on a dualistic philosophy that discerns in 'them and us', 'outside and inside', 'culture and wild'.

These ideas would indirectly suggest that the societies that built these structures were recognising differences and incompatibility more than they accepted a sense of community and integration. Hingley's ideas conclusively point towards a dialectic philosophy of an introspective society, which was not living *with* the natural surroundings and other groups but *in opposition*, perhaps reacting to and creating a hostile climate, socially as well as environmentally.

The main problem with all these interpretations is that they refer to the external appearance and concentrate on complex Atlantic roundhouses which have thick stone-built outer walls with no openings as points of communication to the outside except for the small entrance. Within this interpretation, wheelhouses were regarded as chronologically later and hence seen as the result of social changes reflected in the demise of the construction of complex Atlantic roundhouses. However, recent research (Ascough et al. 2004: 618) suggests that wheelhouses and complex Atlantic roundhouses could have been built contemporary and therefore wheelhouses cannot be excluded from discussion of the social environment that allowed building complex Atlantic roundhouses.

Regarding the manifestation of social isolation, Hingley interprets the thick walls of the houses as symbolic boundary lines to define 'within' and 'outside'. He regards the creation of social isolation as symbolised by the thickness of the wall. This thickness can however not be experienced except when passing through it at the entrance and is put *ad absurdum* by the insertion of cells and galleries that perforate the allegedly massive wall. Far more than the 'symbolic' wall thickness, it is the arrangement of internal space that enables the experience of social isolation and the concentration on an internal centre rather than the external world. Within an additive ground plan that successively reduces access to create private zones furthest from the entrance, distances and boundary lines are created to experience the diametrically opposed concepts of 'in and out'. The agglomerative ground plan visualises the focus around a central area in the very centre of the house. All peripheral space is oriented towards this centre with no reference to the outside; this highlights the boundary line described by Hingley. It is hence the analysis of the ground plans, of levels of access and the character of the space that underpins Hingley's theories and would support the dialectic world view of the societies.

Conclusion

The analysis of Iron Age stone roundhouses in Scotland has demonstrated that there are certain motives behind their designs and that structure and ground plan layout were adjusted accordingly. Stone material was employed because it was readily available, but the way it was used shows that its properties of massiveness and solidity were pushed to the limits to create a sophisticated double wall construction or weightless pier masonry. The limits of timber supply or the different properties of the local stone material were overcome by structural design. The need for central and peripheral space was reflected in the layouts and, although the roundhouses conform to a general circular plan, each structural plan was flexible enough to fulfil its own requirements. The development of additive and agglomerative patterns within similar structures not only displays the flexibility of structure and ground plan, but also the ability of the builder to play with the layout in order to achieve the desired design.

The analysis has been able to highlight the importance of socio-cultural factors as the main motives of design. The inward-looking layout of brochs and wheelhouses, their monumental dimensions of height, wall thickness and internal space reveal how far environmental limits could be overcome or ignored. This uncovers the real potential of the architecture and the people who built it.

In this preliminary statement it is suggested that the physical substance of the roundhouses could generally reflect the relation of the builders to their environment and although the introspective character of these structures does apparently ignore the 'world beyond', the design was still a reaction to it and was always part of it. Therefore, the roundhouse designs reacted to and related with the limits of the environment as well as technology and material supply. Architecture is always the interplay of all factors, social, economic, technological and environmental and no single explanation can be correct to explain the motives of design.

This architectural approach laid out in this interim statement could help providing the archaeological interpretation with new, rather technical, functional and aesthetical arguments by identifying the elaboration and sophistication of building traditions in the Scottish Iron Age. These ideas are developed further in the final thesis and the author would appreciate comments and suggestions.

References

Anderson, J. 1883. *Scotland in Pagan times. The Iron Age. The Rhind lectures in Archaeology for 1881*, vol. 2. Edinburgh: David Douglas.

Armit, I., 1990a. Broch-building in Northern Scotland: the context of innovation. *World Archaeology*, 21: 435-45.

Armit, I., 1990b. Brochs and Beyond in the Western Isles. In Armit, I. (ed.): *Beyond the Brochs: Changing Perspectives on the Atlantic Scottish Iron Age*: 41-70. Edinburgh: Edinburgh University Press.

Armit, I., 1990c. Epilogue. In Armit, I. (ed.): *Beyond the Brochs: Changing perspectives on the Atlantic Scottish Iron Age*: 194-210. Edinburgh: Edinburgh University Press.

Armit, I., 1992. *The Later Prehistory of the Western Isles of Scotland*. BAR British. Series. 221. Oxford: Archaeopress.

Armit, I., 1996. *The Archaeology of Skye and the Western Isles*. Edinburgh: Edinburgh University Press/Historic Scotland.

Armit, I., 1997a. *Celtic Scotland*. London: Batsford.

Armit, I., 1997b. Cultural landscapes and identities: a case study in the Scottish Iron Age. In Gwilt, A. and Haselgrove, C., (eds.): *Reconstructing Iron Age Societies*: 248-53. Oxbow Monograph, 71. Oxford: Oxbow.

Armit, I., 2003. *Towers in the North*. Stroud, Tempus.

Armit, I. and Ralston, I.B.M. 2003. The Iron Age. In Edwards, K.J. and Ralston, I.B.M., (eds.): *Scotland after the Ice Age. Environment, Archaeology and History, 8000 BC – AD 1000.* 169-93. Edinburgh University Press.

Ascough, P.L., Cook, G.T., Dugmore, A.J., Barber, J., Higney E. and Scott, E.M. 2004. Holocene variations in the Scottish marine radiocarbon reservoir effect. *Radiocarbon*, vol. 46 (2): 611-20.

Baines, A. 2002. The inherited Past of the Broch: On Antiquarian Discourse and Contemporary Archaeology. *Scottish Archaeological Journal*, 24 (March 2002), part 1: 1-20.

Barber, J. 1992. Megalithic architecture. In Sharples, N. and Sheridan, A., (eds.): *Vessels for the ancestors. Essays on th Neolithic of Britain and Ireland*: 13-32. Edinburgh: Edinburgh University Press.

Barrett, J.C., 1981. Aspects of the Iron Age in Atlantic Scotland: A case study in the problems of archaeological interpretation. *Proceedings of the Society of Antiquaries of Scotland*, 111: 205-19. Edinburgh.

Bersu, G., 1950. Fort' at Scotstarvit Covert, Fife. *Proceedings of the Society of Antiquaries of Scotland*, 82 (1948-49): 241-63. Edinburgh.

Binding, G, 1999. *Architektonische Formenlehre*. Primus, Darmstadt [4th edition].

Ching, F.D.K., 1995. *A visual dictionary of architecture*. New York: John Wiley & Sons.

Fletcher, R., 1978. Issues in the analysis of settlement space. In Green, D., Haselgrove, C. and Spriggs, M., (eds.): *Social Organisation and Settlement: Contributions from Anthropology, Archaeology and Geography*. BAR International. Series, 47. Part II: 225-40. Oxford. Archaeopress.

Foster, S. M. 1989. Analysis of spatial patterns in buildings (access analysis) as an insight into social structure: examples from the Scottish Iron Age. *Antiquity*, 63: 40-50. Oxford.

Glendinning, M., MacInnes, R. and MacKechnie, A. 1996. *A history of Scottish Architecture: From the Renaissance to the Present Day*. Edinburgh: Edinburgh University Press.

Grant, W. 1941. *The Scottish National Dictionary*, vol. II. Edinburgh: The Scottish Association Ltd.

Harding, D.W. 2000. *The Hebridean Iron Age: Twenty Years' Research*, Occ. Paper Ser., 20. Edinburgh. University of Edinburgh, Dep. of Archaeology.

Hedges, J. 1975. Excavation of two Orcadian burnt mounds at Liddle and Beaquoy. *Proceedings of the Society of Antiquaries of Scotland*, 106: 39-98. Edinburgh.

Hedges, J.W. 1987. *Bu, Gurness and the Brochs of Orkney. Part III, Bu*, BAR British. Series, 165. Oxford: Archeopress.

Hillier, B., Leaman, A., Stansall, P. And Bedford, M. 1978. Space Syntax. In Green, D., Haselgrove, C., and Spriggs, M., (eds.): *Social Organisation and settlement. Anthropology, Archaeology and Geography*, Part II. BAR International. Series, 47: 343-85. Oxford.

Hingley, R. 1992. Society in Scotland from 700 BC to AD 200. *Proceedings of the Society of Antiquaries of Scotland*, 122: 7-53. Edinburgh.

Hingley, R. 1995. The Iron Age in Atlantic Scotland: Searching for the meaning of the substantial house. In Hill, J.D. and Cumberpatch, C. (eds.): *Different Iron Ages: Studies in the Iron Age in temperate Europe*, BAR International. Series. 602: 185-94. Oxford. Archaeopress.

Jones, B. and Mattingly, D. 1990. *An Atlas of Roman Britain*. Oxford: Basil Blackwell.

MacKie, E.W., 1965. The origin and development of the broch and wheelhouse building cultures of the Scottish Iron Age. *Proceedings of the Society of Antiquaries of Scotland*, 31: 93-146. London.

MacKie, E.W. 1977. *Science and Society in Prehistoric Britain*. London: Paul Elek.

MacKie, E.W., 2002. *The Roundhouses, Brochs and Wheelhouses of Atlantic Scotland c. 700 BC - AD 500: Architecture and material culture. Part 1, The Orkney and Shetland Isles*, BAR British. Series, 342. Oxford: Archaeopress.

Marshall, P., Mulville, J., Parker Pearson, M. and Ingram, C., 1999. *The Late Bronze Age and Early Iron Age community at Cladh Hallan, South Uist. Excavation in 1999*, unpubl. Interim Report. Sheffield: Dep. of Archaeology, Sheffield University.

Nieke, M.N. 1990. Fortifications in Argyll: Retrospect and Future Prospect. In Armit, I., (ed.): *Beyond the Broch: Changing Perspectives on the Later Iron Age in Atlantic Scotland*: 131-42. Edinburgh: Edinburgh University Press, Edinburgh.

Parker Pearson, M. And Sharples, N. 1999. *Between Land and Sea. Excavation at Dun Vulan, South Uist*, SEARCH vol. 3. Sheffield: Sheffield University Press.

Piggott, S., 1966. A scheme for the Scottish Iron Age In Rivet, A. L. F., (ed.): *The Iron Age in Northern Britain*: 1-25. Edinburgh: Edinburgh University Press.

Rakob, F.J. 1985. Bautechnik und Ingenieurleistungen der Römer. In Rakob, F.J. (ed.): *Baugeschichte und europäische Kultur I, Forschung und Information*, vol. 37: 83-94. Berlin: Colloquium Verlag.

Romankiewicz, T. 2002 *Opus Caementitium – Zur Einordnung einer Bautechnik in ihre Zeit*, unpubl. Abschlussarbeit, Fachhochschule Köln, Germany.

Romankiewicz, T. in prep. *Roundhouse construction in Iron Age Scotland – an architectural approach*. Current PhD-thesis Berlin: Technical University of Berlin.

Royal Commission on the Ancient and Historic Monuments of Scotland (RCAHMS), 1946. *Twelfth report with an inventory of the ancient monuments of Orkney and Shetland, report and introduction*, vol. 1. Edinburgh: HMSO.

Sharples, N., 1984. Excavations at Pierowall Quarry, Westray, Orkney. *Proceedings of the Society of Antiquaries of Scotland*, 114: 75-125. Edinburgh.

Sharples, N. and Parker Pearson, M., 1997. Why were brochs built?. In Gwilt, A. and Haselgrove, C., (eds.): *Reconstructing Iron Age Societies*. Oxford: Oxbow Monograph, 71: 254-65. Oxford.

Trigger, B. 1978. *Time and Traditions – Essays in Archaeological interpretation*. Edinburgh: Edinburgh University Press.

Watkins, T. 1980b. Excavation of a settlement and souterrain at Newmill, near Bankfoot, Perthshire. *Proceedings of the Society of Antiquaries of Scotland*, 110: 165-208. Edinburgh.

4
Landscape, Material Culture and Social Process along Galician Iron Age: the Architecture of Castros of Neixón (Galicia, Spain)

Xurxo M. Ayán Vila

Padre Sarmiento Institute on Galician Studies

High Council for Scientific Research (Galice, Spain)

Abstract

This article presents an archaeological analysis of Castro Grande de Neixón (Boiro, A Coruña, Galicia) based on what was discovered during the excavations carried out between 2003 and 2007. Our research focuses on the monumental architecture made up by the upper part of the hillfort. Inside a number of storage pits that were used during the fourth and third centuries BC were found. The works carried out in the defensive outside ditches located at the SE entrance of this part of the hillfort have added a great number of pieces of Mediterranean origin (Punic ceramic) and a number of deposits of ritual nature. Taking this record as a starting point, we believe we are faced with architectural scenery from the 2nd Iron Age that was used by some elite groups to negotiate their identity. These elite groups assumed the alocton material culture in an organization into a hierarchy process and a social complexity process.

The biography of a monumental architecture (7th century B.C. – 3rd century A.D.)

The Galician Iron Age covers the period between the emergence of the first fortified settlements (Castros/ Hillforts) during the ninth and eighth centuries B.C., and the roman conquest of August in the nineteenth century B.C. (Sastre 2002; Parcero 2003; Queiroga 2003; González Ruibal 2006a).

In the Northwest Iberian Peninsula, Rias Baixas is the most dynamic region, the most populated and the most open to overseas influences, a region where already in the eighth century B.C. Phoenician seafarers went round in their tin mineral hunt (González Ruibal 2004; 2006). The archaeological area of Castros of Neixón is located in one of these Rias (Boiro, A Coruña). It is the only one of its kind in our country, since two Castros are located on this Ria, one next to the other: the so-called Castro Pequeno at the peninsula end, and Castro Grande located inland (Ayán 2005; 2008).

Within the cultural landscape of the Arousa Ria and the Barbanza mountains, the Neixón End looks like an emblematic place and a true milestone for the rural and sailor communities of the area. In this sense, it is a complex area that was home of important economical activities in the old times (tin mining, wolfram, anchorage for smuggled tobacco) and also nowadays (shellfish gathering, fishing). But at the same time, it is still a symbolic reference. It is used to celebrate traditional festivities like the famous Romaría of Neixón (that takes place in August). It is a natural, economical, social and symbolic area as well as an archaeological site and a patrimonial resource. In this regards, the Hillforts of Neixón are a real historiographic myth in the Galician Iron Age Archaeology) since the first excavation works carried out during the 1920's by F. López Cuevillas and F. Bouza Brey (1926-1927) were used as a basis to establish the first general synthesis of the so-called *Hillfort culture* or *cultura castreña*.

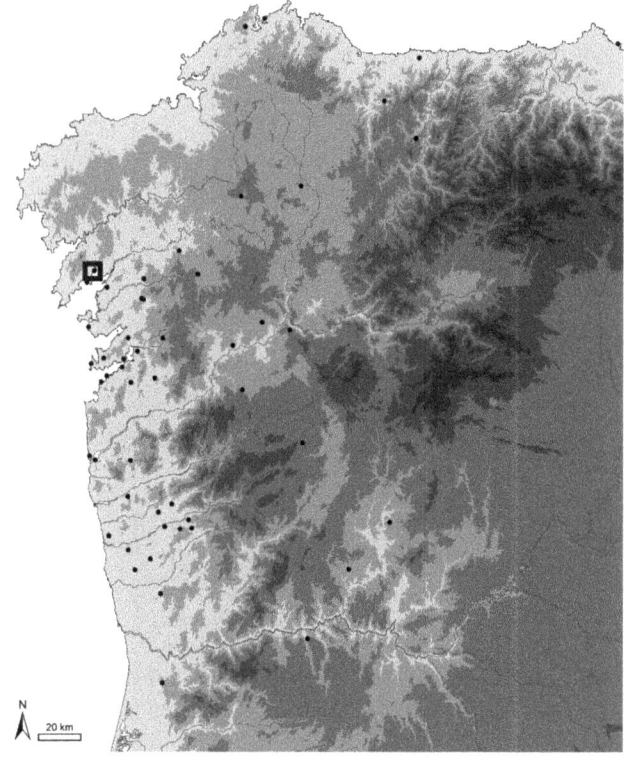

Figure 1. Excavated 2nd Iron Age hillforts in NW of Iberian Peninsula and location of *castros de Neixón*.

The Castros of Neixón are very interesting from a scientific point of view mainly because they allow the study of the changes experienced by local communities throughout 1500 years at a micro spatial scale: the birth of Hillforts, the impact of Carthaginian and Phoenician trade, the social changes that took place during the Second Iron Age, the impact of Romanization, etc... This archaeological potential explains our long-term archaeological project in this area, a project that has been carried out since 2003 in systematic excavation campaigns. These works have made it possible to reconstruct the biography of all this monumental architecture and to understand better the role of Architecture as a tool to reconstruct the reality of society.

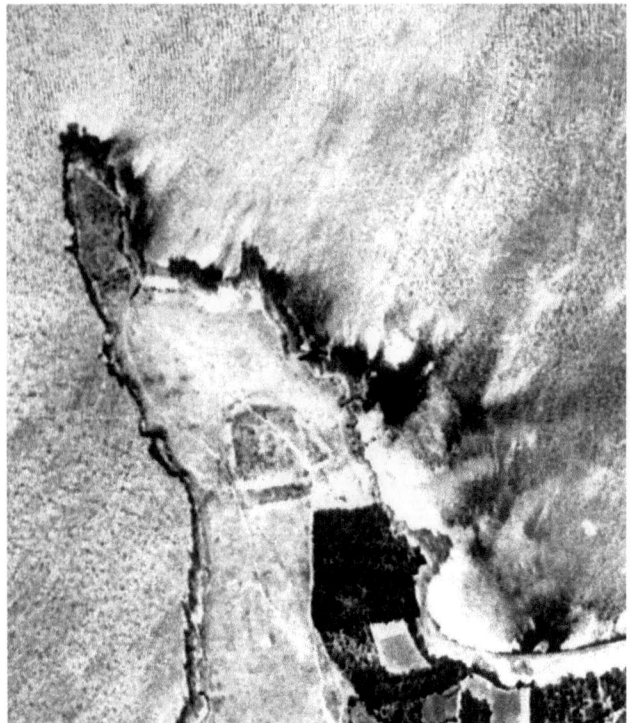

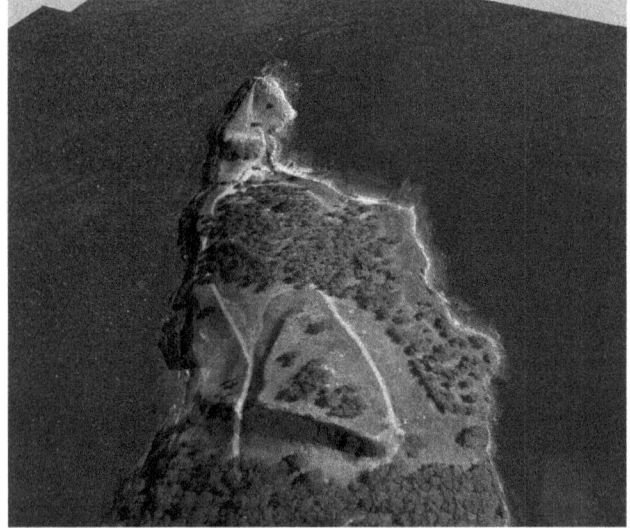

Figure 2. *Castros de Neixón* in 1956 (up), and 3D restitution (below).

Role and sense of an architectural form: Neixón as a central place and architectural scenery.

The Hillfort is the only housing area Known for the whole Iron Age in Galicia; up to now, we have not found any watching posts, or small villages at the bottom of the valley or open hamlets, as it happens in other areas throughout the Iberian Peninsula and Europe (Parcero et al. 2007). There is not much information to support the existence of fortified enclosures specialized in different tasks or that were temporarily used. The excavation works that are being carried out in Castro Grande of Neixón are changing the view outstandingly, and this archaeological area is incorporated into the dynamics of the Atlantic façade during the second Iron Age.

In this sense, the upper part of Castro Grande was put up *ex novo* around the fifth-fourth centuries B.C. following a perfectly defined architectural line. So, the enclosure was surrounded with a huge perimeter ditch. The excavated section of this ditch is about 2.80 m and 3 m deep. In the SE, an access defined by a space in the ditch was fitted out. Originally the defensive system used to have a palisade made of oak posts, which was later replaced by an earth parapet fitting the entry door.

This monumental architecture defended, between the fourth and third centuries B.C., an enclosure with no houses inside it. There were a number of pits to store cereal. Therefore, we are talking about a fortified area used to store the community farming/food surpluses, and it became a real heart for the "Praestamarcos" tribe.

Figure 3. 3D reconstruction of *Castro Grande de Neixón*.

The Castro Grande area can be described as architectural scenery within the hillfort cultural landscape, constituting a polysemous and multifunctional area, symbolically punished by the local community by means of votive deposits and communal ceremonies. In our opinion, it is clear that Architecture is a building technology of reality, a tool that builds material culture, constituting devices of polysemous, multidimensional and multifunctional nature. The walls in Castro Grande of Neixón (like walls in other fortified settlements) are a result of social action, of the group effort to build up a monumental, social and symbolic space. This Architecture had defensive purposes, that is, to protect the enclosure, but at the same time it demarcated the social welfare area, it became a control and constraint tool of the community itself, and constituted a monumental element, built to see and to be seen, conceived as the materialization of the settlement prestige image.

But this monumental and multifunctional area had a specific task, related to the rationality pattern of the people living in the Castro Grande of Neixón. In this sense we can say after four excavation campaigns in the upper part of the site, that these areas were in their origin, during the second Iron Age, not only a storage area, but also a symbolic place where several activities of social and/or ritual nature took place.

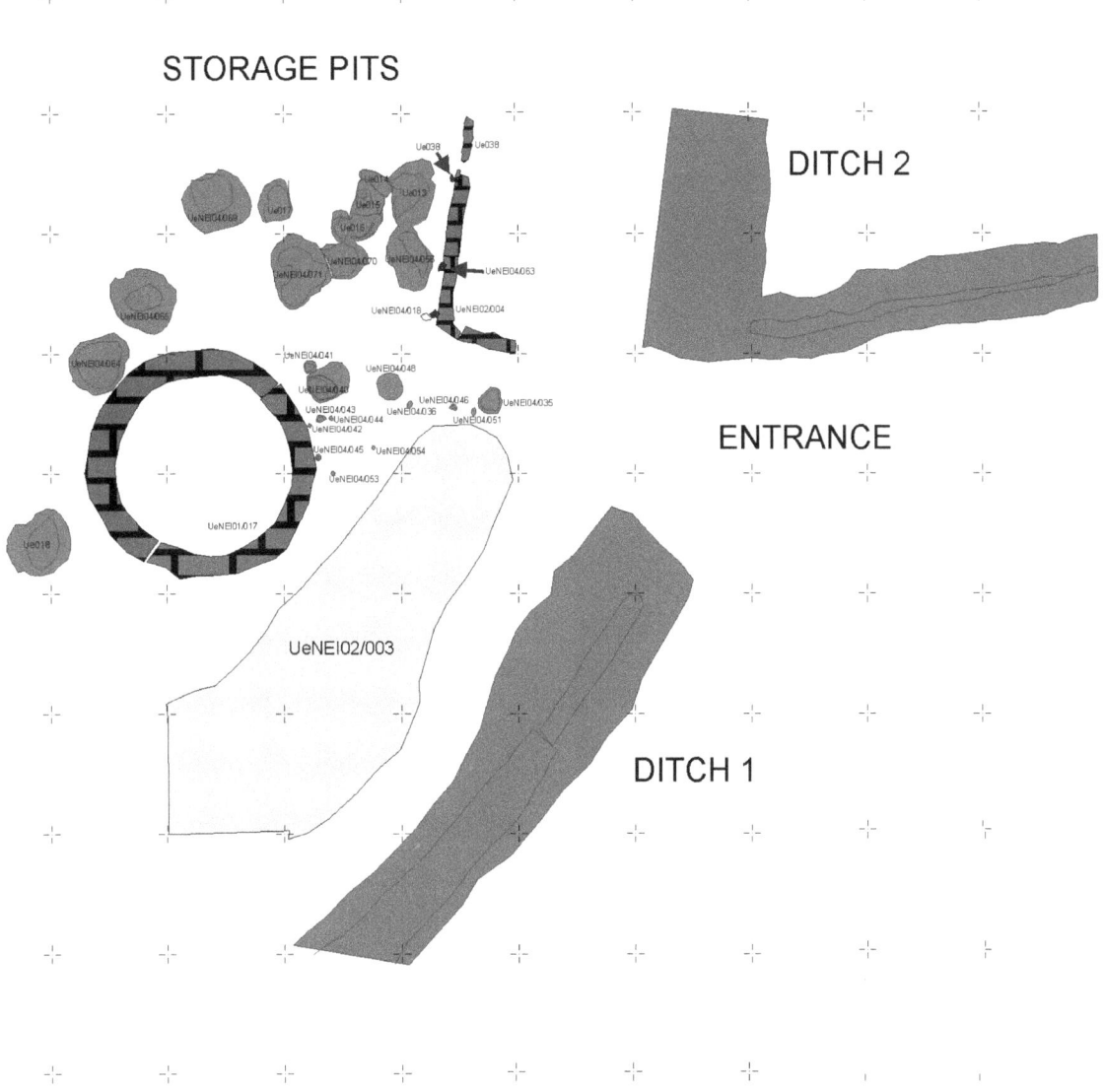

Figure 4. Castro Grande de Neixón: 2nd Iron Age entrance.

A place for business, a landscape to find their identity

During this period the use of these storage structures is a fact. An early recovery of the ditch can be seen throughout the second Iron Age. This fact makes us think that at the end of the second century B.C. the pit was totally clogged, losing its defensive nature. Therefore, the pit section 01 shows an intentional filling deposit at the bottom made of big schist blocks. Successive layers of shells were placed on it, originating an intentional deposit made up of additions, next to the entrance. Between the fourth and second centuries B.C. the filling was completed with two big ceramic deposits, where some Punic materials are mixed with indigenous ceramics. The Punic ceramic that was exhumed in the pit is that of ritual type (*kalathos*, *pithoi*, urns and *askós* from Ibiza) whereas the one found in the filling is of domestic nature (small jugs and amphorae).

All this documentation related to Punic ceramic and other products from the East, like an Aribalo vessel dated the fourth century B.C. or (aryballos) or the records of indigenous imitations of the alocton material culture, prove that this was an area greatly influenced by the Mediterranean culture. These people controlled their trade exchanges and renegotiated the group identity through material culture (architecture, ceramics, metallurgy).

The materials of Punic origin exceptionally documented in the site may indicate the role of Neixón as a distribution centre of these products during the second stage of Punic trade, that is, between the fifth and second centuries B.C.

On the other hand, the imported ceramic found in the ditch which we have called rituals, related to malacologic remains, to a dog burial, and to indigenous ceramic used to drink alcoholic beverages (*Toralla* jugs), may indicate the practice of communal ceremonies, maybe as a social unity mechanism and a establishment of the indigenous elite power, materialized by the celebration of a ritual banquet, following the parallels documented in nearby sites like A Lanzada (González Ruibal 2004: 37).

Figure 5. Storage pits (IV-III cal. BC).

The combination of all these evidences leads us to consider the use of that entrance and, by extension, the use of the whole upper part of Castro Grande as a social area of ritual nature. Everybody knows about the symbolic nature of the settlement and village entrances during the European Protohistory and the Classical Period (Parker Pearson 1999).

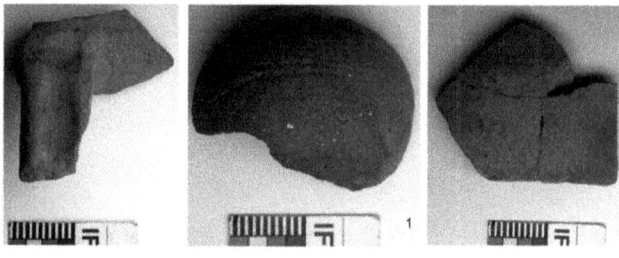

Figure 6. Punic pottery discovered into the storage pits. Number 1 is an indigenous imitation of punic pottery.

These preliminary areas (facing the sunrise, a metaphor of life reproduction and of social body) were symbolically punished with the erection of elements of apotropaic nature, like the well-known statues of Galician warriors. Some were found *in situ* or *in loco*, linked to some hillforts doors (Bettencourt 2003). Along this line, just a slight look to Recent Prehistory and to Protohistory adds many parallelisms regarding the use of these pit sections related to monumental enclosures entrances (Hingley 1990; Hill 1996).

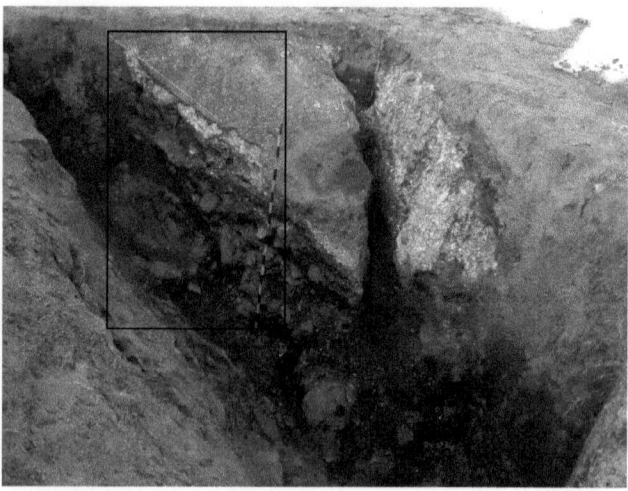

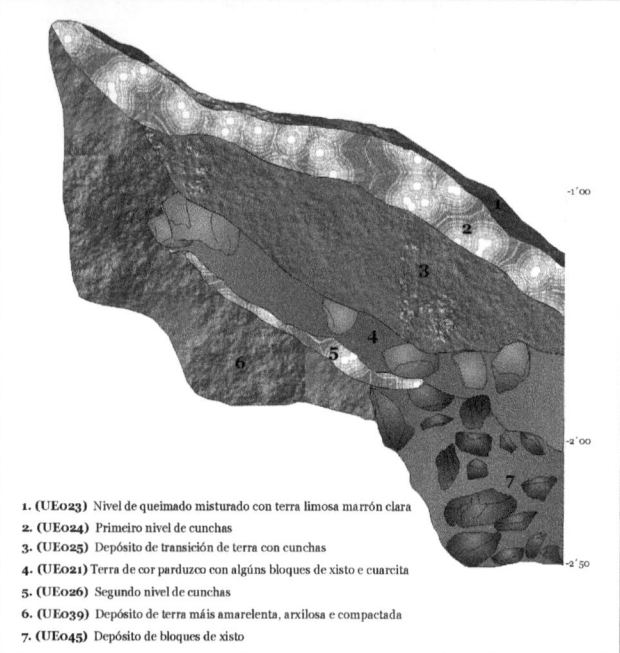

Figure 7. Ditch 1: stratigraphic profile.

Therefore, for instance, during the Neolithic period and the Bronze Age these enclosures were very often used in social celebrations of ritual nature and domestic materials of votive nature, materials related to daily work routine of these communities were placed on them (Owok 2005; McFadyen 2006). In this regards, material culture is seen as a tool to build the social reality. This fact has been stated in the Atlantic and Central European cultures, where elite warriors used alocton material culture (Greek, Phoenician and Carthaginian ceramic) as prestige elements, in rituals, feasts and banquets where alcoholic beverages were drank (Arnold 1999).

The finding of all these Punic materials at the SE entrance, as well as the probable burial of a dog and the votive deposit of material culture elements of unusual nature (hafted cervid horn, iron axe, ceramic ampoule, bronze fibula) suggest a ritual use of this architecture which demarcates the upper part of Castro Grande.

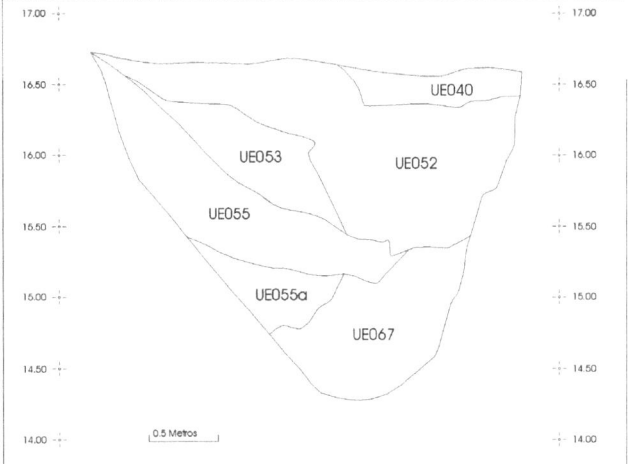

Figure 8. Ditch 2: stratigraphic profile.

Figure 9. Ditch 2: prestige elements of material culture.

Consequences: new architectural scenes for a complex society

Finally, it is quite suggestive to see this monumental enclosure as another example of the architectural scenes that arose in the Northwest hillfort communities since the first Iron Age. So, for example, the upper part of the Asturian hillfort acropolis of Chao Sanmartín suggests a cultural and architecturalized space. Its entrance was symbolically punished by the votive placement of a human skull (a woman's skull probably) (Villa and Cabo 2003). Another example is the upper part of As Laias (Ourense), with a huge number of silos and structures of communal nature used to store cereal (López and Alvarez 2000). These examples may be the precedent of those enclosures located on top of Phase III big hillforts, like Monte Mozinho, San Cibrán de Lás or Coaña, enclosures that were not used as housing areas but as social, religious and communal areas.

Regarding Castro Grande, the building practice probably dates back to the silos that were characteristic of open villages during the Late Bronze Age in South and North Galicia (Lima and Prieto 2002). It helped the sedentarization process of the communities during the First Iron Age and originated a tendency to store the surpluses, which ended in the Second Iron Age.

The social and economical complexity of the Second Iron Age in the peninsula and in the Atlantic context can be seen in the agricultural practice and in the storage system that is now found in specialized areas. Its aim was to protect and guarantee the surpluses. These *storage pits* have been documented in British and Irish fortified settlements, and therefore there are many examples. The most outstanding is the *Danebury site*. Its central part has pits and silos with great storage capacity (Cunliffe 2004: 45, fig. 43). The storage pits documented in *Conderton Camp* are another good example. They are spatially linked to the parapet and to the enclosure entrance (Dyer 2003: 58-9, figs. 37-38). Sometimes a great number of granaries are found inside the fortified enclosure, between the houses and the defensive system, like the well-known *Moel and Gaer* in Wales (Dyer 2003: 34, fig. 22; Champion et al. 1991: 369, fig. 9.11). This fact led part of the investigation group to believe that grain storage was one of the main functions of this type of settlements (Cunliffe 1978: 268).

The silos, just like warehouses-houses were part of the communal storage systems that became quite popular during the Iron Age in the Mediterranean Iberian Peninsula (Buxó 1997: 253). Although these silos are located outside the settlements, near the fields and rivers, in the Northwest Iberian Peninsula, on the contrary, the documented storage structures of communal nature are placed inside the fortified area. In this regard, the evidences exhumed in Castrovite are a good example (contemporary with the upper part of Castro Grande) of the presence of cereal storage devices, with a specific terrace with storage and processing structures, some mills and burned cereal (González and Carballo 2001) and also in Laias (López and Alvarez 2000). This last site has in its upper part, some silos made of vegetable frameworks covered with clay, as well as some containers insulated by clay paving, boards and cork.

and redistribution in a certain political region (González Ruibal 2006-2007: 317-20). Like in *Danebury*, we have to imagine that these areas were central places where fundamental activities for social reproduction of a community scattered around the area took place. Likewise, in the case of Neixón this facet would be increased since it probably redistributed imported alocton materials from Punic trade.

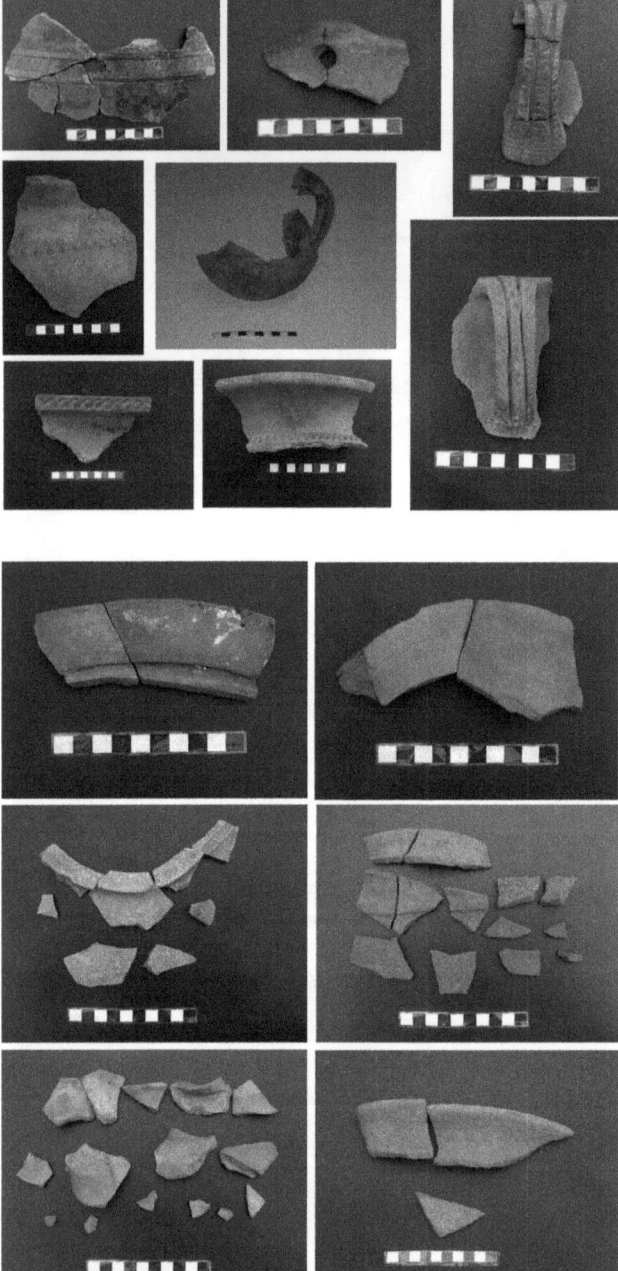

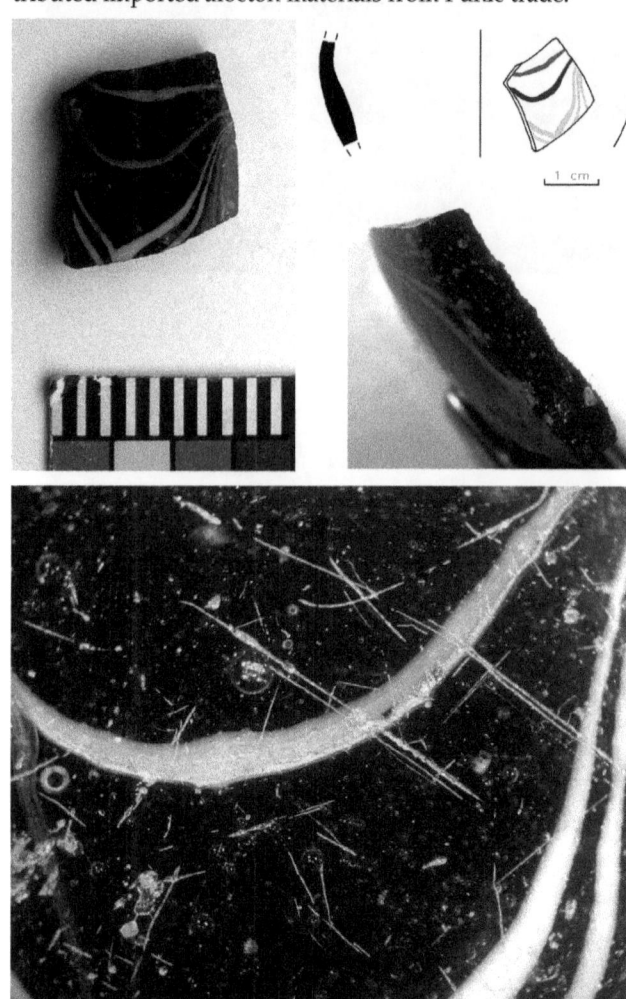

Figure 11. Punic aryballos of Castro Grande de Neixón.

Figure 10. Ditch 1: indigenous pottery (up) and punic imported pottery (below).

In a period of economic growth such as the fifth and fourth centuries B.C., the surpluses increase originated the need to have more specific installations in certain sites for trade and commercial exchange. These places would become real central post of aggregates; In A. González Ruibal's opinion, Castrovite or Laias were places for storage

Figure 12. Ditch 1: *Toralla* jar (IV-III BC). Decoration is influenced by mediterranean punic patterns.

Appendix

	Datation Code	Material	BP Age	Calibrated 2 sigmas
MU040825J02	Ua-34405	Charcoal	3400 ± 40	Cal BC 1779-1607
MU040825J08	Ua-34406	Bone	2530 ± 50	Cal BC 803-508
MU050802J01	Ua-34407	Charcoal	2 250 ± 35	Cal BC 322-205
MU050808J01	Ua-34408	Charcoal	2 220 ± 35	Cal BC 382-202
MU060824J01	Ua-34409	Charcoal	2 235 ± 35	Cal BC 329-204
MU060829J04	Ua-34410	Charcoal	2 110 ± 35	Cal BC 206-43

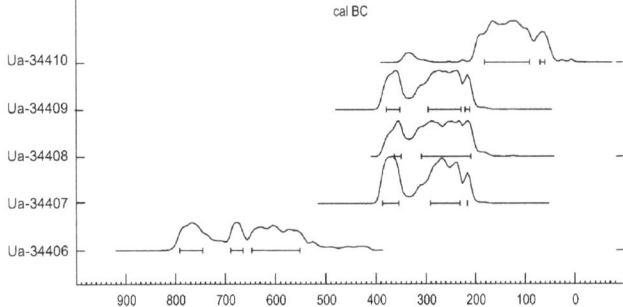

Figure 13. Castro Grande de Neixón. Calibrated dates distribution.

References

Álvarez González, Y. and López González, L. F. 2000. La secuencia cultural del asentamiento de Laias: evolución espacial y funcional del poblado. *Actas do III Congresso de Arqueologia Peninuslar* (1999, Vila-Real): 523-30. Porto.

Arnold, B. 1999. 'Drinking the Feast': Alcohol and the Legitimation of Power in Celtic Europe. *Cambridge Archaeological Journal*, 9:1: 71-93. Cambridge.

Ayán Vila, X. M. (coord.). 2005. *Os castros de Neixón*. Serie Keltia, 30. Noia: Toxosoutos.

Ayán Vila, X. M. (coord.). 2008. *Os castros de Neixón, II: de espazo natural a paisaxe cultural*. Serie Keltia, 39. Noia: Toxosoutos.

Ayán Vila, X. M. 2008. A Round Iron Age: The Circular House in the Hillforts of the Northwestern Iberian Peninsula. *e-Keltoi. Journal of Interdisciplinary Celtic Studies 6: the Celts in Iberian Peninsula*: 903-1003. http://www.uwm.edu/Dept/celtic/ekeltoi/volumes/vol6/6_19/ayan_6_19.pdf

Ayán Vila, X. M. and Blanco Míguez, D. 2008. Presentation of the creative, relativist and multicultural blog of the castros de Neixón archaeological Project (Galicia, Spain). *Archaeolog*. http://traumwerk.stanford.edu/archaeolog/2008/04/presentation_of_the_creative_r.html

Bettencourt, A. M. S. 2003. Expressôes simbólicas e rituais da Idade do Ferro do Noroeste de Portugal. En *Arquitectando Espaços: da natureza à metapolis*: 131-150. Porto-Coimbra.

Buxó, R. 1997. *Arqueología de las Plantas*. Barcelona: Crítica.

Carballo Arceo, L. X. and González Ruibal, A. 2003. A cultura castrexa do NW da Península Ibérica en Galicia. *Boletín Auriense*, 33: 37-75. Ourense.

Champion, T., Gamble, C., Shennan, S. and Whittle, A. 1991. *Prehistoria de Europa*. Barcelona: Crítica.

Criado Boado, F. and Parcero Oubiña, C. (eds.). 1997. *Landscape, Archaeology, Heritage*. TAPA (*Traballos en Arqueoloxía da Paisaxe*) 2. Santiago: GIArPa.

Cunliffe, B. 1978. *Iron Age Communities of the British Isles*. London; Routledge and Kegan Paúl.

Cunliffe, B. 2004. *Iron Age Britain*. London: English Heritage

Dyer, J. 2003. *Hillforts of England and Wales*. Shire Publications Ltd.

González Ruibal, A. 2004. Facing two seas: Mediterranean and Atlantic contacts in the North-West of Iberia in the first millenium BC. *Oxford Journal of Archaeology*. Volume 23 (3). August 2004: 287-317. Oxford: Blackwell Publishing.

González Ruibal, A. 2006. Past the Last Outpost: Punic Merchants in the Atlantic Ocean (5th-1st centuries BC). *Journal of Mediterranean Archaeology*, 19(1): 121-150.

González Ruibal, A. 2006a. House societies vs. kinship-based societies: An archaeological case from Iron Age Europe. *Journal of Anthropological Archaeology* 25: 144-73.

González Ruibal, A. 2006-2007. Galaicos: poder y comunidad en el Noroeste de la Península Ibérica: (1200 a. C.-50 d. C.). *Brigantium* 18-19. A Coruña: Museo de San Antón.

Hill, J. D. 1996. Hill-forts and the Iron Age of Wessex. En T. C. Champion y J. R. Collis (eds.): *The Iron Age in Britain and Ireland: recent trends*: 95-116. Sheffield: Sheffield Academic Press.

Hingley, R. 1990. Boundaries surrounding Iron Age and Romano-British settlements. *Scottish Archaeological Review*, 7: 96-113.

McFadyen, L. 2006. Building technologies, quick architecture and early Neolithic long barrow sites in southern Britain. *Archaeological Review from Cambridge*, 21.1: 117-134. Cambridge.

Owok, M. A. 2005. From the Ground Up: Agency, Practice, and Community in the Southwestern British Bronze Age. *Journal of Archaeological Method and Theory*, 12 (4): 257-281. New York.

Parcero Oubiña, C. 2003. Looking forward in anger: Social and Political transformations in the Iron Age of the north-western Iberian Peninsula. *European Journal of Archaeology*, 6(3): 267-99.

Parcero Oubiña, C., X.M. Ayán Vila, P. Fábrega Álvarez and A. Teira Brión. 2007. Arqueología, Paisaje y Sociedad.

In F.J. González García (coord.) *Los pueblos de la Galicia Céltica*: 131-258. Madrid: Akal.

Parker Pearson, M. 1999. Food, Sex and Death: Cosmologies in the British Iron Age with Particular Reference to East Yorkshire. *Cambridge Archaeological Journal*, 9:1: 43-69. Cambridge.

Queiroga, F.M.V.R. 2003. *War and castros. New perspectives in the Iron Age of north-western Portugal.* B.A.R. International Series. Oxford.

Sastre Prats, I. 2002. Forms of social inequality in the Castro Culture of north-west Iberia. *European Journal of Archaeology*, 5 (2): 213-248.

Several authors. 2006. *Guía de castros de Galicia e NW de Portugal.* Santiago: Xunta de Galicia.

Villa Valdés, A. and L. Cabo Pérez 2003. Depósito funerario y recinto fortificado de la Edad del Bronce en el castro del Chao Sanmartín. *Trabajos de Prehistoria*, 60(2): 143-51. Madrid: CSIC.

5
The ordinary medieval house:
the use of wall stratification in French preventive archaeology of built space

Astrid Huser

I.N.R.A.P., France

Abstract

Our work improves the traditional framework where the preventive french archaeology has been moving in, presenting the study with archaeological methodology of the Heritage built from the Archaeology of Architecture parameters. An example of this approach is the analysis of the *Chirac Town-House* in the medieval heart of Montpellier. The works developed in this building show the methodological tools used to go into the history of a living domestic architecture, of a house which tells us about everyday life of its inhabitants, about a medieval urban population and about the historic context they are in as a material expression.

Introduction

The speed with which the "urban built framework" is being transformed in France in the past twenty years has rendered indispensable the increase of preventive excavations. These have led to the exploration of unknown parts of the city. The ordinary medieval house as a result is presently perceptible and has become the most important historical witness of past everyday life of the town. Present-day analyses now begin directly at the subsoil and work up the buildings in elevation, thus validating a global archaeology. It modifies and enlarges our knowledge of the urban world, until recently mostly limited to its public or religious structures. Non-monumental, it asks for approaches other than formalist or typological ones. A complete new field of research has opened with the archaeological study of built space.

This impulse is not isolated, but roots itself in new perspectives opened up by fundamental works of historians and archaeological program research.

Archaeological approach to a medieval house

A single example will be chosen to illustrate the richness and the complexity of a preventive study of built space. Known as the «Chirac Town-House» it is located in Montpellier, a medieval city in the south of France.

This building is part of a neighbourhood inside the Protector District of the city. Whereas legislation in France allows a relative control of all reconstruction projects within the boundaries of such a perimeter, it is not so outside of it, particularly in the villages where the lack of a clear-cut municipal policy and collective disinterest permit a lot of destruction and anarchic renovations.

The present operation was prescribed in 1999 by the regional Service of Archaeology to the National Institute of Preventive Archaeologies (INRAP). The professional framework was an intervention of limited duration before drastic transformations of the "Chirac Town-House" were to be performed. The project was completed thanks to collaboration between various competences and institutions.[1]

Figure 1. The *Chirac Town-House* classical façade, on the side of the *Rue de l'Aiguillerie* (view by A. Huser/INRAP).

---

[1] The operation was placed under the responsibility of P. Alessandri (INRAP) with A. Huser (INRAP) for archaeology of built space study, with the collaboration of J.-L. Vayssettes (Regional Service of Inventory); drawings (P. Alessandri, C. Bioul, F. Guyonnet, A. Huser/INRAP), historical researches J.-L. Vayssettes (R.S.I.); drawing of the façade, 1995, by S. Bonnaud (INRAP).

The ordinary medieval house: the use of wall stratification in French preventive archaeology of built space

Evidences of a classical town-house with facades of the beginning of the 18th century are the starting point of the study (fig. 1). After examining the different strata and incessant recastings that these coatings hid, several intricate medieval units eventually became apparent.

What are the scientific techniques required for such archaeological study of built space?

This way of investigation is not a different type of archaeology. It is the same method and the same registration applied to verticality; i.e. peeling the memory of walls as stratified levels. As such, it makes possible a global archaeology, combining the digging of foundations as well as of elevations.

It took some time to stop searching exclusively for the primitive state of the building and to recognize the fundamental importance of proceeding with a logical and methodical "décroûtage" (i.e. stripping, peeling) from the last tapestry to the naked wall, as well as the registration of every single pellicle of distemper, as layers stratifying the history of the wall -- and this, in relationship with space in a permanent three-dimensional analysis. A "décroûtage" without registration is the death of the archaeological purpose because it definitely ruins the understanding of the evolution of the structure itself.

By using the correct process, the ordinary medieval house is apprehended in all its historical and spatial density. The practice of systematic vertical soundings is the basis for a stratigraphic analysis of the volume. The detailed study of maconneries (which includes disturbances, prints in negative, blockages or pinnings) requires their graphic translation and the creation of a data base for normalized registration in a preventive context.

This type of approach to the house is also ethnographic with the technical study of:

- the bonds, mortars and coatings of the ceilings;
- the use of local or exterior ressources, of stone, wood or earth in the construction;
- the typological evolution of the openings, both functional and decorative elements; and all the numerous amazing details that one can collect about its successive inhabitants.

Finally, it is essential to study the way in which the building is integrated topographically into the urban space and street network, also to discover its evolution as a constructed space within the entire built framework.

This precise evolution, established at first in a relative chronological scale, can be completed in an absolute chronological scale by having recourse to other sciences such as dendrochronology. Two medieval painted ceilings were thus discovered in the "Chirac Town-House" and were able to be dated: one from the first half of the 13th century, the other from the second half.

Particular attention is also given to archives. We are at present becoming increasingly interested in bills of construction or repairs, sales contracts mentioning common ownership and disposition of the interior, inventories, etc.

A huge operation of regrouping, undertaken at the beginning of the 18th century by Pierre Chirac in view to recasting different units into a classical town-house, is precisely registered in the city archives and is graphically visible in the general plans of the same period.

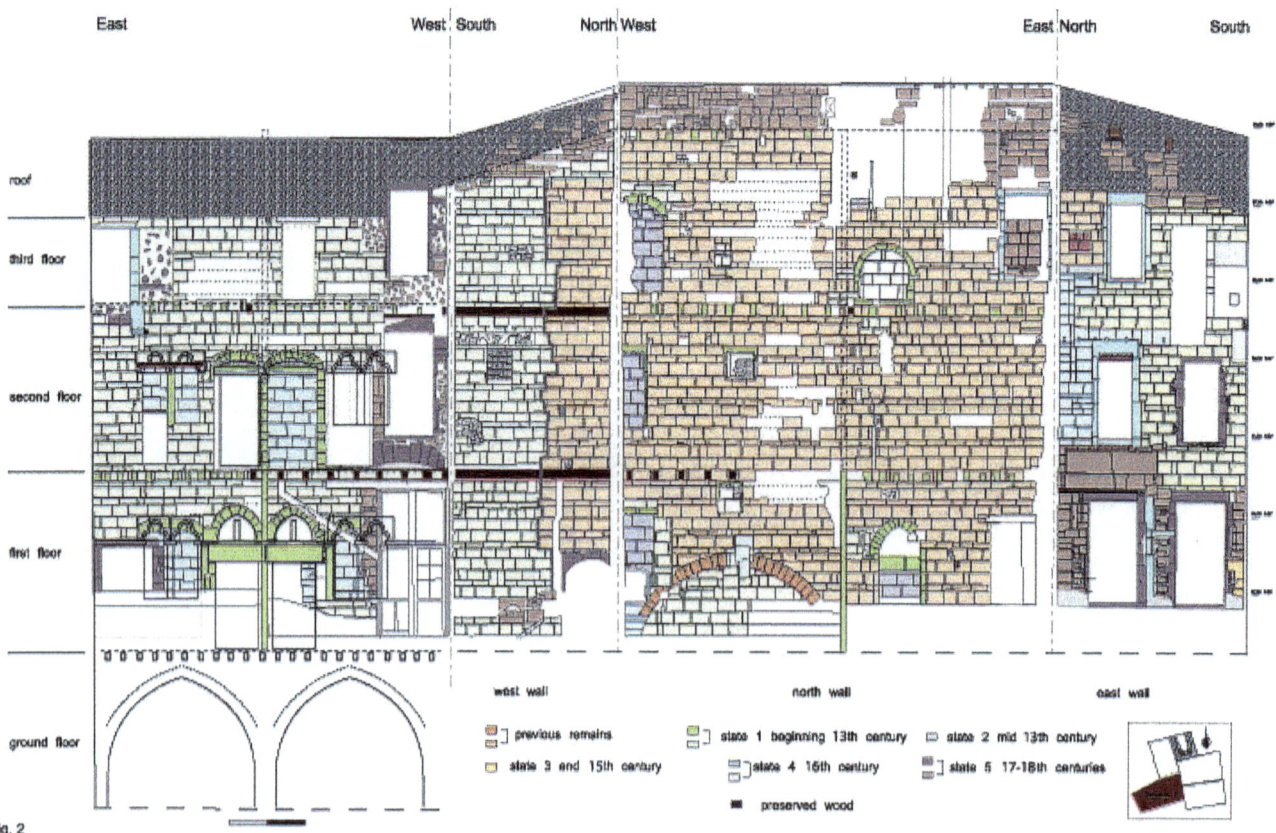

Figure 2. Setting up of the inner walls of House 1 with the superposition of the outside of the façade (drawing P. Alessandri, C. Bioul/INRAP; DAO C. Bioul; phasing A. Huser/INRAP; setting up X. Chadefaux/INRAP)

As a result, we are following the destiny of three interwoven medieval units in five major stages : based on previous remains, a first coherent state is dated from the first half of the 13th century; then, different variations of regrouping of the units are perceptible until the unfinished remodelling as a town-house at the classical period.

This chronological evolution can be summarized by a stratified diagram of the elevations (which is also an indispensable means to check the established registration).

An inn in a merchant town

Only one unit (House 1) has been studied on all four faces (Fig. 2). It gives a precise idea of an ordinary medieval house - but one with a peculiar function! The context of the two others could only be estimated (Houses 2 and 3), their full perimeter being beyond the limits of our study. Here, then, is a short exposition of our archaeological study of what is classified as House 1.

The choice of building walls is technically based on a model called "appareil de Montpellier" because of its widespread use in the city. The term designates a bond of alternate stones, headers and stretchers on face. The stone quarries are local : they delivered standard module and the same type of material throughout all of the Middle-Ages (limestone for the main structure and sandstone for the different openings).

Three of the four walls of the building present a regular alternative of three headers for one stretcher. The facade has a mixed system of two, three or four alternative courses.

The west wall presents a particularity, a suture from the bottom to the top (Fig. 3). This implies a gap of stone courses. On the east side, though greatly transformed during the 16th century, a similar scenario is perceptible. This irregularity, added to a difference of binding mortar, suggests that the unit was built on a former structure after the front wall was pulled down to modify the building's organisation. House 1 does not rise from an empty space and keeps all that could be preserved from the preceding construction. The creation of a front yard along the street implies the total reconstruction of the facade, homogenized as the same unit by ceilings and roof. As often, the primitive topography only survives in the walls.

The plot belongs to the first constitution of Montpellier which occured, like other towns without antique origins, around the 10th century, at the same time as the first villages.

Since the end of the 11th century at least, fortifications grouped together the principal economical, political and religious functions into four main sections (Fig. 4). But under a strong economical impulse at the beginning of the 13th century, the limits of the first fortifications were rejected for new ones, called the "commune clôture". This implies the extension and remodelling of numerous areas.

Such is the case of our plot. Its initial morphology was changed probably to satisfy new functions. Destruction was reduced to a minimum and the hanging of the facade was carried out with care, the same building method being applied. The first visible state is thus scaled as a homogeneous unit with a complete wall frame. The ceilings indicate that it dates from the first half of the 13th century.

Figure 3. Suture in west wall (view by A. Huser/INRAP).

The house is structured by a ground floor, two floors above and a third one which is directly under the roof. The interest of the study is the particularity of its organisation, as interpreted from the reading of the remains.

Preceded by the front yard, the facade gives a clear reading of the inner structure (Fig. 5): the bays are symmetrically disposed on a median axis which corresponds to a division wall from ground to top. At each level, a room is situated on each side of this partition.

As to the ground floor, it is an extension of the yard with its two Gothic arch doors covered by a ceiling (Fig. 6). The interior symmetrical organisation rules the openings on the first and second floors with two entrance doors and two twin windows on each side. The third floor has only two doors in the alignment of the windows. If the general composition is well-balanced, the volume as a whole translates a hierarchical conception of the house to the benefit of the first floor with a higher ceiling (4,50 m), whereas the same measurements are given for the ground, second and third floors (3,75 m). The degree of elaboration of the external signs of decoration also underlines this preference.

Figure 4. *Plan des Iliers*, Notre-Dame des Tables district, City of Montpellier, mid-XVIIIth century (collection from the Archaeological Society of Montpellier).

All the assets are concentrated on the first level : the openings reveal excellent workmanship. The doors are skillfully drawn by engaged piers covered by a monolith lintel in limestone which is relieved by an ogival arch with a pierced tympanum inside! A head band underlines the floor (Fig. 7).

The composition of the twin windows forms a well-balanced structure on each floor but differs from the front to the back : on the outside, the figure is precise and decorative with two monolith lintels carved with a trefoiled form. Their junction lays on a central engaged pier. On the back, however, there is just a relieving arch to support the openings.

Even though the same organisation of the openings and the distribution is used on the second floor, some technical details are modified such as the recourse to cheaper material : here the doors are only covered with a fine lintel topped by a small relieving arch. The twin windows and their decorations are simply sustained by a back-lintel in wood.

The third floor retains a minimum of the symmetrical organisation with two doors on the same level.

How does the distribution work? The facade gives us the clue : alignments of holes on each floor are visibly the prints for beams of an outside distribution with staircases and galleries, serving even the third floor (Fig. 8). Such a combination is costly. It means that this particular space is not simply a mere room, but that it has a specific function (otherwise a ladder from the inside would be enough).

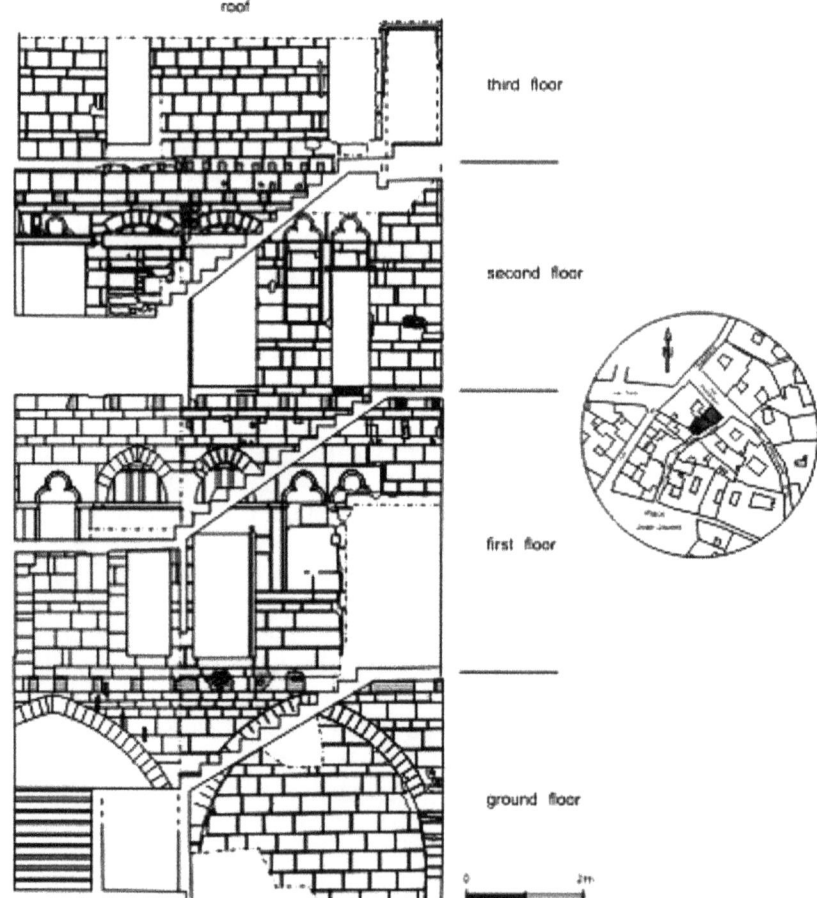

Figure 5. Façade on courtyard of House 1 (drawing by S. Bonnaud/INRAP, 1995)

Figure 6. Gothic archs doors of the ground of House 1 (view by M. Descossy/General Inventory, ADAGP).

Figure 7. Doors and windows of the first floor, House 1 (view by A. Huser/INRAP).

Figure 8. Beam holes of the outside gallery (distribution), first floor, House 1 (view by S. Bonnaud/INRAP).

Inside, the ground floor is visibly functional but carefully paved: a bore indicates the first level of circulation. Another one in the recent first floor shows prints of holes from a previous ceiling before a groin vault was installed during the 16th century.

The attributes of wealth concentrated on the first floor are significant : the highest rooms, the quality of decoration of the openings on the outside as well as the inside, the delicately painted ornaments on the ceilings and the fragments of deep red pigment on the walls and openings, which could be part of possible decorative patterns. The second floor is still a qualified space but contains fewer details and lower ceilings like the ground and third floors. If pigments are visible on the walls, we know nothing about the decorative possibilites of the ceilings which no longer exist. The third floor has no windows but still has a massive sink topped by a semi-circular arch and a vertical system of stone canalisation embedded in the wall. These factors classify the space as being less important, but still as an habitable room.

This type of ordinary house is rare. Considering its unusual interventions, such as a symmetrical organisation of the openings with an external distribution right up to the top floor, it can be identified as a medieval inn, having a potential of (at least) six rooms with hierarchic status.

This inn emerges at a period of Montpellier's splendour, at the time when it is dependent on the Aragon Kingdom and becomes a kind of trade republic enriched by the energy of its business with the Mediterranean, Levant and Champagne Fairs.

The topographic position of the inn is excellent because it is just behind the heart of the economic center of the city and very close to one of its main access routes, which is also an ancient and famous pilgrimage route. It welcomes foreign merchants with its front yard for horses and carriages. Its symmetrical rooms, served by an external and independent staircase, can cater to every social level.

An evolving urban islet

What do we learn about the connection between the different plots and their evolution? (Fig. 9).

Two neighbouring lots did exist in the first half of the 13th century. We have described House 1 which is a unit. The other one, House 3, has been modified enormously. Initially, it was linked to the first one by a common wall. We do not know much about the primitive shape of the lot which is back-to-back with House 1 and communicates by different doors at the north. The lack of windows can indicate that an earlier structure existed here too.

On this very same spot, some 50 years later, a house appeared (House 2), attached to House 1, thus condemning the shared openings. It is based on ogival vaults whose construction broke a section of the common door. The height of the floors varies from one unit to another : this is typical of Montpellier which, being built on a hill, has different street levels! The walls are not connected to House 1 and may imply that the original building was totally destroyed in order to build a new house. Judging from the one room we studied, we do know that it was part of a patrician house because of its size, of the quality of its decoration and its monumental chimney. The same frescos have been found on the next parcel which still has a visible medieval facade. Visibly, the two units probably belonged to the same house.

House 1 and 3 therefore became part of a regrouping of lots in the 15th century, but did not undergo structural changes.

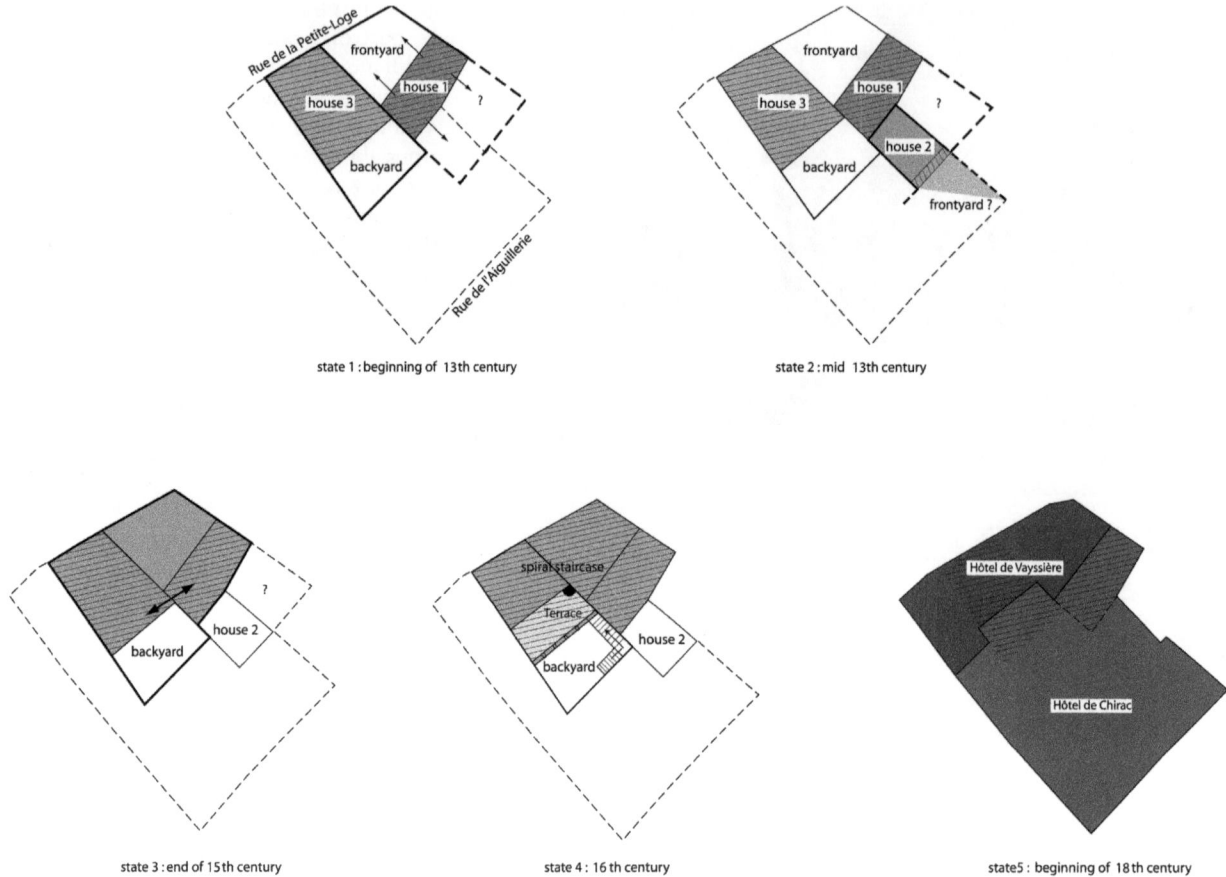

Figure 9. Evolving urban islet (reconstitution by A. Huser/INRAP and J.-L. Vayssettes/ SRI)

Deep modifications in the 16th century suggest the breaking up of a part of House 3 to create an open space with a terrace and a turret within a spiral staircase (Fig. 10). Huge casement windows were built in House 1. All the medieval openings, with the exception of one door on each floor, were condemned : it means that the front yard was built at that time and that the entire system of openings and distribution was modified.

By the beginning of the 18th century, Pierre Chirac, the owner, had not managed the total remodelling of his townhouse. Although he had destroyed completely the medieval lay-out to build up the facades, whole pieces of ancient constructions were preserved behind the structure.

The scenario reconstructed on the basis of the elements we collected through a stratified "décroûtage" provides just a glimpse into the comprehension of primitive urban built framework and its evolution. Nevertheless, it does suggest some answers to the fundamental research begun on the subject, mainly since 1990, by the works of the Inventory Service for the City of Montpellier.[2]

---

[2] Sournia, Vayssettes 1991 ; 1994, Fabre, Lochard 1992

The historical frame can be resumed thus : the 13th century constitutes a definitive turn in the typology of the ordinary and patrician houses which is complete by the middle of the 14th century. The 15th century translates the efforts of renovation with the preservation of pre-existent structure. At the same time, a new structural logic settles down and destabilizes, from the inside, the former architectural system right into the classical period. It marks an essential mutation : the passage from discontinuous and additive space construction, typical of the medieval town, to a homogeneous urban built framework under the leadership of the classical architect.

This evolution is slow and resists in many ways, as it is often limited only to appearances : our town-house looks homogeneous on the front but it remains disconnected and additive on the inside...

Conclusion

The ordinary medieval house escapes all monumental rules and is based on a knowledge of recycling, accompanied by constant inventiveness and a do-it-yourself response to functional necessities. Through these studies of domestic architecture, we have now the methodological tools to obtain a much more subtle vision of the local/regional practices and changes. It is time to get rid of "descriptive archaeology" and to try to get into a "producer or consumer arc-

Figure 10. Backyard, terrace and spiral staircase, XVIth century (view by A. Huser/INRAP).

haeology". From this point of view, the medieval building becomes a "social motor" as well as a "reflector" of its time.

Beyond simple monography, it is possible to define vernacular aspects from other sources than our knowledge of the art of building, which is mainly derived from monumental reference. It is symptomatic that the translation of "arc plein-cintre" in English is "Roman arch" and that "arc brisé" becomes "Gothic arch". These terms give a false vision of the facts. The definition of "arc plein-cintre" is simply a technical solution designed to cover up a large opening. In the middle of the so-called Roman period (mid-12th century), in Cahors for example, these "Gothic arches" were used to cover up shop windows - thus they had a specific function!

In some cases, of course, a return to aesthetic considerations is evident by the decision to cover up an opening with a so-called Roman or Gothic arch. The facade of our study-case reveals the significance of such a choice, for on the first floor, where all the wealth attributes were centralised, the openings were covered with an up-to-date Gothic arch, whereas a Roman arch was kept for those on the second floor.

In fact, a same architectural element is the fruit of different simultaneous approaches (aesthetical, structural and functional).

In order to grasp these social "transitions", a fundamental registration of all the aspects of the house, regarding its conservative or innovation choices, must be established. But this implies other methods and a new vocabulary, distinct from those used for the traditional monumental concept which is formalistic. Technical uses and aesthetical effects must be kept separate in the reasoning (Journot 1999).

Field archaeology of built space is no longer experimental. It has transformed our vision of the habitat by giving irrepleacable data to historical problematics. It opens huge perspectives of understanding domestic architecture, and through it, that of a society in its every day life-history.

Acknowledgments

Special thanks for translation help to Doris Orrett-Huser.

References

Fabre, G. and Lochard, T. 1992. *Montpellier: ville médiévale. Cahiers du Patrimoine*, 3. Paris: Imprimerie nationale Editions.

Journot, F. 1999. *Archéologie du bâti*. In Bessac, J.-C. ; Journot, F., Prigent, D., Sapin, C and Seigne, J.: *La construction: la pierre* : 133-63. Paris: Errance.

Sournia, B. and Vayssettes, J.-L. 1991. *Montpellier : La demeure médiévale. Cahiers du Patrimoine*, 1. Paris: Imprimerie nationale Editions.

Sournia, B., Vayssettes, J.-L. 1994. *Montpellier : La demeure classique. Cahiers du Patrimoine*, 38. Paris: Imprimerie nationale Editions.

6

Concepts dominants en construction ancienne de maisons d'habitation de la zone forestière de la région de l'Oural ouest

Elisaveta Tchernykh

Abstract

The archaeological study of the old housing areas in Kama region, in the western Urals, is the central topic of this work. We start from an ethno archaeological comparison with communities living nowadays in the same land. From this premise, we analyze the distribution of space and an interpretation from a semantic point of view of the Kama region settlements during the Metal Age, highlighting the cosmological patterns which ruled the domestic architecture of these communities.

La présente communication a pour but de dépasser le cadre d'examen bien ancré dans les esprits de chercheurs selon lequel la recherche sur l'habitation ancienne était axée surtout sur l'étude de sa fonctionnalité et de son schéma constructif. Or, étant l'un des symboles-clés culturels, l'habitat mérite une étude plus dépouillée.

Les recherches dans le domaine de l'« archéologie d'habitat» ont manifesté de façon convaincainte que les stéréotypes de construction régionaux ou locaux à l'époque primitive sont un critère solide. Ils résultent non seulement de l'action de facteurs d'adaptation (adaptation de l'éthnie à son milieu d'habitation), mais aussi du fait d'interprétation par la société primitive de sa place dans le monde environnant. Ceci se traduit à travers des cérémonies rituelles inspirées par coutumes et traditions. L'ethnologie nous apprend la lenteur avec laquelle ce système se transforme. L'habitat actuel est plein de rites, sans parler de l'époque plus éloignée.

Figure 1. Zone forestière de la région de l'Oural ouest.

Ceci est dit pour argumenter une reconstruction culturologique de l'habitat que nous proposons et notamment l'aspect conceptuel de l'habitat ancien/primitif. Certes, la sémantisation des significations objectivées dans les fragments qui restent des constructions anciennes demande de la prudence . Il faut aussi tenir compte du manque de repères méthodologiques dans ce nouveau domaine de recherche, à la différence de la procédure de reconstructions paléoéconomiques et sociales riche d'expérience positive. Elle nous demande souvent de nous référer aux études ethnologiques et culturologiques intéressantes. Le recours à des parallèles ethnographiques nous parait justifiée seulement au cas où il s'agit de sociétés à un même type économico-culturel sur un territoire où le développement archéologique n'est pas perturbé pendant une période très longue et où les monuments archéologiques sont attribués de façon évidente par le matériel historique à une éthnie concrète. Le territoire de la région de la Kama (fig.1,2), lieu le plus ancien d'habitation des peuples de Permie (komi et oudmourtes/votyaks) correspond, à nos yeux, exactement à cette définition (Tchernykh 1995). Avec cela on est en quête de faits illustrant de façon très nette la culture socionormative et spirituelle de la société primitive.

L'archéologie de la région de la Kama et des régions avoisinantes connait actuellement beaucoup de faits qui permettent de donner des caractéristiques de la sphère rituelle de la construction d'habitat primitif. Ma communication porte sur les particularités les plus importantes de l'organisartion et de l'interprétation sémantique de l'espace d'habitation des peuples de la région de la Kama à l'âge des métaux. Cette tâche a demandé une récolte minutieuse et une systématisation de tous les éléments qu'on a à notre disposition en ce qui concerne la construction d'habitat. L'étude a fait découvrir certains éléments d'habitation constamment répétitifs au cours de millénaires, donc une certaine tradition, grâce à quoi il est possible d'utiliser telles méthodes comme analogie et construction de modèles. Celle-ci est justifiée, si on accepte la thèse que le modèle d'habitat et les rites de construction reflètent en général les représentations cosmogoniques. Cette approche nous donne un schéma conceptuel de départ, à savoir le recours au modèle du système de l'univers, qui est - grosso modo - universel. L'universalité du modèle cosmique (cosmogonique) consiste avant tout en sa verticalité réunissant trois mondes – céleste, terrestre et souterrain/sous-marin, ou haut, milieu et bas, dont la cohésion est assurée par l'axe du monde, ou «l'Arbre du monde», autour duquel se déploie l'espace horizontal. L'horizontalité s'exprime par l'orientation aux quatre parties du monde. Ce paradygme serait propre au stade d'élaboration de la tradition de construction d'habitat. Il se retrouve, malgré l'apparente variété de types d'habitation de la région de la Kama à l'âge des métaux, dans leurs traits communs : rectangularité préférée de formes qui avait déterminé la stabilité de la tradition technologique. Il n'y a aucun doute que les murs d'habitation correspondent aux quatre parties du monde. Trente pour cent de maisons sont orientées par leurs murs de flanc au nord-sud, cinquante pour cent au sud-ouest et au sud-est de rhumb. Cette orientation, compte tenu des conditions d'insolation et des vents dominants la rose des vents, est une expression de la fonction profane de l'habitat pour protéger le mieux la collectivité du milieu naturel. Néanmoins, le bien-être des maitres de la maison dépendait de sa cohérence à leur vision du monde. Elle se révèlerait dans la topographie de l'axe central, défini dans l'horizontalité des maisons ouralo-paléoasiatiques comme « entrée – foyer – sanctuaire » (Aroutunov et al. 1991 : 29). Notre matériel d'investigation permet de concrétiser ce schéma. L'entrée des habitations de la région de la Kama se trouvait généralement dans le mur de flanc, c'est-à-dire donnait sur le sud. En même temps cette disposition coincidait avec l'orientation vers le cours d'eau. J'ose supposer que cet emplacement est dû non seulement à l'esprit pratique des anciens, mais aussi à leur pensée mythologique. Je rappellerais l'Image du fleuve cosmique qui traverse les trois mondes de l'Univers en les réunissant (Vladykine 1996: 219). L'entrée d'habitation dans ce modèle correspond toujours au bas qui est un équivalent de l'enfer, du monde souterrain. Il est opportun de rappeler l'orientation au cours d'eau des tombes de plusieures cultures archéologiques du bas bronze et de l'âge du fer. Ainsi la foi assez convainquante des khantys (en Sibérie) que la maison où toute la famille est morte doit être poussée dans le cours d'eau (c'est ça enterrer pour eux). Le mur opposé à l'entrée – celui du nord – comme la partie avant de la maison passe aux yeux de beaucoup de cultures finno-ougriennes pour pur et sacré. C'est là la place du maitre de la maison et des réliques. Il est très rare, ce qui n'est pas dû au hasard, de trouver des traces de lits du côté nord de la maison (12,5% de cas). Les fouilles effectuées sur des sites de la région de la Tcheptsa, fin du premier – début du deuxième millénaire de notre ère (Idnakar, Porkar de Malovenij), ont révélé des amas de cendres et d'os calcinés près du mur de la partie nord dans presque toutes les habitations. Il n'est pas inintéressant de se référer à un témoignage d'ethnographes oudmourtes : on ne jetait pas le cendre et les os de la construction d'été (kouala) dehors (le foyer étant considéré comme saint). On les mettait dans une caisse spéciale. Il y a des études dépouillées de complexes de culte des maisons du site Zayumtchirsk I à la Moyenne Kama (fin du deuxième – milieu du premier millénaire avant notre ère). Ils comprenaient, en règle générale, des crânes de chevaux, des pattes d'ours, des récipients, des pointes de flèches, des bobines de quenouilles aux symboles solaires et démarquaient des foyers spéciaux ou des creux à proximité du mur nord de la maison (fig.3-2,3). Un ensemble d'artefacts impressionnant, comme vous voyez. Je citerai un exemple curieux des fouilles d'une construction haut moyenâgeuse du site de Postol (Oudmourtie du Sud). Les fouilles effectuées par T.Ostanina de la partie nord non chauffée de la maison ont découvert la trace d'un pilier d'un diamètre considérable (42 centimètres) (Ivanov and Ostanina 1983: 118). Il serait douteux de prétendre qu'il était utilisé dans la construction de la maison. L'archéologue croit plausible de l'interpréter comme pilier de totem. Une situation planigraphique analogue est fixée par V.Semionov lors des fouilles d'une construction de culte du site Polomski 1 de la région de la Tcheptsa (Semionov 1979 : 131). Ici la vocation du pilier est bien déterminée par la destination de la construction. Dans l'imaginaire des oudmourtes les représentations sur le pilier de vorchoud («воршуд-йыбо» en oud

mourte), selon mon collègue ethnographe Vladimir Vladykine, peuvent être typologiquement liées au pilier de totem et à l'Arbre du monde, les deux notions correspondant au culte de koula. Ceci dit, il est évident qu'on peut parler d'un ordre intérieur de l'espace habitée, fondée sur le schéma conceptuel de départ.

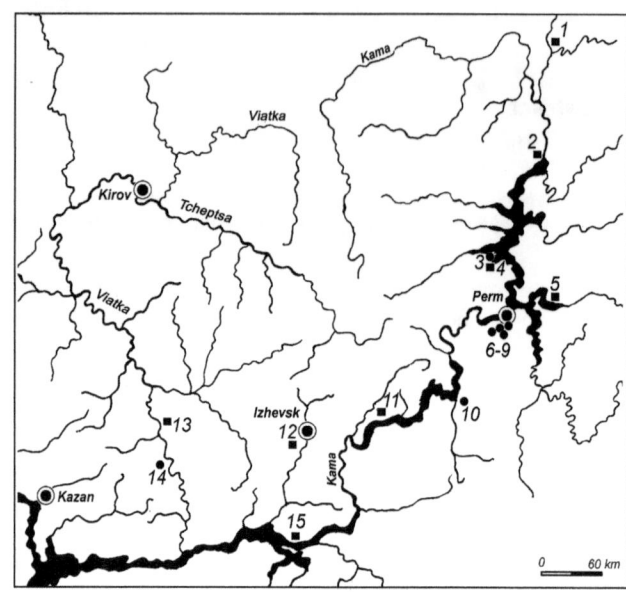

Figure 2. Lieux d'habitation à dominante rituelle: 1 - cité d'Iskor; 2 - cité d'Esper; 3 - Zarodiata, village; 4 – Opoutiata, cité; 5 - Salomatovo, cité; 6-9 - Zayurtchim I, VI, Polovinnoïe, Zaossinovo, lieux d'habitation; 11 – Stepanovo I, cité; 12 – Tchoujialovo, cité; 13 - Arguyn, cité; 14 – Izran, lieu d'habitation

L'articulation de l'espace habitée tient compte aussi de la structure de sexe et d'âge, donc de la dualité sociale comme traits universels de l'époque primitive. Ils sont exprimés par la culture traditionnelle dans les oppositions binaires essentielles: avant – derrière, gauche – droit, masculin – féminin. Elles sont souvent complémentaires, car la partie gauche est, de règle, censée féminine, la partie droite masculine, à moins d'être inversées. La spécificité des vestiges archéologiques de lieux d'habitation ne permet pas de solutionner ce problème une fois pour toutes. Il y a des ouvrages qui tentent de discerner les parties féminine et masculine à base d'assortimernt d'objets trouvés. Pourtant le matériel à analyser ne s'y prête pas toujours. Souvent les archives ou publications ne mentionnent pas de données cartographiques d'objets de fouilles. Dans ce cas il est à essayer de recourir à un autre repère, celui de l'emplacement du foyer. Il ressort des recherches ethnographiques qu'on pourrait parler de foyers masculins et féminins. Or, il est à noter que chez certaines populations le feu se présente dans l'image de femme et c'est près du feu qu'elles attrribuent à la femme sa place. Ne pourrait-on pas utiliser ce lien (femme – foyer) pour expliquer le déplacement du foyer de l'axe central vers le mur ou le coin? A coup d'oeil, dans les habitations de la région de la Kama le déplacement des foyers dans deux tiers des cas s'effectue vers la droite. Apparemment dans ce cas nous avons affaire à l'inversion chez lez finno-ourgiens, d'autant plus qu'il y a des observations analogues de E. Gorunova faites au sujet du plan de la maison Volossovo du

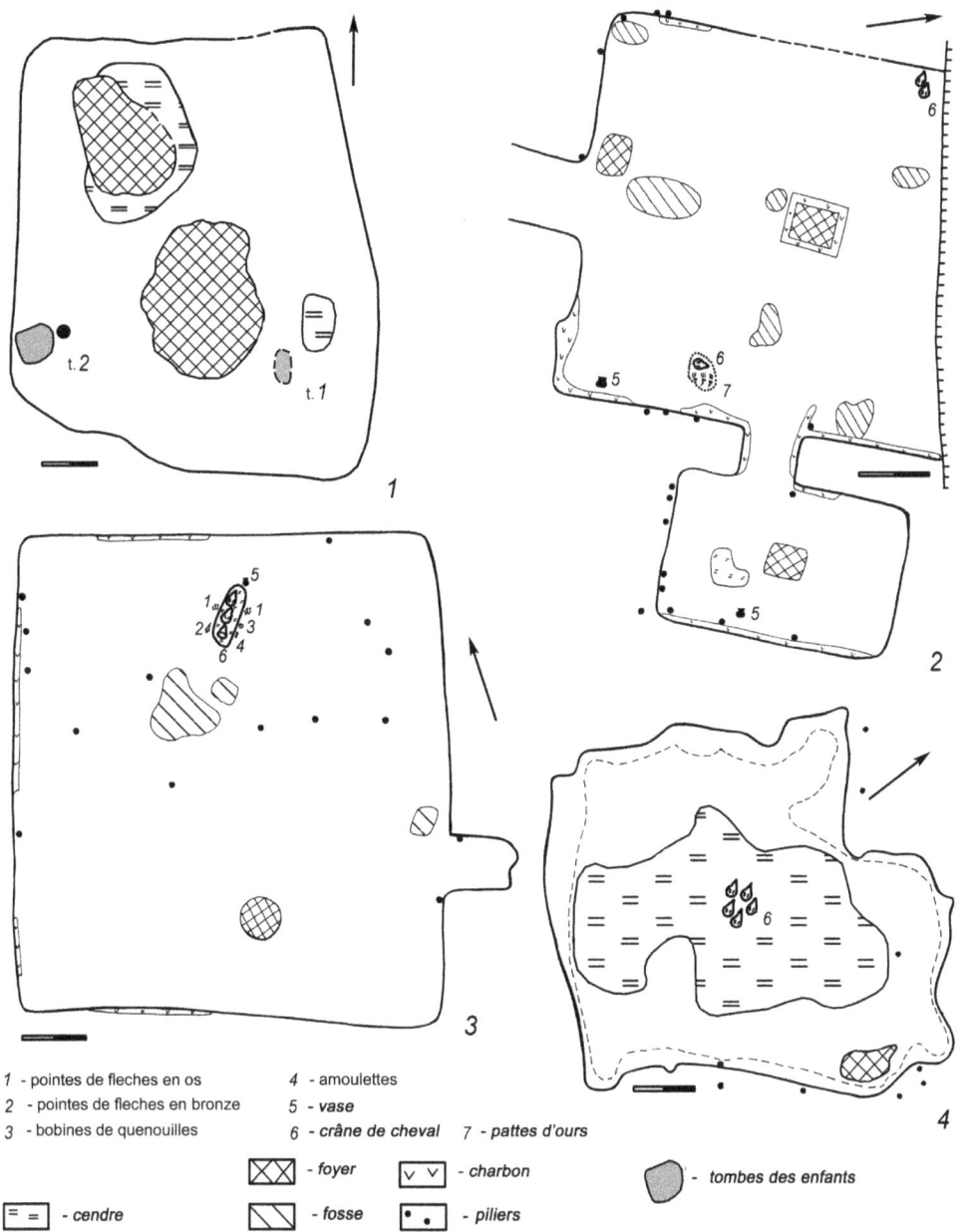

Figure 3. Habitations de la région de la Kama avec des onjets rituels de l'intérieur: 1 – Zouyevy Kloutchi, cité; 2,3 – Zayurtchim I, lieu d'habitation; 4 – Zayurtchim VI, lieu d'habitation.

site de Panfilovo (culture de type énéolithique) (Goriounova 1963: 134-5). Ou, par exemple, le fait de placer le fondeur dans l'habitation de culture Azeline (culture du bassin de la Viatka des troisième - cinquième siècles de notre ère). La fouille d'une habitation à plusieurs foyers (n.5 du site Bouillsky sur la rive de la Viatka) réalisée par L.Achikhmina révéla un foyer à revêtement de pierre, différent des autres à usage domestique non seulement de par construction, mais par l'inventaire d'objets trouvés. Celui-ci mentionne un moule pour bijoux de femme, il y avait à côté un complexe de culte sous forme d'amas de pierre, de mâchoires d'ours et de pointes de flèche en os. Les artefacts de culte font penser à la sacralisation de la fonte de cuivre, tandis que l'emplacement du foyer de production dans la partie droite de l'entrée est, de toute évidence, à examiner en fonction du rôle joué dans la société Azeline des femmes fondeuses (Guéning 1963: 67).

Un témoignage de plus d'importance de l'habitat comme élément du schéma cosmogonique se retrouve dans les complexes rituels marquant le début et la fin de fonctionnement de la maison. Il est surtout difficile de fixer archéologiquement la fin de fonctionnement de l'habitat. C'est, manifestement, le fait d'enterrement de 19 personnes dans le foyer de la maison (site Lougovskaia 1 de la Basse-Kama). Le « début » de la maison lié dans la cosmogonie au corps de sacrifice est fixé plus souvent. L'attribution des complexes rituels comme « sacrifices de construction » demande une argumentation supplémentaire. Pour le faire il est nécessaire de respecter plusieures conditions : 1) le complexe doit se trouver à l'intérieur de l'objet examiné; 2) il doit correspondre stratigraphiquement au niveau inférieur au sol et contenir des dépôts culturels dans la maison; 3) si le complexe se trouve dans une fosse, celle-ci ne doit pas révéler de traces d'utilisation secondaire. La fouille la plus ancienne de ces complexes re-monte aux habitations de cultures de la région de Kazan et d'Erzovskoié de l'âge du bronze. Les complexes de culte que nous intérprétons comme « sacrifices de construction » se caractérisent par l'emplacement dans la partie nord de l'espace habitée ou à l'entrée. Ceci a des parallèles paléoethnographiques étonnants. La planigraphie pareille a des correspondances évidentes avec la sacralisation horizontale de l'espace habitée. Le nord, comme nous l'avons déjà dit, est d'habitude associé au pays de la mort, au monde d'au-delà. La disposition des sacrifices à l'entrée marque les notions du mien et de l'autre/étranger. Les « sacrifices de constructions » des habitats de l'âge du bas bronze sont présentés essentiellement par des crânes de chevaux (fig.3-4), plus rarement par des restes d'ossements d'ours et de porc. Le cheval des complexes rituels du bas bronze et surtout à l'époque d'Ananino où il est largement répandu témoigne de façon évidente l'apparition du culte de cheval. Pour les finno-ougriens il est intimement lié aux cultes agraires. C'est à cette période que l'économie de production s'affirme et se développe dans la région de la Kama. Mais de l'autre côté, le cheval symbolise à la fois le soleil (la vie) et l'eau (la mort). Cela veut dire que dans son image se reflète la structure tripartite de l'univers. Les monuments plus récents ne portent pas de signes de transformation de ce rite. Dans les complexes d'offrandes le rôle essentiel revient aux images de taureau et de cheval. Les transformations plus substantielles se produisent dans la deuxième moitié du premier millénaire de notre ère, où on retrouve en qualité de sacrifice le chien dont le crâne et les os sont mis sous les détails porteurs des constructions, c'est-à-dire dans les lieux à charge fonctionnelle maximale. Il est à noter que les complexes sacrificatoires comportent des objets tels que petits récipients, pointes de flèches en os ou en bronze, quenouilles à ornement solaire, râpes à grains. Cette panoplie d'artefacts est traditionnelle pour les sanctuaires et les lieux de sacrifices de la région de l'Oural à partir du mézolithique jusqu'au bas moyen-âge et témoigne de l'existence de tout un système complexe de croyances et de représentations sur l'organisation idéale de la vie quotidienne et de l'univers en général.

Bibliographie

Aroutunov S., Vassiliev V. and Djarylgassinova R. 1991. Parallèles ethnographiques anciens entre la région de l'Oural et l'Asie de l'Est (à base d'habitation) // Ethnographie soviétique. 1991. №2. P.29. (en russe) – Арутюнов С.А., Васильев В.И., Джарылгасинова Р. Древние уральско-восточноазиатские этнографические параллели (на материалах жилища) // СЭ. 1991. № 2. С.29.

Goloubeva L. 1984. Femmes fondeuses (sur l'histoire de la fonte artisanale par les femmes chez les finno-ougriens) // Archéologie soviétique. 1984. №4. P.75-89 (en russe) - Голубева Л.А. Женщины-литейщицы (к истории женского ремесленного литья у финно-угров) // СА. 1984. №4. С.75-89

Goriounova E. 1963. L'évolution de l'habitat chez les mordves // Etudes sur la culture matérielle du peuple mordve. Oeuvres d'expédition ethnographique mordve. N.2. Moscou, 1963. P.134-135. (en russe) - Горюнова Е.И. Развитие жилища у мордвы // Исследования по материальной культуре мордовского народа. Труды мордовской этнографической экспедиции. Вып.2. М., 1963. С.134-135.

Guéning V. 1963. La culture d'Azelino des IIIe-Ve ss. Izhevsk, 1963, P.67. (en russe) - Генинг В.Ф. Азелинская культура III-V вв. Ижевск, 1963. С.67.

Ivanov V. and Ostanina T. 1983. Sur le problème de Bakhmoutino et de Mazounino (études d'habitations // Habitations et logements de tribus primitives de l'Oural du Sud. Oufa, 1983, p.118. (en russe) - Иванов В.А., Останина Т.И. К вопросу о бахмутинско-мазунинской проблеме (по материалам поселений) // Поселения и жилища древних племен Южного Урала. Уфа, 1983. С.118.

Semionov V. 1979. Le matériel concernant l'histoire de l'habitat et des constructions auxiliaires d'oudmourtes du VIème à la première moitié du IXème ss.// Le matériel de monuments archéologiques de la région entre la Kama et la Vyatka. Izhevsk, 1979. p.131 (en russe) - Семенов В.А. Материалы к истории жилища и хозяйственных сооружений удмуртов в VI - первой половине IX вв. // Материалы археологических памятников Камско-Вятского междуречья. Ижевск, 1979. С.131.

Tchernykh E. 1995. Des résultats d'études de l'habitation de la région de la Kama (fouilles de sites du premier millénaire avant notre ère à la première moitié du deuxième millénaire de notre ère) // Etudes finno-ougriennes. 1995. №3-4. P.88-115. (en russe) – Черных Е.М. Итоги изучения жилищ Прикамья (по материалам поселений I тыс. до н.э. – первой половины II тыс. н.э.) // Финно-угроведение. 1995. №3-4. С.88-115.

Vladykine V. 1996. La vision religieuse et mythologique de l'univers chez les oudmourtes. Ijevsk : Udmurtia, 1996. P.219. (en russe) - Владыкин В.Е. Религиозно-мифологическая картина мира удмуртов. Ижевск: Удмуртия, 1996. С.219.

7

The fortress of Rocha Forte and European military building trends
A concentric castle (14th century)

Xosé M. Sánchez Sánchez

Medieval Documentation Area of the Archive-Library of the Santiago Cathedral (Galice, Spain)

Abstract

Medieval fortress of Rocha Forte is one of the most important deposits related to military and feudal world and power in medieval Galician history, in Hispanic NW. In this article, with the light not only of the archeological sources, but with the enormous information and help of the medieval texts, we try to do an reconstruction of one of the most important moments in the history of the building and deposit: the reconstruction with the archbishop Berenguel de Landoira, at 1317-1330. Considering this reconstruction we will find parallelisms of Rocha Forte in Wales and in Holy Land and we will determinate the morphology of the castle as a concentric castle and the application of the most advanced French techniques military architecture.

Abbreviations

ACS	Archive of the Santiago Cathedral
ASV	*Archivio Segretto Vaticano*
HBL	*Hechos de don Berenguel de Landoira*
¹TFL	Tabera-Fonseca Lawsuit
²AR	Archaeological Record

Introduction

After my participation, in 2002, in a project of investigation developed by the Santiago de Compostela University that investigated, brought out the light and reconstructed the medieval happening and the history of the Compostelan fortress of A Rocha Forte,[3] I have maintained a line of investigation that during this time has not separated to me from the deposit. From A Rocha, with a morphology already defined since the 15th century by the historical sources, and that has not done but to confirm itself at the present time, after several campaigns of excavation (Casal et al. 2004, Casal et al. 2005 and Casal et al. 2006), there are diverse questions that reduce to define. They are, some of them, as we're going to see, those that will occupy the following pages.

Our conceptual frame has been already defined in the volume derived from mentioned investigation project and is in this one in which we reaffirm ourselves. Thus, and as a synthesis of that frame, we have to establish a series of premises. From our point of view the data and information of the AR could solely be processed, in which to investigation and medieval archaeology it takes about, within its context and located in the historical evolution of the Middle Ages; an affirmation that, although seems evident, not always is completely assumed (Sánchez, 2005: 65-6). It will not be sufficient to bring to light the vestiges of the past, the material culture, the structures and walls, but to develop a complete and complex interpretation of such, locating them of an exact, coherent and rigorous way in the ample chronological and evolutionary panorama of the medievalism; something for what the historical knowledge and of the textual sources is revealed as fundamental.

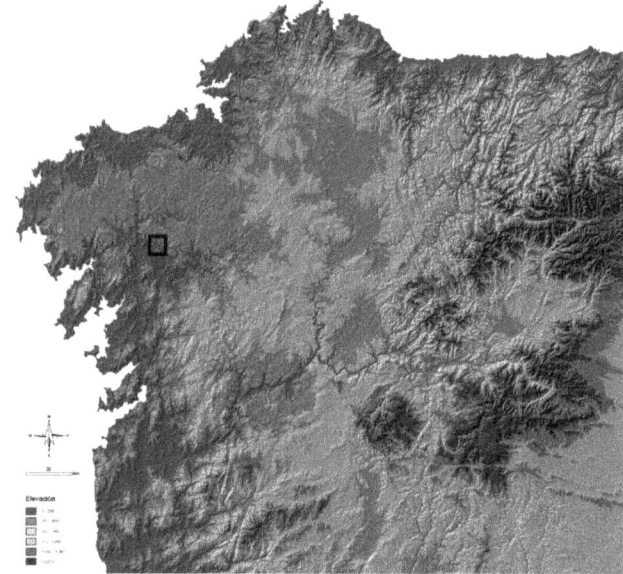

Figure 1. Location of Rocha Forte in Galicia (NW of Spain)

The data of the AR will not be sufficient by himself, as in many occasions – something of which so many times we, the medievalists, have complained– the written references are also incomplete. Only overlapping perfectly both types of sources we will reach the objective that, from the medievalism, like from historical science in general, it is persecuted: the creation of historical knowledge, as we say, rigorous, devoid of speculations –hypothesis is not equivalent to speculation–; a knowledge marked by a serious methodological exposition, guided by a series of asks and questions to solve and that, after our investigation, has to receive his fulfilled an-

---

[1] Several authors: *Hechos de don Berenguel de Landoira, arzobispo de Santiago*. Santiago de Compostela, 1983.

[2] RODRÍGUEZ GONZÁLEZ, Ángel, *Las fortalezas de la mitra Compostelana y los «irmandiños». Pleito Tabera-Fonseca*, Santiago de Compostela, 1984.

[3] Project of investigation of which a volume has emanated that collects and interprets textual information relative to the castle, giving an historical interpretation of the fortress that does not forget the material rest (Portela et al., 2004).

swer. Medieval archaeology will not be reinforced because of making more interventions, but to remove true and rigorous yield to its results, by valid and critic interpretations for the knowledge of the medieval world.

The incipient definition of the morphology of the fortress, as we have expressed, does not make but confirm the data that the historical sources, since end of 15th century, offers to all that wanted to listen them and that in no way are exhausted, but more and more loaded of reason. Well; today, from the present writing, we want to make, following the path indicated with that first investigation, a reconstruction of the military architecture of A Rocha Forte at 14th century, through a series of interpretations that we hope will serve as base for future works and help to a clearer conception about the morphology of the strongest fortress of his time in the Kingdom of Galicia.

An study that, as we are going to see, are fruits of an investigation that has thrown surprising results, transporting to us in a trip by Syria and Wales of centuries 13th and 14th.

A Rocha Forte. Constructive phase with Don Berenguel de Landoira and insertion in the European military constructive currents. A concentric castle

In the title of the present epigraph we make a reference to a *concentric castle*, a very concrete type. As we are going to see, the morphology of the fortress has confirmed, after our investigation, an extremely interesting and unpublished information that locates the architectonic advances and applications of the 14th century in such type of building.

As we will be able to appreciate next, the construction, or, rather, the second constructive phase in the construction of A Rocha, that we had already defined previously (Portela et al. 2004: 69), developed with Don Berenguel of Landoira, at the 20's of the 14th century, can be integrated, unlike which it has come affirming traditionally and lately, in a much more general constructive current. A constructive current that applies the last advances in architecture and medieval military construction. In fact, the consideration of the fortress of Rocha Forte from the point of view of the architectonic military middle-medieval advances can suppose a certain change respect to consideration of delay of the fortresses in the peninsular northwest towards 13th and 14th centuries in relation to the own French and English fortifications –remarked delay, sometimes, even for the set of the hispanic-christians peninsular constructions in general.[4]

Any affirmation, denying the existence of any parallel of A Rocha Forte, makes no sense since the moment in that, as we are going to see, its morphology is directly related with fortresses from Holy Land to the welsh coast, locating itself in a very concrete moment with equally concrete constructive and defensive traditions and methods, at level of western medieval Europe.

The type denominated *concentric castle*, corresponds, with all probability, to the most outstanding and strong model of the medieval fortifications, as well as to one of most complex. Let us make, in the first place, a characterization in abstract.

Figure 2. The two *cercas* or walls of *A Rocha Forte* at the south corner with circular tower in the inner and space opened between both.

Generally such type is defined as a castle within a castle or a fortification within a fortification, maintaining the sense of the word «concentric», that is to say, with only one center. Such concept, morphologically, is shaped in a fortification characterized by the presence of an outer wall of smaller height, with drum towers in the corners, that surround to the inner fortification, more elevated (Gravett, 2006: 51), generally with square or quadrangular plant and with the towers fit in the wall. The plant is made most symmetrical as possible, facilitating the defense.

Between both walls not only stays a reduced distance (Gravett, 2006: 51), but the space *interwalls* is divided and segmented with cross-sectional walls, so in case the first defense were broken, the enemy, in its penetration, see disabled its movement, remaining confined in an relatively reduced spaces (Hopkins, 2001: 148) and at the mercy of the first fortification, more elevated and with higher power of attack-defense.

The defense of such types of fortifications is relatively simple, maintained by its great strength and military constructive advances, so that, generally, it was decided on long sieges in which the war machine played a fundamental role in the attack.

---

[4] In words of Mora-Figueroa (1988: 21), towards century 13 such fortifications of the peninsular christian space "aún perfeccionándose respecto a los tres siglos precedentes, acusan ya incuestionablemente un notable retraso cualitativo respecto a las homólogas occidentales" without support comparisons with the fortresses emanated of the reigns of Felipe II Augusto (1180-1223) or of Eduardo I Plantagenet (1272-1307).

Figure 3. Outer wall and circular bucket of S corner tower. Ther is appraised, in background, the inner wall.

Figure 4. Western corner circular tower.

Is a basic principle the fact of the difference of height between the inner walls, higher, and the outside, so, this way, from both of them a defense could be maintained reliable by means of archers, without obstructing in any case the firing line (Gravett, 2006: 51). The enemy would see itself, thus, harassed by two firing lines that affect him directly with a defense of the inner wall that perfectly observes the movement of the attackers (Hopkins, 2001: 148).

Although in the fortress of A Rocha Forte we cannot consider, in the elements of the AR, the heights of the *cercas* (the walls) (Cooper, 1998: 56), such aspect will be at least fundamental if we put it in relation with the image that of the castle offers to us the Tumbo B, book contemporary to the prelature of Don Berenguel, to the reform of A Rocha in 14th century and to all these innovations.

In addition, in the concentric castles, we can see in the buildings technical advances like the circular towers in the angles, so that, on the one hand, blind angles were eliminated for the defense and, by another one, the projectiles sent against them were rejected better. The square angular towers had presented a bigger problem of structure by the corners and a greater weakness, resolved, towards end of 13th century and beginning of the 14th, with the circular towers. It allowed, on the other hand, a better circulation of the defenders throughout the building and a better firing line.

This type of fortification is marked too by its great size, in contrast with the previous minor castles and other constructions, reason why the concentric castles contained a greater number of troops lodged in the complex.[5]

Finally, diverse constructions were added too, that reinforced the weakest points of the building, as it could be the entrance, in which located lateral towers to the door and a barbican like first defensive element, along with the pit and the drawbridge and *portcullis*, iron door that rose as a rake.

Defined already the theoretical archetype, as second step let's make specific such characteristics in concrete examples, real parallels of the castle of Rocha Forte, in spite of the distance that separates them; let's follow the line that leads us from Syria and Wales to Compostela and A Rocha.

The first castle that we can denominate concentric, is the one of Caerphilly, near Cardiff, in Wales; at least the first that properly initiates its construction in that style *ex novo*. Its construction begins in 1268, being at its moment the hardest castle of all Great Britain. Is a construction of the nobility, carried out by order of one of the main welsh nobles, Gilbert of Clare, *earl* of Gloucester. Caerphilly, as we are going to see, constitutes a plant and a type of fortification that, truly, can be considered concentric (Saunders, 1998: 111).

But the origin of the concentric castles was even further and previous. In the Holy Land, after the crossed expeditions and throughout the ample Christian establishment in the zone, there were built, among others, diverse and considerable concentric fortresses that served as model for the European, with one specially remarkable case: the Krak of the Knights, in Syria. The Krak comes from an Muslim establishment occupied by Raimundo of Tolosa towards 1099, in the First Crossed; on this base, already in Christian hands, at 1142 it is yielded at the service of the Hospital Order, which establishes in him its seat. From here, the enclave will begin to being fortified, to became the strongest Holy Land castle; after the destruction, by natural causes, towards beginnings of 13th century of that fortifications, defensive elements are constructed again, although of greater power. It is then, already towards 1202, when it begun to be built the enormous wall that surrounds it, taking advantage of orography, and conforming a concentric castle.

The crossed and the noble knights took good account of such model and plants for the construction of fortifications, as well as of their effectiveness, and carried such military advances to Europe, not only to construct new fortresses but to modify the already existing ones.

It is for that reason why we refer Caerphilly as the first concentric castle *ex novo*, although coexists with other modified previous fortresses. This one is, also, the case of the Krak.

---

[5] Something common to many low-medieval European fortresses. (Turnbull, 1995: 94).

Figure 5. Quadrangular tower in the middle of the S-W wall.

But this is not, simply, an inference. The British monarch Edward I participates actively in the campaign of San Juan of Acre, in 1271-1272, and will be during this stay in the Holy Land when he realizes of the effective of the Krak and its plant, carrying such idea to England. His campaign of siege in Wales begins shortly after, with devastating campaigns in 1276 and 1277 and with the construction of multitude of fortresses in the last quarter of 13th century –when A Rocha were already built since the 30's of the century, by the archbishop Juan Arias– to seat his dominion in the British West, military establishments marked by its power and its strategic location (Saunders, 1998: 111). Of such fortresses several of them were made following the concentric model;[6] among them the most perfect example of concentric castle: Beaumaris, begun its construction in 1295 and, in fact, never finalized. Beaumaris predominates with other three fortresses of Edward I on all those of the moment: Harlech, Conwy and Caernarfon, constituting, Beaumaris, the most perfected.

The importance that Beaumaris has for our case, comes given not only by its plant, which, as we are going to see, it could resemble to the one of A Rocha, but by the equipment of construction that raises it. The constructive technique, design of plant, etc. of the main fortifications of the welsh campaign of Edward I were developed by French architects, emphasizing one on all of them: James of Saint George d'Esperanche (†1309),[7] architect of the locality of Saint George d'Esperanche, near Vienne, person in charge of more than 10 of the 17 Edwardian castles in Wales and person in charge of the construction of Beaumaris, perfection of the concentric castles, in addition to other European fortifications, like the castle of Yverdon, for the count of Saboya, in the 70's of 13th century (Pounds, 1990: 178).

So, let's summarize this second step. Fortresses of concentric type in the Holy Land; the Frank and British crossed take good account of the effectiveness of these plants and defensive systems; they carry such models with them to apply them in their castles in Europe or to construct other ones *ex novo*, among them Edward I, following the example of the Krak of the Knights; it crystallizes such tendency in fortresses as Caerphilly or, in a more perfect way, Beaumaris; and those are French architects the ones that perfect that kind of construction, specially the greater military architect of the transition of 13th to 14th centuries, James of Saint George d'Esperanche, person in charge of Beaumaris.

Figure 6. Cross-sectional wall *interwalls*, in one of the corners towers, that delimits the space, reducing the attacking mobility; own defensive system of the concentric castles.

But making specific, do true similarities exist in A Rocha? Can we really speak about a general constructive tradition? Can we consider, with the existing data of the AR, that Rocha Forte was conformed at 14th century as a concentric castle, applying important architectonical advances of French influence? After the analysis that we have made, the answer to all those questions is, without a doubt, affirmative.

The structures and rests of the deposit are overlapped perfectly with the textual information –mainly the Tabera-Fonseca– and the draws of the Compostelan documentation and, as we are going to see, with the considerations of the present article, we fitted a new piece of puzzle, starting of the raises that has guided this line of work since the 2002 project.[8]

Most of the principles that we have already theorized and applied to European and crossed cases are perfectly visible in A Rocha.

---

[6] The Edwardian fortresses in England and Wales are: Beaumaris, Raby, Harlech, Aberystwyth, Caerphilly, the tower of London, Leeds, Queensborough. There are other fortresses that follow partially the concentric model: Conway, Denbigh, Carew, Kidwelly, Goodrich and Dover.

[7] Personage studied deeper by A. J. Taylor (1950: 433-57). It is remarkable the concentric castle of the birth locality of James, Esperanche, although of smaller complexity than the welsh examples (Taylor, 1953: 36-9).

[8] An idea that we have had introduced at Portela et al. 2004: 63, when, making a reference about a possible cooperation of French architects on the building of A Rocha, we affirm that "no es imposible que en esa tarea, contribuyeran a la difusión de los modos de la arquitectura militar francesa, fenómeno conocido en la Europa de la centuria del doscientos".

Figure 7. Narrow space between walls, delimited by the circular corner tower, inner, the second wall, outside, and the cross-sectional wall.

Let's consider, in the first place, the plant and the defense. As we had referred, the concentric castles are marked by the existence of, *ad minimum*, two concentric walls and a quadrangular plant marked by the symmetry; it happens in the main considered fortresses, like Beaumaris or Caerphilly.

In case of A Rocha Forte the information emanated of the Tabera-Fonseca lawsuit, with one question exclusively about A Rocha, refers the existence of three diverse defensive walls, called *cercas*; in concrete *three çercas around [...] and says this witness that the çercas of the fortress was battleled*;[9] although there are multiple references in this source that corroborates such configuration we will not go deep more in them, till present is not a study centered in the textual sources, although, as we will see, its information is completely truthful and trustworthy.

Such descriptions suggest already, as we see, that this is a plant of a concentric castle, and, confirming such consideration, the successive campaigns of excavations have brought out to light two of the referred walls, now perfectly visible. Considering the aerial photography the plant that is observed (Portela et al. 2004: 35, 42), as well as in a simple observation on the land, it is perfectly quadrangular. At the first wall, the interior, we find two circular plant towers, at least in the excavated sectors, the corners, and one quadrangular plant tower in the middle of the wall, three of the nine towers that, following the textual low-medieval sources, would have the fortress. Nine towers located two arranging the entrance, another four, one in each corner, and another three, one in the center of each wall; and it must be added to them the *bara de casa* or donjon. The second wall, the exterior one, presents drum towers (circular) in the corners and a quadrangular bastion in the center, in correspondence with the towers of the first enclosure. We verify here the application of the defensive system of circular plant in the corner towers, avoiding or trying to diminish the damages of an attack, thus like blinding angles to possible enemies. The assumption of such advance, in addition, is demonstrated, also, in the fact that the central tower of the wall, at least the bastion of the outer one, needing a deeper excavation of the own tower, presents a quadrangular plant; they are the corner towers those that are made on circular plant, technical resource developed in the transition between 13th and 14th centuries and oriented, as we said, to the deflection of the shots of level trajectory (Cooper, 1998: 56).

The information, as much the textual information of the Tabera-Fonseca as the extracted ones of the AR, allows to infer a plant marked by the symmetry, with an entrance flanked by two quadrangular plant towers, although of smaller power than the ones of the corners, and almost without a doubt a tower in the middle of the wall opposed to the entrance.

Figure 8. Cross-sectional wall delimiting, perhaps, a space, as a defensive system, between second and third close.

It would be conformed, thus, in plant, that "castle within a castle", which, more ahead, we will examine in a more graphical way, considering the parallels already referred.

Between both *cercas* or walls there opens a reduced space interwalls; a sufficient space for the movement of the defenders but that, in case of being broken the outer enclosure of defense by the attackers, it would become for them a mouse hole. This is possible in order to the cross-sectional linen cloths of wall that limit the space, reducing the capacity of movement of the invader and leaving him at the mercy of archers and defenders in the inner enclosure. An innovator system applied in the Krak of the Knights, in the welsh fortresses and here in Rocha Forte. There are perfectly clear defensive elements that we had suspected, and, among them, such cross-sectional walls that delimit the intermediate space, in a new application of military constructive advances at level of western Europe in 14th century.

There is even the possibility, although only a deep and rigorous archaeological work will be able to confirm it, of which the linen cloth of wall that is observed cross-sectionally one of the corner circular drum towers of the outer enclosure, corresponds with one of such constructions that would divide the space between second close and third, referred by the Tabera-Fonseca, as well as reflected in the illustration of the for-

---

[9] *Tenia tres çercas alderredor [...] e dize el dicho testigo que las dichas çercas de la dicha fortaleça heran almenadas de sus almenas.* Answer of Fernán de Roán. TFL, pages 117-118. Also clear results other answers, as the one of the clergyman Gonzalo García of Baamonde.

tress made at the Tumbo B.¹⁰ One third wall which would be further of the castle and that would go until beyond the pit. This one is, as we say, a hypothesis that only with work will be clarify.

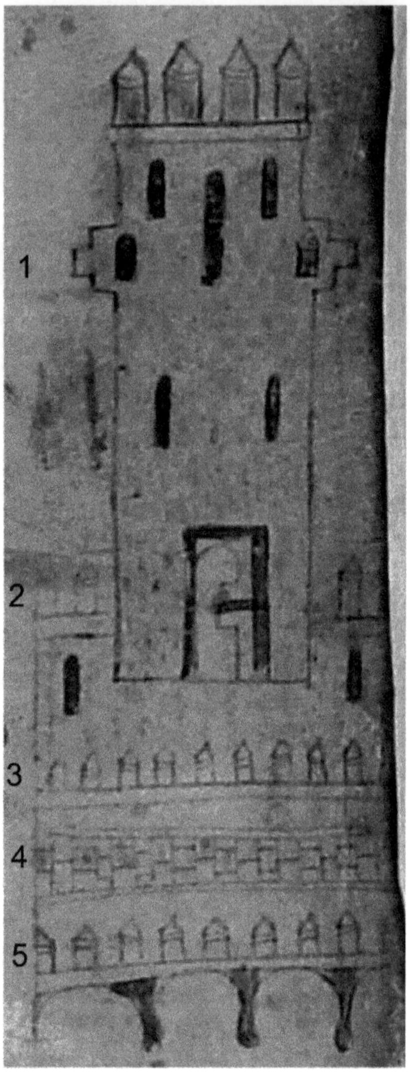

Figure 9. Miniature of the *Tumbo B* representing the strength of Rocha Forte. Possible interpretation to the light of AR: 1.Donjon; 2. Towers of the first wall (elevated over the wall); 3. First wall; 4. Second wall; 5. Pavement; 6. Third wall.

As we have had indicated, relative with the defense –and morphology– of the concentric castles was fundamental the difference of altitude between both enclosures,¹¹ allowing in the defense the activity of archers on each one of them without interfering each other; from each one of them the firing line would be clean, allowing the defense from both. Certainly, we do not have a complete wall, *in situ*, that rises from its base to the battlement, so we solely will be able to make inferences about the heights. But other sources come in our aid;

again the Tabera-Fonseca and, in a graphical way, the illustrations of the Compostelan Tumbo B.

Figure 10. Identification of constructive elements in SW wall: 1. Towers of the first wall; 2. First wall; 3. Second wall; 4. Pavement.

As we expressed, we will not do here one draining of the documentary sources, nor make a complete history of the place; such work is already done and published, within reach of any investigator. We will consider, simply, extremely illustrative descriptions, like already referred of Fernán of Roan and Gonzalo García of Baamonde, some of the more graphical of the lawsuit. First it affirms that *la torre de bara de casa* (central donjon) *muy alta que hera de quatro sobrados en alto [...] las quales dichas nuebe torres eran altas sobre la dicha çerca que tenian cada una un sobrado*¹² and the second that there was, in the middle, *una bara de casa e torre de omenaje e dentro su fuerte que hera de quatro sobrados*.¹³ They make, thus, reference to the different height between towers and close.

The existence of those three walls, as well as its different height, along with the greater elevation of a central donjon and an medium height of the towers fit at the first wall, is reflected perfectly in the miniature that initiates the Tumbo B. The elevation of the towers over the linen cloths of walls is considered, along with the application of round towers cleared in the corners and with the change in the location of the fortresses –location from moats and elevations to level geographic spaces– as one of the main innovations in the military construction of 14ᵗʰ century (Cooper, 1998: 56-7).¹⁴

---

¹⁰ ACS, CF 33, fol. 2v°.
¹¹ Signed, in the case of A Rocha, in Casal et al. 2006: 200 giving to it the sense of "para dificultar el acceso a las partes nobles del castillo".
¹² TFL, page 35.
¹³ TFL, page 36.
¹⁴ In particular, and in relation to the elevation of the towers, a current "más notable en Castilla en castillos que parecen ser del siglo 14 que en ninguna otra época". Such elevation is attributed, also, at general level, to the development of the war machine in that century, counting on passages that cross the towers and of great elevation to allow the transit of the men and the displacement of such machinery (Cooper, 1998: 57, 60).

Figure 11. Pavement located in the humid pit, the one that responds, maybe, with the pavement of the miniature in the *Tumbo B*.

Figure 12. Humid pit outside the second wall. Fortress of Beaumaris (Wales).

So, in a more graphical way, and extending the set of our sources, we observe the Compostelan building in this illustration, that, in the Compostelan Tumbo B, reflects the fortress of A Rocha, shaping an episode of the *Facts of don Berenguel de Landoira*. A miniature made in that 14th century, not much later, without a doubt, of the rebuilding of the castle with don Berenguel, to which more ahead we will make reference. In fact, considering the previous data about the construction of concentric castles and intercrossing them with the image, we can get to understand better such representation; a case in that there are the written sources those that allow us to document the reality, beyond any partiality.

In such illustration, there is a possibility that the three walls are not only represented in perspective, that is to say, to a different distance with respect to the center, the donjon, but represented, similarly, the altitude difference among them.

Even, considering the vestiges of the AR, we can get to close identify the pavement that in the Compostelan miniature is drawn between second and third walls the pavement that indeed was extra walls of the second close; pavement that is located just in the middle of the pit. It could to make no sense, unless we consider the information of the Tabera-Fonseca, in which it alludes to a pit half dry and half humid, that is to say, only partially full of water: the fortress *tenia dos cabas, la una llena de agoa que no se le podía quitar y otra seca e que le paresçe que tenia su barbacana*.[15] The pavement could allow, without a doubt, the transit by the own pit, already was in its dry part, like towards the humid part.

It does not constitute some singularity; the fortress of Beaumaris presents an identical defensive system.[16] An outer wall of smaller height, with a pit, half dry half humid, and an higher inner wall more elevated with towers in the own fence, following a well-taken care of symmetry in plant.

In Rocha Forte, if we consider the information of the documentary sources of the low Middle Ages, third wall it has not been identified yet; we must verify –among other aspects– if the arches represented in the miniature of the Tumbo B corresponds with some real constructive system of the fortress or, on the contrary, responds to a esthetic or imaginative criteria of the cotrack or drawer.

To such innovations are added elements like the battlement of the walls, referred already in the documentary sources, like the declaration of Juan of Silva, who, in reference to the fences affirms that all *toda hera almenada*.[17] Walls of such potency that some of the witnesses affirms that *hera alderredor cercada que paresçia una çiudad*,[18] comparing the castle with an fortified town, in a testimony referred to 15th century but because of a construction, as we see next, developed in the 14th.

As we have referred, we consider Rocha Forte like one more example of a constructive military current developed in the transit of the 13th century to the 14th, with influences of the Holy Land, France and the British Islands. But such affirmation will be more comprehensible if we consider the plants of the mentioned fortresses. As from aerial photography as in plant, the comparison of A Rocha with the other castles, about distribution of the space, application of defensive and military constructive techniques and morphology of the fortresses, it does not leave another possibility that to fit it in the same constructive current of concentric castles, emphasizing, specially, the parallel of Beaumaris.

---

[15] TFL, page 63. Declaration of Pedro Gómez, Compostelan clergyman.
[16] Plants and images of Beamaris and Caerphilly, source: www.castlewales.com.

[17] TFL, page 179. Declaration of Juan de Silva. Corroborated by other declarations, as the one of Alonso Cerdeira. TFL, page 223.
[18] TFL, page 228. Declaration of Jacome Alonso of Faxilde.

The fortress of Rocha Forte and the european military building currents. A concentric castle (14th century)

Figure 13. Dry pit outside the second wall. Fortress of Beaumaris (Wales).

The walls, concentric, the bastions and drum towers in the outside wall, the towers in the interior wall, the disposition of them, the angular ones and the quadrangular one, the fortification of the entrance with towers to each side, the circular plant of the angular towers, all of them are revealed like common and fundamental factors to consider the history of A Rocha Forte in 14th century and to interpret, correctly, the AR.

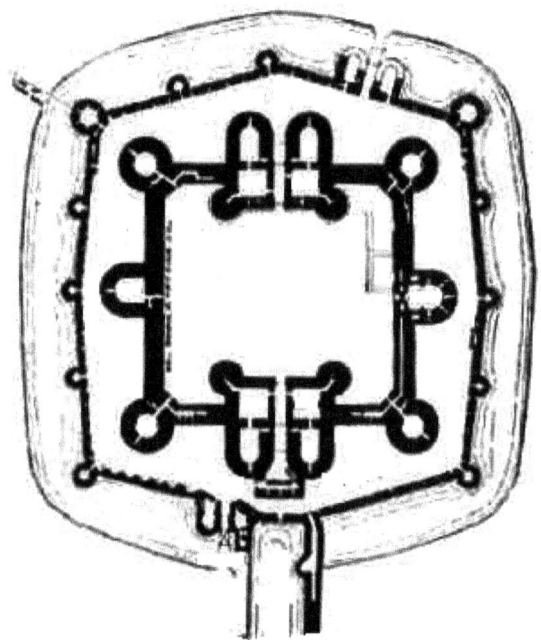

Figure 14. Plant of Beaumaris fortress (Wales).

Certainly fortresses of Beaumaris and Caerphilly present a greater potency, demonstrated, for example, in a greater space *interwalls*, but the constructive conception, purpose and technique grown from the same trunk. In the case of the Krak of the Knights all of it is magnified, specially this constructive potency, inner spaces, and towers and drum towers and bastions of enormous power, but again, and favor to Edward I among others, this conception drinks of the same sources that, *mutatis mutandis*, Rocha Forte.

The Krak of the Knights, as precedent, is revealed as a first moment of the construction of concentric castles, for that reason the similarities with the model that we are establishing are minor than in parallels like the welsh Edwardian fortresses.

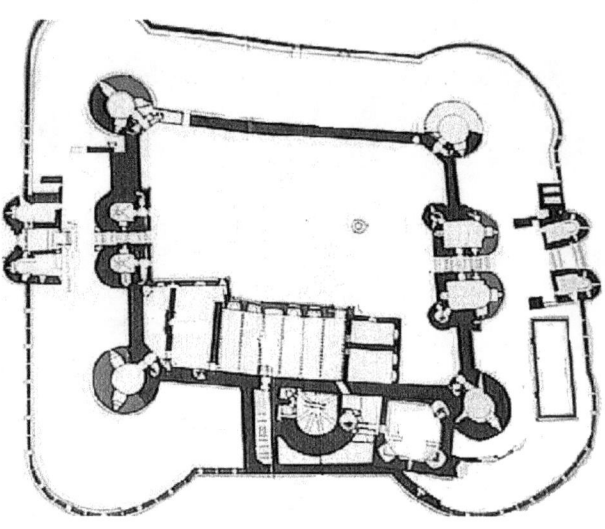

Figure 15. Plant of Caerphilly fortress (Wales).

In Rocha Forte the first and second walls are separated by a smaller distance, but, with such precisions, the partial consideration of the right longitudinal wall of Beaumaris seems to see itself reproduced in the Galician fortress. In both cases we can observe clearly the same succession of defensive structures, in the same order: *pit-second wall-interwall space-first wall*; and the same we could say about Caerphilly.

Similarly, the entrance in both fortresses, A Rocha and Beaumaris, present undeniable similarities, conforming both castles, as we are affirming, clear examples of concentric castles and fitted in the same chronological and constructive frame. An entrance protected by a barbican, or defensive structures, in front of the access, structure that in the case of A Rocha is not confirmed yet, and with two towers arranged one to each side. It although we found some differences, like the ample defensive structure intrawalls in Beaumaris, pertaining to the barbican, whereas in Rocha Forte the two outer towers are solely documented, or the fact that in Beaumaris these towers are semicircular, whereas in A Rocha seem quadrangular.

What it is doubtless is that Rocha Forte presents all the defensive elements, as far as its access, observable in the concentric castles and that were developed, mainly, in the fortresses of 14th century. The written medieval sources, again, of outstanding form the lawsuit Tabera-Fonseca, and the comparison with other cases, gives us the reason.

It is a fortress that counted with a barbican as protection in its entrance; a barbican that perhaps is under the slope that is located in front of the own access of A Rocha.

Figure 16. Plant of A Rocha Forte in aerial view.

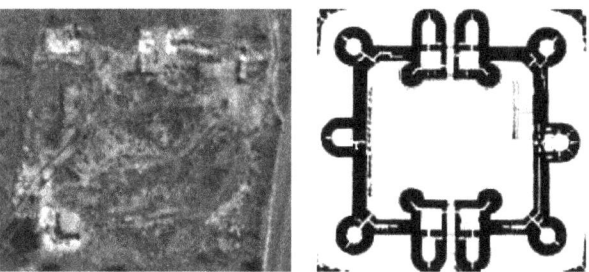

Figure 17. Comparison of A Rocha-Beaumaris plants.

The existence of a pit implies the presence of a drawbridge that makes the transit possible towards the inner space; one bridge referred, also, by the people that had observed the castle at the end of 15th century, like Fernán of Roan who refers its *barrera y cava alderredor con su puerta llebadiça*.[19] Everything is united the existence of a *portcullis*, an iron door or grate elevated from inside, exerting a limitation in the own access and a defense, a barrier *que benia debajo de las dichas dos çercas*.[20] Everything is oriented, evidently, to make more difficult the penetration of attacking and enemy contingents in the fortress; this way, the weakest access, the door, is controlled and assured.

There is a possibility that some of such elements were reflected in the Compostelan miniature of Tumbo B. The representation of the access door to the fortress presents a strange outline that feels to us like a schematization of some defensive system in the own door or access; we are not able to define if it is located in the close inner one, with the towers to both sides, or in the *bara de casa*, or donjon, which would imply a modification of our hypothesis.

We have to add the presence, already referred, of a tower to each side of the door and we can obtain a complete image of the system of access to the fortress of Rocha Forte. Particularities? None; at least none if we considered the Compostelan castle like one more in a low-medieval constructive tradition as which we are defining. As we have verified in the analysis of the plants, as much Beaumairs as Caerphilly has that defensive elements: the drawbridge, *portcullis*, one defensive structure in front of the access, making more difficult the attacks and the penetration of hostile troops, and the towers flanking the own door. In the case of the Krak, its location conditions the morphology, as far as defensive elements, so that it lacks a pit to the use, although presents, also, defensive structures reinforcing the access.

The parallels of A Rocha are not only these, but, in last case, we could establish them, also, with fortresses like the one of Saint George d'Esperanche, concentric castle although much more simple. But it is certain that, the referred ones constitute the clearest parallelisms.

Advances and constructive systems, everything, that made Rocha Forte the main fortress of the Kingdom of Galicia, strong and impressive, that "beautifull candel and jewell" for one of its contemporaries.[21]

Figure 18. Aerial view of the Krak of the Knights (Syria). Are appraised the two concentric walls, the towers in the walls and the outer buckets. It is not so evolved as Beaumaris or Caerphilly, but we have to consider that is a point to begin.

Plant, disposition of walls, disposition of towers, accesses, military, defensive and constructive conception, architectonical advances... Characteristics, all of them, not only common between A Rocha and the referred fortresses in Syria and Welsh, but archetypical of the European and Holylander concentric castles, that begins to be built in 13th century and seen their apogee in the 14th. All of it with two incontestable conclusions:

The first one is that Rocha Forte, after the repair of 14th century, is conformed as a concentric castle, being of this moment the architectonic innovations and constructive development that today is observed, remote and separated already of its moment of construction, with don Juan Arias in first half of 13th century; and the second one is we have located the morphological parallels of the fortress in its European sisters.

---

[19] TFL, page 117. Declaration of Fernán of Roan.
[20] TFL, page 242. Declaration of Alonso of Souto.

[21] TFL, page 218. Declaration of Fernando of Mini, senior.

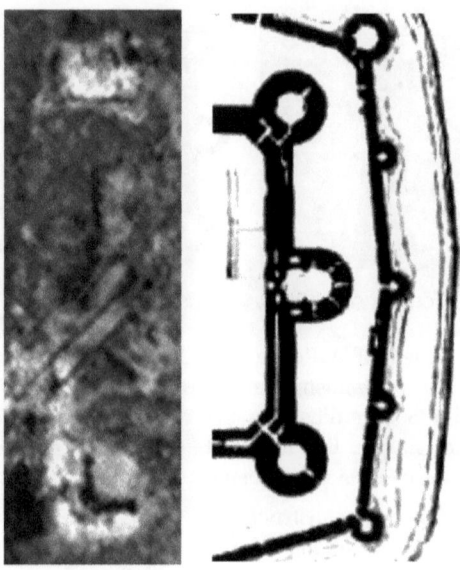

Figure 19. Longitudinal left wall of A Rocha and longitudinal right wall of Beaumaris.

But there is another final question to determine: the way in which such constructive and innovating methods, are applied in a fortress in the Galicia of the 14th century; I mean, how such currents arrive here from European military architecture and leave his track.

The rebuilding of A Rocha Forte like concentric castle in 14th century. Don Berenguel of Landoira, carrier of european constructive currents

So, as any other scientific asseveration, the affirmation of A Rocha Forte as a concentric castle cannot be made avoiding a contextualization. The previous references and dissertations of anything serve if they are not possible to be located and to be fitted, perfectly, in the medieval history of Galicia and Iberian Peninsula; as we have said, only in this way the medieval archaeology has full sense and fulfills its function of generating of historical knowledge.

The application of such military architectonic innovations to the fortress of A Rocha is clear; in fact, one of its contemporary ones, Alonso García of Parga, in its declaration in the Tabera-Fonseca lawsuit, offers us the key: the fortress *hera nesçesaria para la dicha santa yglesia de Santiago e dize que si la dicha fortaleza no fuera nesçesaria para la dicha sancta yglesia de Santiago que a ella no la hizieran como la hizieron por quel dicho testigo dize que oyo dezir que la dicha fortaleza de la Rocha Fuerte hera una cosa muy rezia y fuerte más que fortaleza de alderredor;*[22] we complete such sense with the eloquent phrase of the Compostelan clergy Pedro Gómez: *aquella fortaleza hazia estar quedo a los de la çiudad e de la tierra*[23] (that fortress made to be quiet to those of the city and the land). The castle of A Rocha adjusts, about its functionality, to which, from the high Middle Ages, in the terminology of the peninsular post-Carolingian territory denominates *domus*, a constructive set always composed by a variety of constructions that served as residence and refuge (Farias, 2002-2003: 38). But, at the same time, and probably in a more outstanding way tan the previous motivation –at least at 15th century–, A Rocha exerted a function of reinforcement of the feudal power of the Compostelan church on the city, constituting one of these centers of power characteristic of the feudalism (Portela et al., 2004: 61).

Figure 20. Entrance. Beaumaris.

Surely the rebuilding that suffer Rocha Forte during the prelature of don Berenguel, could have been less important and bottoms destined for it, but, being in that way, the castle were lost their sense: a truly unconquerable enclosure for protection of the Compostelan archbishop and members of the church in case of necessity and that it impressed the inhabitants of Compostela. Specially after the events which the archbishop don Berenguel, just named and arrived from France, had to face, with the city of Santiago in revolt and with A Rocha like only refuge. If that situation were repeated, at least he would be prepared. Like had affirmed Lopez Ferreiro, and as we have paraphrased other times: the Castell Sant'Angelo of Compostela.

The arriving of don Berenguel of Landoira to the Compostelan prelature was not, far from it, calm and quiet. After the death of the prelate don Rodrigo of Padrón, towards 1315, and after a split in the cathedral chapter, an urban revolt rises in Compostela, with the butler of the city don Alonso Suárez of Deza at the top. The pontiff John XXII, trying to tide up, names to one of his men of confidence, that in that moment managed peace between Flandes and the French monarch Philip V: the General of the Dominican Order, Berenguel of Landoira. His origin will not be trivial, as we are going to see; French, he was member of the house of the counts of Rodez and son of Arnaldo of Landoira, landlord of Solomiech (López Ferreiro, 1903: 12).

Figure 21. Entrance of A Rocha and quadrangular tower arranging it.

---
[22] TFL, page 144. Declaration of Alonso García of Parga.
[23] TFL, page 63. Declaration of Pedro Gómez.

Don Berenguel is named archbishop of Santiago by John XXII in 1217. With a city raised in arms against the archbishopric and with the cathedral and the own city closed, to his arrival he did not have more solution than continue his way and to take refuge in the fortress of the archbishops of Compostela, the Rocha Forte.

There he was under an intense siege, where, as the Chronicle of the facts of Don Berenguel says, the attackers *destrozaron completamente las edificaciones situadas dentro [...], les prendieron fuego en varios puntos y quemaron por entero las habitaciones del arzobispo*.[24] A situation that stayed until the well-known episode of the murder of the rebellious Compostelans, with Alonso Suárez de Deza to head, and the end of the revolt.

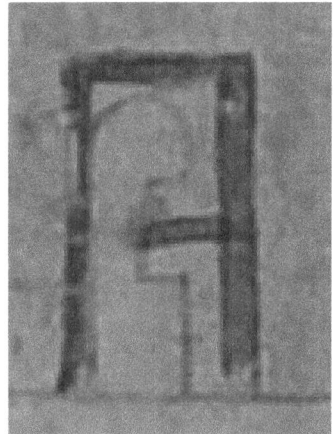

Figure 22. Representation of the access in A Rocha Forte (ACS, CF 32, fol. 2vº. Tumbo B).

The remodeling that needed the fortress was considerable, as much that don Berenguel passed to history, for some people, as the first builder of the castle, *ex novo*, case of Fr. Bartholomew, witness of the Tabera-Fonseca lawsuit and that *oyo dezir que la abia echo el arzobispo don Beringuel*[25] (he had listened to don Beringuel had built it). The reconstruction work, without a doubt, was long and expensive, but, in view of the convulse situation that the Compostelan church have had lived was necessary for the prelate to have a truly safe and strong fortress, that could support long sieges and that became guarantor of the integrity of the archbishop and the church chapter.

It is for that reason why don Berenguel, without a doubt put all means necessary so that the rebuilding of the Rocha responded to such characteristics of force and security. He could not allow that one situation as already happened were repeated, but, in case that happen, he would be prepared to resist. The one of don Berenguel constitutes, so, the second constructive time truly outstanding of Rocha Forte, after its construction by don Juan Arias, in 13th century, near the 30's (Portela et al., 2004: 64), and at the moment when the French architectonic innovations are truly applied.

---

[24] HBL, page 97. To beginnings of 1318 John XXII writes to Alonso Suárez de Deza in order to release the city and the fortresses that had took to the archbishop. ASV, Reg. Av. 9, fol. 109.
[25] TFL, page 58.

The fortress, without a doubt, was not collapsed as a whole, because throughout the conflict, many times it was used to pass the night by the prelate. With all probability to the flaws, that yes they would be numerous, was united the will of don Berenguel to fortify much more the enclave, obtaining a truly unconquerable bunker. This way, to the rebuilding of damaged structures would be united the addition of new constructive elements that completely change the appearance of the fortress.

Taking one more step, if we consider the origin of don Berenguel is completely coherent that the techniques that apply in the new construction of A Rocha are those he considered more advanced, following the French models that, probably, he had known. We must remember that don Berenguel comes from the zone of Rodez, very next to Isére, where, to 30 km SW of Lyon, locates Saint the Georges d'Esperanche, birthplace of the architect James of Saint the Georges, builder of Beaumaris, among others, in addition to build one concentric castle in this locality of Saint George.

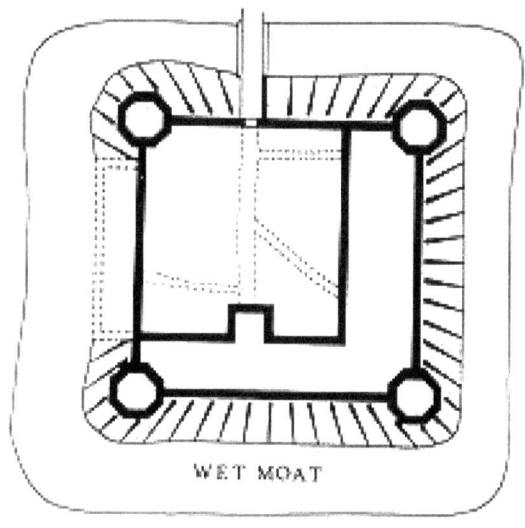

Figure 23. Plant of the fortress of Saint George d'Esperanche, forming a simple concentric castle built by James of Saint George.

Although we will not risk, at least while we do not count on new information, to say that the team of architects and constructors who rebuilt the Compostelan fortress was French, yes we can infer, without fear to be mistaken, that some architect of French influence was demanded and contracted by the Compostelan prelate to direct or to counsel the fact of the work. It is as well as it is explained that the constructive models of places and so different constructions are so similar.

The main advances in the European military architecture were being applied in Galicia, which already we have considered, and, indeed, don Berenguel is the nexus that explains such application: the fact of being the most important remodeling that suffered the fortress in its history, until the point to pass to history, for some, like its constructor; the fact that techniques developed in the transit of 13th to 14th centuries are applied; the fact of having documented this second constructive stage; the exact coincidence with plants of fortresses developed by the French school. It is the conjunction of such factors the one that conducts us to affirm that it was with don Berenguel, as a result of the destruction and later remodeling of Rocha Forte by the Compostelan rise, when the fortress is formed like a concentric castle, getting up to the most advanced European constructive currents.

Conclusions

We have not treated, in the present text, to apply principles of interdisciplinarity but of multiplicity of sources, intercrossing many different references and removing the greater possible yield to the existing information. We so understand and defend, thus, as already Jorge Eiroa has expressed, the existence of only one Medieval History susceptible to be studied taking as base several sources of very different origin (Eiroa, 2004: 113).

It is a rigorous critical procedure towards the written medieval sources, in the same way that it is towards the archaeological ones, which allows us to affirm its total validity as historical methodology itself. A critic that is solely serious and valid if it is made from the own medievalism, and the knowledge of his structures and of the treatment of his more basic sources. And it is in this context where we must insert the information that the AR provides to us and that, intercrossed with the textual ones, gives rise to the historical and scientific knowledge of the Middle Ages.

We have solely tried to conjugate the multiple sources whereupon we count for the study of the Galician Middle Ages, applying them to one of the most impressive deposits open in the last years: the fortress of A Rocha Forte.

We have been able to verify how, to the thread of the prelature of don Berenguel of Landoira, since 20's of 14th century, the fortress has been rebuilt. In the important conflicts the prelate finds at his arrival to Compostela and the important flaws they take place in the castle, its reconstruction was vital.

In agreement with the origin of don Berenguel, at the moment of making the repairs French models are followed, applying new constructive techniques and military architecture, developed already from second half of the 13th century by the French architects, specially by those employees by the English monarch Edward I in their campaigns of fortification of conquered Welsh territories.

Following such relation we found several parallels of A Rocha in Europe, mainly the Welsh castles of Beaumaris and Caerphilly, and, like more chronological and geographically further precedent, the Krak of the Knights in Syria.

Such parallels allow to infer the rebuilding of A Rocha following the models of the concentric castles, marked by a symmetrical plant and with several concentric walls, the existence of several heights in the walls, the circular corner towers, the pit presence and defensive systems in the accesses, like barbicans and *portcullis*. Everything we have been able to identify it in A Rocha.

We maintain, therefore, a line of investigation already initiated in 2002, that has been revealed deeply fruitful, giving rise to this new contribution about the fortress. We hope, from the present study, to contribute to the deeply knowledge of which it was more outstanding fortress of the Compostelan archbishopric and, probably, in the light of our considerations, the strongest fortress of the Kingdom of Galicia in 14th century.

Acknowledgments

Special thanks to Marina Novás Pérez for her help in the correction and writing of the present text, and to Sonia García Rodríguez for some graphical material.

References

Blanco Rotea, R. and García Rodríguez, S. 2005. Paisaje arquitecturado y arquitectura en el paisaje: la fortificación del territorio en época moderna en el Baixo Miño. *Arqueo-Web*, 7(2): september-december. 2005. (www.ucm.es/info/arqueoweb)

Casal, R.; Acuña, F.; Vidal, L.; Rodríguez, Á. and Nodar, C. 2004. A Fortaleza de Rocha Forte (Santiago): campañas de intervención 2002-2003. *Gallaecia*, 23: 195-204. Sada: Ediciós do Castro.

Casal, R.; Acuña, F.; Vidal, L.; Nodar, C.; Rodríguez, Á. and Alles, M.J. 2005. La fortaleza de A Rocha Forte (Santiago de Compostela): campaña de 2005. *Gallaecia*, 24: 193-218. Sada: Ediciós do Castro.

Casal, R., Acuña, F., Vidal, L., Nodar, C., and González, G. 2006. Fortaleza medieval de A Rocha Forte (Santiago de Compostela): campaña de 2005. *Gallaecia*, 25: 147-72. Sada: Ediciós do Castro.

Cooper, E. 1998. Los castillos de Castilla en el siglo XIV: un esquema para su estudio. In *El castillo medieval español: la fortificación española y sus relaciones con la europea*: 45-60. Madrid: Editorial Centro de Estudios Ramón Areces.

Eiroa Rodríguez, J.A. 2004. La relación entre documentos escritos y Arqueología en el estudio de la Edad Media en Europa: reflexiones para un debate teórico y metodológico. *ÁGORA*, 10(1/2): 113-27. Santa Cruz do Sull (Brazil).

Farias Zurita, V. 2002-2003. Las fortificaciones medievales del Vallés (siglos IX-XIII). Un inventario a partir de las fuentes escritas. *Acta historica et archaeologica medievalia*, 23/24: 23-49. Barcelona.

Lilley, K., Lloyd, Ch. and Trick, S. 2005. Mapping medieval urban landscapes: The design and planning of Edward I's new towns of England and Wales. *Antiquity*, 79(103): project gallery#3.

López Ferreiro, A. 1903-1905. *Historia de la Santa A. M. Igloesia de Santiago de Compostela*, VI-VIII. Santiago de Compostela.

Montjoye, A. de. 2002. La maison médiévale en brique (XIIe-XIVe Siècles) en France méridionale. In *La maison au Moyen Âge dans le Midi de la France* : 109-28. Toulousse.

Mora-Figueroa, L. de. 1998. La fortificación hispano.cristiana en el contexto europeo de los siglos IX al XIII. In *El castillo medieval español: la fortificación española y sus relaciones con la europea*: 15-22. Madrid.

Pounds, N.J.G. 1990. *The medieval Castle in England and Wales. A social and political history*. Cambridge.

Portela, E., Pallares, Mª. C. and Sánchez, X. M. 2004. *Rocha Forte. El castillo y su historia*. Santiago de Compostela.

Sánchez Sánchez, X. M. 2005. Castrizán: a fortaleza vixiante do sur. 1477-1478/9. *Seminario de Estudios Redondeláns*, 2: 63-94. Pontevedra.

Saundes, A. 1998. The castres of the norman conquest of England. Contrast and similarities with the "Reconquista". In *El castillo medieval español: la fortificación española y sus relaciones con la europea*: 101-112. Madrid.

Taylor, A. J.L 1950. Master James of St. George. *English Historical Review*, LXV: 433-57.

Taylor, A. J.L 1953. The castle of Saint George d'Esperanche. *Antiquaire Journal*, XXXIII: 36-9.

8

The Archaeological impact of the Lisbon earthquake (1755): the Archaeology of Built Space applied to the monastery of Santa María de Melón (Galice, Spain)

Rebeca Blanco Rotea
University of Santiago de Compostela

Begoña Fernández González
University of Santiago de Compostela

Abstract

This article summarizes the methodological process used, as well as the most outstanding results of the Architecture Archaeology study carried out in Santa María de Melón monastery (Galicia, Spain). Our project combined the stratigraphic analysis of paraments, the medieval Archaeology, the systematic casting of medieval and modern documentation as well as a typological and iconographical analysis much more common in Art History. This work has made it possible to identify the different stages of a building, as well as to reveal the existence of a number of structural improvements carried out during Modern age as a result of the 1755 Lisbon earthquake, also known as the Great Lisbon. In this respect, our work represents one of the first approaches carried out in Archaeology regarding the impact of this natural disaster on our country Heritage.

Introduction

In August 2002 the General Directorate of Tourism of Galicia's autonomous government, the Xunta, chose three independent working groups to carry out initial studies prior to designing the intervention project for the rehabilitation and conversion of the ancient Cistercian monastery of Santa María de Melón (Melón, Ourense) into a hotel and spa. Three specific types of study were requested: an archaeological company[1] was hired to carry out a series of soundings in various parts of the monastery. A team from the University of Santiago de Compostela, directed by Begoña Fernández Rodríguez, was hired to carry out a historical and artistic study of the building, involving the analysis of historical sources that refer to the monastery. Finally, a team from the Archaeology Laboratory of the 'Padre Sarmiento' Institute of Galician Studies directed by Rebeca Blanco Rotea was commissioned to carry out a stratigraphic analysis of the building by applying the Archaeology of Architecture.

The work of the last two teams started in August 2002 and came to an end on 31 January 2003. Although these studies were independently commissioned for each team, the need to work jointly on them meant that there was constant communication between all three. However, there was a much higher level of collaboration between the teams responsible for the historical and artistic investigation and the stratigraphic reading. In fact, the discovery of the impact caused upon the building by the Lisbon earthquake was a result of this collaboration.

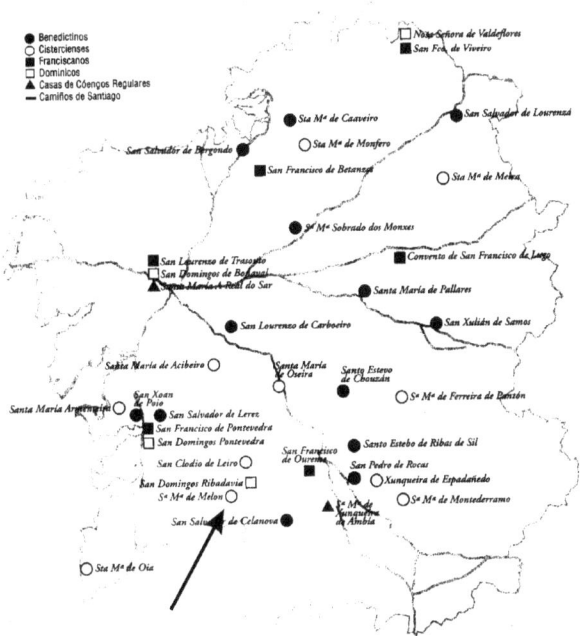

Figure 1. Geographical location of the monastery of Santa María de Melón (Ourense, Galicia).

In the study entitled *A Historical and Artistic analysis of the Monastery of Santa María de Melón*, it was requested that investigations be carried out into the real situation of the monastery and the role it played at the heart of the Galician Cistercian monasteries, which implied consulting numerous documental and bibliographic sources. This investigation was completed with an analysis of the building in terms of Art History, studying the different conserved parts of the building from both a stylistic and formal point of view. Simultaneously, in a study entitled *Stratigraphic Analysis and graphic documentation in the Monastery of Santa María de Melón* a stratigraphic reading was requested of some parts of the building that would help uncover their chronology and func-

---

[1] This work was carried out by the company "*Prospectiva y Análisis Arqueólogos*" directed by the archaeologist Andrés Bonilla Rodríguez.

tion. After an initial visit to the monastery, it was decided that a more general study be carried out covering the building as a whole, as although it was observed that the building had been made in different periods, it all belonged to a single unified complex forming a single entity, which had to be considered as such.

Description

Situation

The Monastery of Santa María de Melón is situated in the north-western Iberian peninsula to the south of Galicia, on the border between the provinces of Ourense and Pontevedra, between the hills of Faro and Carvelo, the Cortela and Bouzas rivers, and close to the mouth of the river Cerves. The building, as is typical in Cistercian monasteries, was built at the bottom of a deserted, lonely valley, suitable for spiritual contemplation, with some type of watercourse. The monastery at Melón overlooks a panorama of distant mountain ranges and pine woods (Torres Balbás 1954:19), perfectly in line with the type of location expected by the Order.

In 1134, one of the Order's guidelines stipulated that their houses should be set apart, in *"lonely places that are not frequented by man"* meaning that they generally chose valley floors with difficult access, allowing the community that settled there to concentrate on their monastic life. Closeness to watercourses was also sought (Torres Balbás 1954: 18), to guarantee the perfect development of community life within the monastery.

Description of the monastery and its internal organization

The remaining structures of the monastery are a church, part of the cloister and two wings of the Hospice Cloister (figures 2 and 3), as well as other common areas in both cloisters, and structures on nearby plots of land (dovecote, granaries, terraces for growing crops, etc.) The whole monastery complex is surrounded by a wall of large granite blocks combined with smaller stones, with a house to the west of the monastery today in private hands, but which was once monastery property.

The Church

The church of the Monastery of Santa María de Melón is laid out in the shape of a Latin cross whose naves (long since vanished) would have been divided into three main naves in seven sections (the organisation of which may still be seen today on the inner section of the southern wall, conserving the lateral southern nave), and whose central nave, following the traditional style, was twice the width of the side naves. There is a wide transept, divided into three main sections (arms to the north and south and transept), in which it is possible to observe evidence of restructuring work that took place in the monastery according to new stylistic movements, following its incorporation in the 'Congregation of Castille'. However, it still conserves remnants of its Mediaeval layout, with the northern wing including enclosures with primitive crossed vaults, whereas the eastern walls have two chapels displaying a clear influence from the Burgundy region.

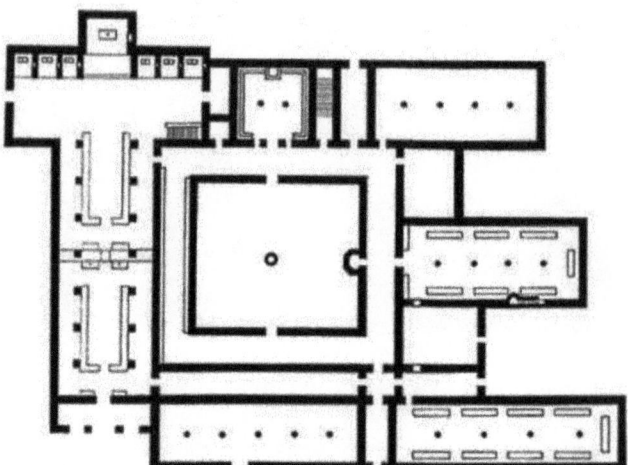

Figure 2. Standard layout of a mediaeval cistercian monastery.

Although something uncommon in Cistercian churches, as the majority chose to remodel their temples after joining the 'Congregation of Castille', the church at Santa María de Melón has a typically Mediaeval top section, organised around an ambulatory leading to three radial chapels, meaning that it has a close relation with other examples found today in the region of Galicia.

Apart from the chapels mentioned above, in the northern arm of the transept, communicated with it via an access door (referred to in Mediaeval times as the *Door of the Dead*), is a chapel with a single nave divided into two sections, finished off with a semicircular apse preceded by a straight section which forms the presbytery of the chapel and which was used for funerary purposes.

The church has undergone serious alterations around its naves, and lost a significant part of its surface area after being struck by lightning and affected by a storm at the end of the 19th century, which lead to the reconstruction of the western gable end of the temple in modern times.[2]

Parts of the monastery

The Cistercian Order appeared at the end of the XI century, when a group of Benedictine monks, affected by the chaotic situation of the regular clergy and a distancing from the original tenets of the Benedictine order, decided to return to the lifestyle propounded by St. Benedict; their basic statement of rules for the Cistercian order are the Regula Benedictini. This conceives monasteries as spaces that should remain completely independent from the rest of the world, and be organised as closed spaces in which the monk has contact with the rest of the community but remains cut off from the outside world. To do so, the monasteries were built around a common space (the cloister), around which a number of rooms were built in which the monks carried out their shared and private activities.

---

[2] See Cameselle Bastos 1990.

Archaeotecture: Second Floor

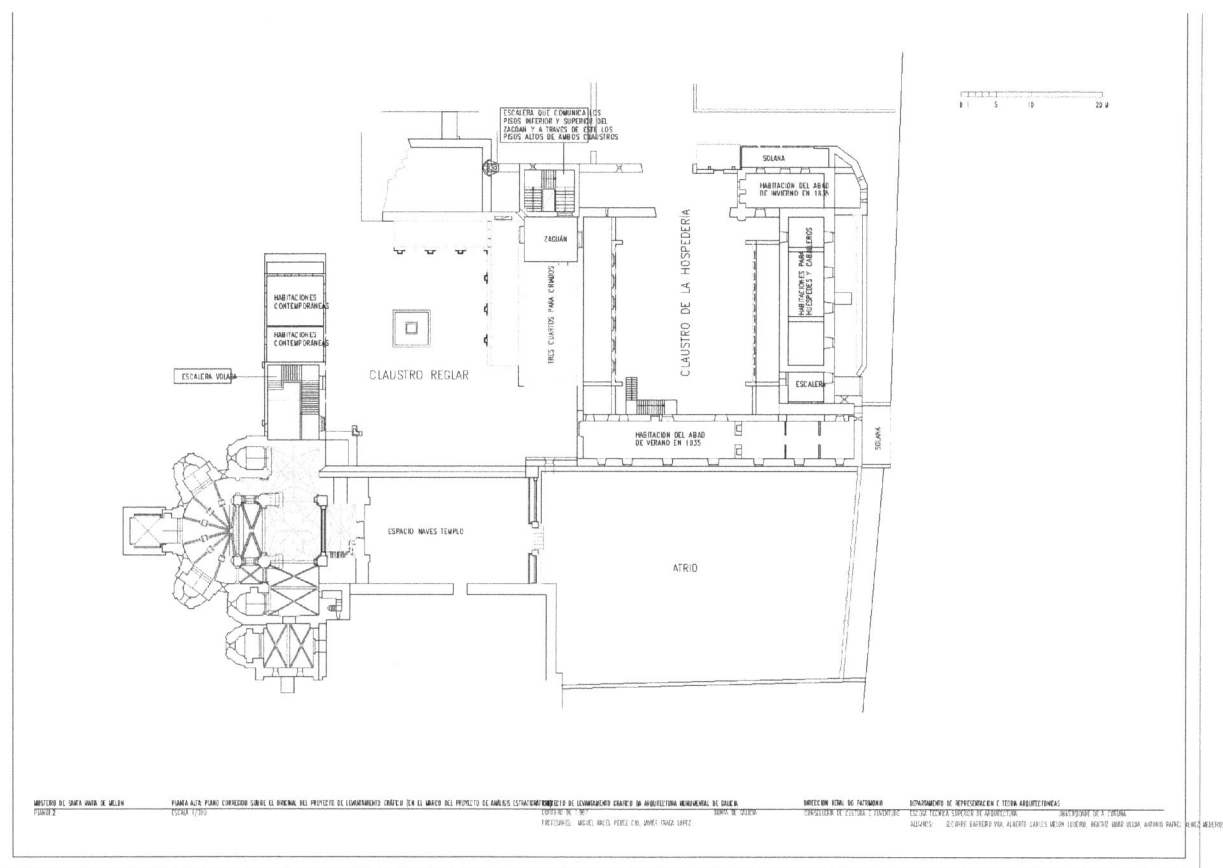

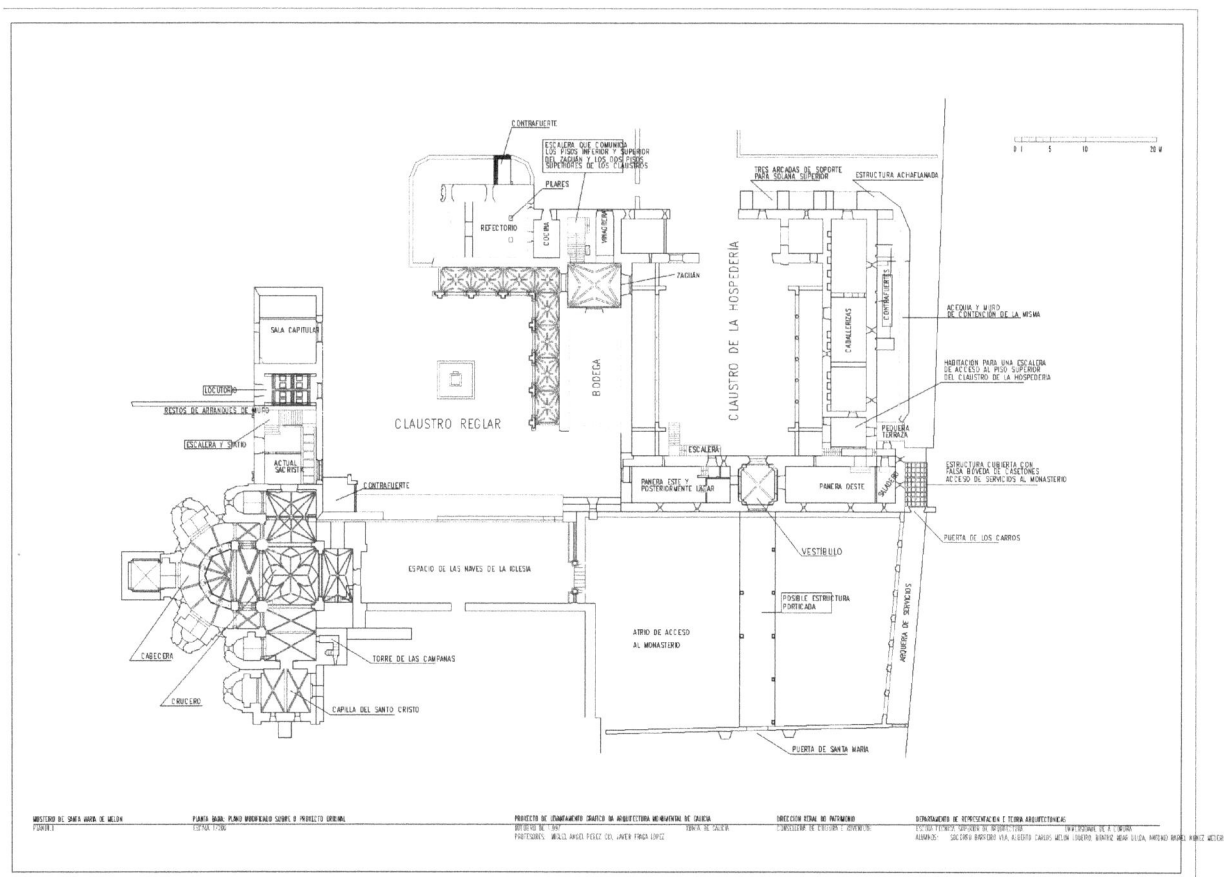

Figure 3. Upper and lower of the monastery of Santa María de Melón.

It is possible that this organisation around a single cloister continued in Melón until 1506, when the monastery was incorporated into the Congregation of Castille, and as a result of this underwent a series of reforms that eliminated the old Mediaeval structures replacing them with structures that were more in line with the trends of the time, growing in size and opening up to the exterior with a new cloister (The Hospice Cloister), around which other new constructions arose. However, it is not possible to confirm this until excavations are made around the building that make it possible to define the layout and structures that were present in the building at that time.

Figure 4. General photographs of the monastery of Santa María de Melón.

The monastery, at the time of starting work, despite being in ruins and completely abandoned, was a clear example of a structure that had been modified in modern times. It was set out in two cloister spaces; the first, the Processional Cloister, only retained its walkway to the south and west, opening up into a series of rooms which were not interconnected. The second cloister is the Hospice Cloister, which is in considerably better condition than the other, and conserves its four wings and has rooms in a much better condition that the previous area. It would appear that both cloisters and their rooms were organised over two floors, and with the exception of the other structures which today are in the garden (the dovecote, silos or terraces which divided the garden into different areas for cultivation), there was no indication or evidence of any other type of construction within the monastery that was suitable for investigation.

Also, in the interior of the monastery and defined by the wall, before entering into the monastery itself, there was a large atrium divided into three clearly separated spaces. The first was in front of the monastic rooms, featuring a symmetrical axis that lead directly from the Door of Santa María to the entrance to the vestibule of the Hospice Cloister. This space is flanked by another two: on its left, and separated by a small stone balustrade, is a rectangular atrium (occupying the space previously occupied by the naves of the temple), leading to the church and cemetery. To the right is another rectangular space, which runs longitudinally and is separated by an archway of the main atrium and leads to the 'service area' of the monastery, access to which was via its own entrance in the monastery's wall.

Initial proposals and analytical methodology

Initial proposals

When investigation work started at the monastery, the first explorations involved a series of visits, as well as examination of published bibliographic works and reports kept at the General Directorate of Cultural Heritage from the Department of Culture, Communication and Tourism of the Xunta, Galicia's autonomous government, on possible intervention work that had taken place at the monastery. This made it possible to establish a series of initial hypotheses, which, as well be seen in some cases, were proved incorrect once work started. The initial proposals, based on these visits and explorations of written documents, were as follows:

> The monastery was ruined, abandoned and covered in vegetation.
>
> The building belonged to the Cistercian Order.
>
> Its origins were in Mediaeval times, around 1195.
>
> The monastery underwent transformations in modern times, as a result of being incorporated into the 'Congregation of Castille' in 1506.
>
> The building was abandoned around 1835, at the time when church lands were sold off.
>
> After this date the building underwent a series of changes: it was split up between different owners; and in 1885 lighting and a storm knocked down the church's naves and left it in its currently ruinous state.

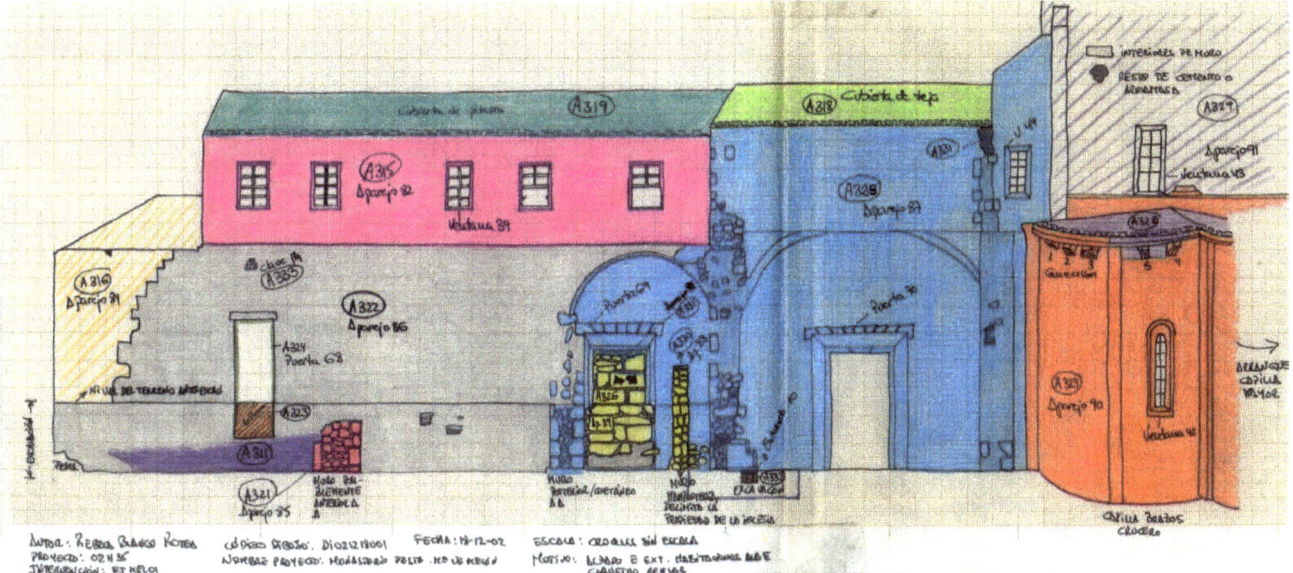

Figure 5. Sketch of the eastern elevation of the monastery, showing the different activities that took place there.

Analytical methodology

1. Bibliographic study of different works selected according to content
2. Study of documentary sources referring to the ancient Cistercian monastery. This study was carried out in different public bodies and historical archives at local, regional and national level.
3. Simultaneously, in order to contrast the different hypotheses that were suggested, specialists examined the different aspects of the building, making it possible to affirm the time periods involved, and allowing work to advance despite the condition of the building itself.
4. To establish connections with other monasteries, both Benedictine and Cistercian, from the same period. An exploration was made to determine periods, analyse structures and distributions, carrying out visits to other Cistercian monasteries to examine the types of structures used, construction methods and use of space. Despite the fact that many of them have undergone restoration work, they are still basic references for the study of the structures, forms and stylistic resources used in Cistercian architecture throughout the modern period.
5. The study, periodization and formal analysis of the Mediaeval stage of the Monastery of Melón, which is mainly seen in its temple. Creation of plans with chronological information. This study, despite being marginal to the project, has made it possible to establish a whole series of links and relationships between parts of the monastery that were considered to be Mediaeval and which have served as a criteria to confirm or reject these hypotheses.
6. The study and analysis of the monastery, analysing the different formal elements and grouping them according to type, not only establishing and seeking contacts with other elements in Melón, but also in other monasteries, at the same time as exploring the stylistic and constructional methods that were developed there, grouping them firstly according to styles, and then by chronological development.
7. Establishing the first hypotheses, in contrast to the data from the stratigraphic analysis and with the results obtained from archaeological soundings, which have made it possible to evaluate the information obtained, to progress with and ratify hypotheses, without which we would have continued with merely hypothetical foundations.
8. Photographs have also been taken of the different structures and spaces present at the monastery, although here, and thanks to the policy of co-operation established between the different teams, the graphic material produced by the team responsible for the Stratigraphic Study has been used, in order to make comparisons and bring together criteria that make it possible to unite or differentiate positions in the case of different points of view existing over one single reading, an objective which in most cases was highly successful, and which has been of great benefit to the Monastery of Melón and its restoration project.

Methodology used in the stratigraphic analysis

1. Study of bibliography and consultation of other documentary resources. This work started in July 2002, whilst awaiting the signing of the agreement, although this was abandoned as work progressed, as it was one of the tasks that had been carried out by the previous team.

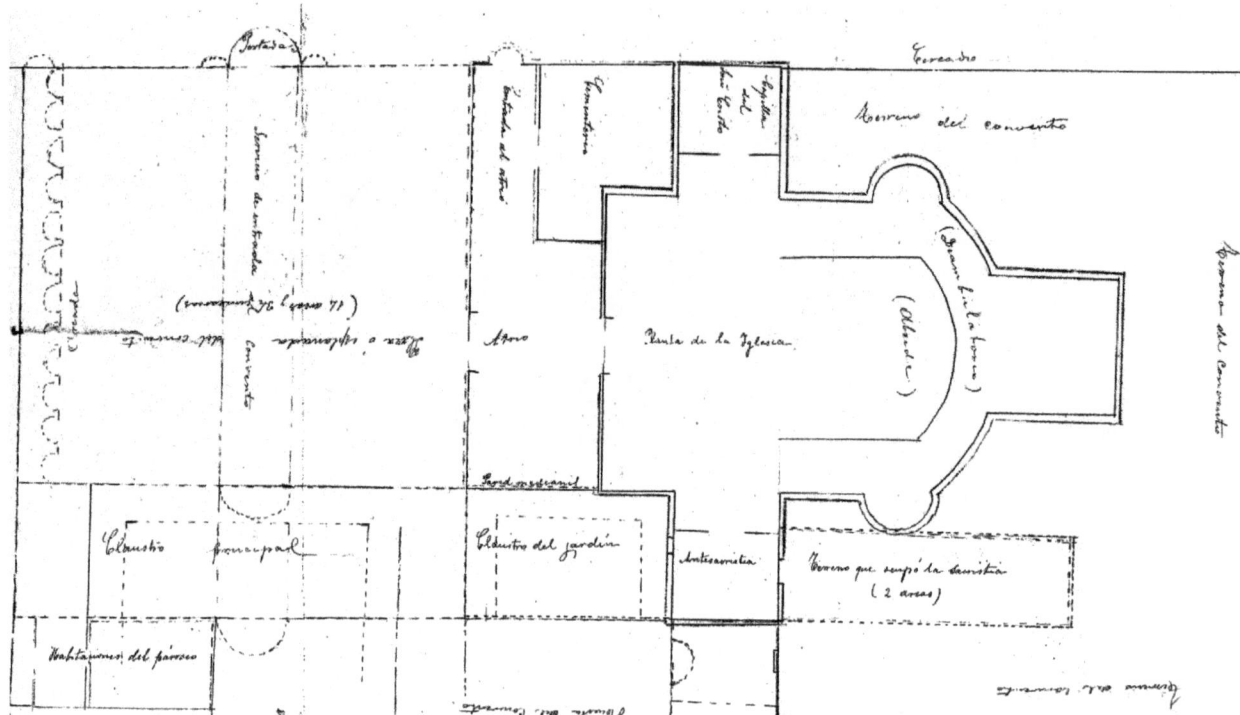

Figure 6. Plan of the Monastery of de Santa María de Melón (Melón, Ourense. Galicia), held at the Cathedral Archive in Tui (Tui, Pontevedra, Galicia), dated from the end of the nineteenth century.

2. Graphic documentation

Compilation of old photographs from inhabitants of the Local Council of Melón.

Taking digital photographs of the entire monastery before clean-up work started.

Correction of the survey provided by official bodies on starting work.

Drawing illustrations of all of the constructions still conserved within the monastery.

Taking digital photos of the entire monastery after cleaning and repointing.

Taking topographic points in the east and west wings conserved in the Hospice Cloister, of the southern and western wings conserved in the Processional Cloister and in the circular tower joined on to the southern façade of the monastery. The purpose is to rectify the photos taken in these three areas, in order to carry out an architectonic survey of all of them.

Taking photogrammetric pictures in order to produce a survey of the four façades of the atrium leading into the monastery.

3. Analysis of the construction methods used.

Stratigraphic analysis of the building, by differentiating units using the manual illustrations of all of the conserved construction elements, and creating analytical reports.

Differentiating different types of construction materials, constructive and decorative methods. Creating descriptive reports.

After differentiating and describing each of these units and elements, groups were then formed of all coinciding elements, taking into account the interfaces that existed between them. Summary processes were also started, attempting to interrelate some units with others, and other singular elements with others.

Process of summarising, correlation and periodization.

4. Documentary analysis: in the final stages of analysis, work started to compare the data taken from the stratigraphic reading with that from the documentary investigation, as well as that provided by the team responsible for the historical and artistic analysis.

Apart from the work described above, all of which had a direct relation with the project that was initially presented, other work was carried out that was required as the process developed. These were: controlling work on repointing and cleaning, to avoid it from affecting the construction itself; writing reports throughout the period of field work, in order to provide information to the relevant authorities about events that took place on the site (such as the western wing of the Hospice Cloister falling down) or to provide information that could be included in the project whilst being created.

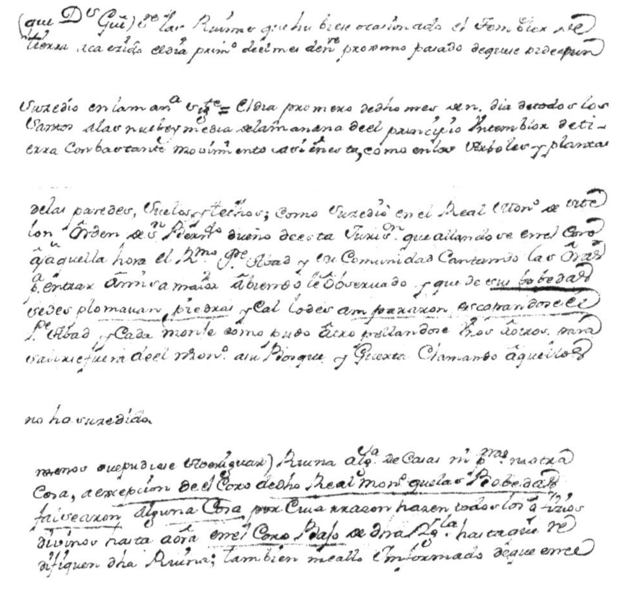

Figure 7. Document sent by the legal authorities of Melón in response to a questionnaire commissioned by King Fernando VI, to ascertain the damage caused by the earthquake in Spain.

First evidence

While work was underway, a series of issues arose that contradicted the information that had been initially used. These revealed the existence of a serious problem that had lead to considerable destruction in the building, before being abandoned by its monks, as a consequence of the selling of church properties in the nineteenth century. These problems were:

- The presence of a series of cracks with horizontal displacement of foundation blocks, which could not be explained by the settling of structures.
- The presence of walls that indicated that this destruction had not been produced at the same time, for example in the enclosing wall of the lateral nave of the epistle (which conserved part of its internal layer, but not the outer layer); the buttress in the north-eastern section of the Processional Cloister (its presence explains the state of conservation and maintenance of the domed structure of the first section of the nave of the temple).
- The conservation of a series of structures which indicated that a number of emergency repairs had been carried out in the building: a supporting structure/buttress built against the southern façade of the rooms of the eastern wing of the Processional Cloister; pillars in the interior of the Refectory.
- Also, the interruption which took place during an important phase of construction work.

All of these factors indicated that the monastery, in the middle of the eighteenth century (a date established thanks to stratigraphic investigations and historical/artistic studies), had suffered serious damage to its structures which forced it to reposition its different spaces and planned construction work.

Preliminary results obtained from investigations

The evidence described above largely contradicted the initial starting hypotheses, supported by bibliographic and documentary sources studied in the initial phase. These would appear to indicate that the monastery was abandoned and fell into disrepair for two reasons: the process of abandonment came about as a result of the sale of church lands that affected the monastery in 1835, and as a result of the destruction of the naves by a bolt of lightning and a storm in 1885 (Cameselle Bastos 1990).

However, as surveying and analysis work continued at the monastery, the data indicated that construction work had been paralysed around the middle of the eighteenth century. Around this time a series of structures had appeared that indicated building work had increased in the monastery, motivated by functional changes, in particular a desire to beautify the building, particularly its exterior, characteristic of the Galician Baroque style. These changes were:

- Modifications made to the main façade of the monastery (N) and the opening of five balconies in the façade.
- The construction of a series of arches that separates the service area from the area that leads directly into the monastery from the atrium, and modification of the open space to the west of the monastery, by construction of a terrace in the western section of the garden to provide more space. This meant it was necessary to build a containing wall for the terrace and to modify the structure and vaulted roof of the room that leads to the 'service area'.
- The construction of a bevelled structure to embellish the southwestern corner of the outer façade of the rooms in the Hospice Cloister. The bevelled form of this structure makes it possible for carts to turn around in the area, and also hides the sewer that runs under the monastery, guaranteeing its safe use.
- The construction of a sun gallery, today greatly altered, in the southern façade of the rooms in the southern wing of the Processional Cloister.
- Construction of large staircase in the room to the southern end of the transept of the church. This room communicates the space with the Processional Cloister and with a new space now situated on the eastern side of the monastery.
- Modifications to the room initially identified as the *Locutorio*.
- In the eastern façade of the room that contains the large staircase are the bases of the two walls that run the whole height of the façade, as well as the outline of an arch that would have possibly lead to a large dome between these two walls. On the other

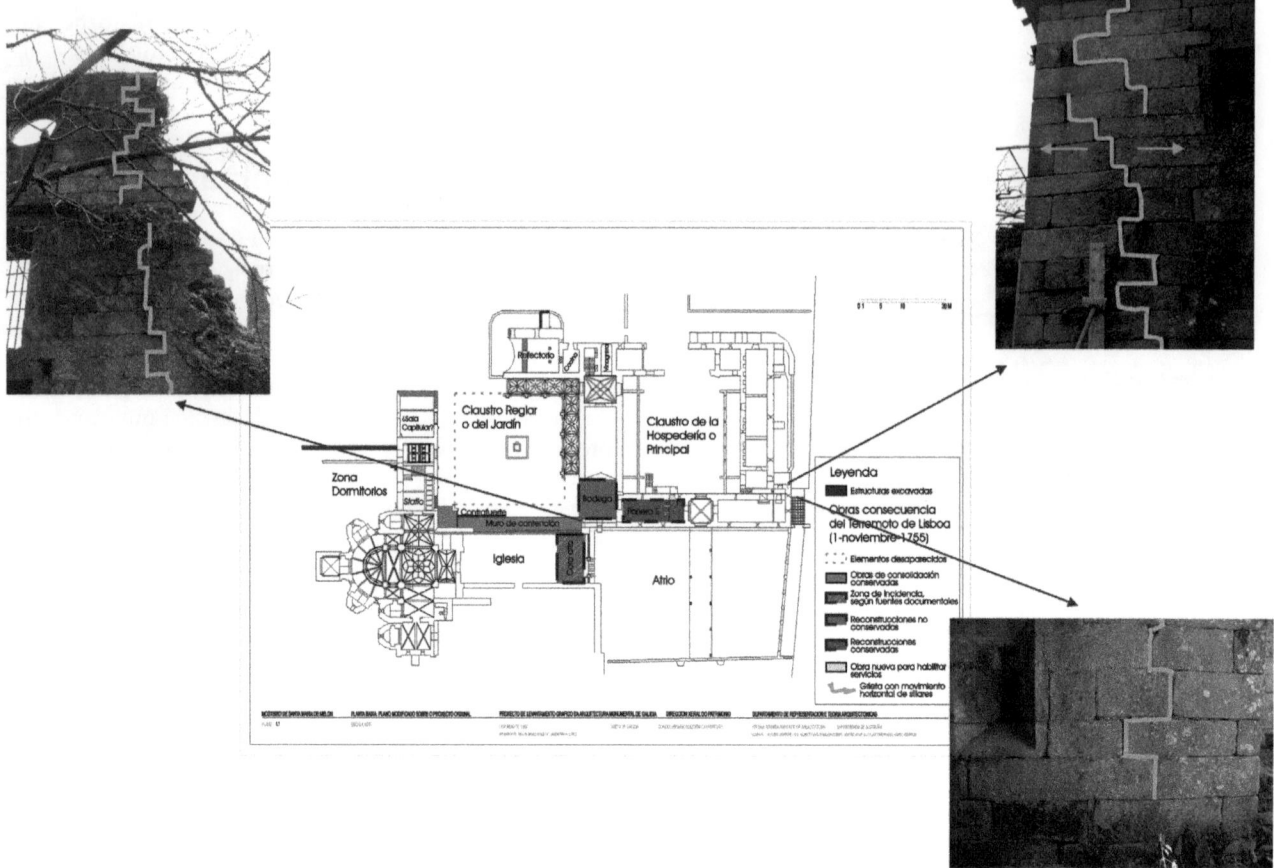

Figure 8. Cracks produced in the monastery of Santa María de Melón due to horizontal movement of stone blocks.

side there are also the bases for a smaller wall, connected to the southern post of the eastern door to the possible *Locutorio*, which contained the groove for another arch that joined the base of the wall to the south.

This evidence lead to the suggestion of carrying out archaeological soundings in the area, as all of the indications pointed to the existence of rooms in this area of large dimensions which were unknown until that moment. In effect, the soundings[3] revealed the existence of a room which opened out to the east of the *Statio*, of which the south-western corner was excavated, formed by a series of walls with very high quality stonework, perfectly seated and raised over a stone base of equally high quality. Judging by the dimensions of the room, the remains of a possible vault and the quality of the workmanship, it was considered that the room would have served some purpose within the monastery. Due to the nearness of the temple, the absence of a sacristy, and the change in function of the room where the chamber was found, now converted into a *Statio*, it was suggested that it was itself used as the Sacristy.

Another sounding was made in the area where the base of a lower wall had been detected. Here another wall was found with very high quality facing and of considerable size, over 20m long, and perfectly finished at its eastern end, although without appearing to enclose any type of space. Finally, the sounding also discovered that there had been a considerable collapse of material.

This data indicates two events. Firstly, it would appear that the first of these rooms was used as the Sacristy, which had not been found until this moment. This fact could finally be affirmed with total security, when in the latter stages of the inspection of documentary resources, a plan was found dating from the end of the nineteenth century in the Cathedral Archive in Tui (Pontevedra), with the area defined as "*sacristy (occupying two areas)*". It would also appear that the wall following on from it never actually took place, but indicates that there were important reforms to the eastern section of the monastery. In light of this, it was decided to close off the door to the possible *Locutorio*, which was the situation found when work started.

The condition of this wall, as well as the 'reinforcing' structures that had been documented and previously indicated (a buttress connected to the NE corner of the Processional Cloister that prevented circulation through its ambulatory; a buttress-like structure connected to the southern end of the room identified as the *Sala Capitular*; or pillars documented in the interior of the *Refectorio* supporting the cannon vault), lead to a rethinking of the initial hypotheses, as work of this kind, the consequence of an important destruction, was not in line with the 'repairs' that had been documented and dated after the time of the selling off of church land or the destruction caused by the lightning bolt.

---

[3] Carried out by the archaeological company *Prospectiva y Análisis* and directed by the archaeologist Andrés Bonilla Rodríguez.

Archaeotecture: Second Floor

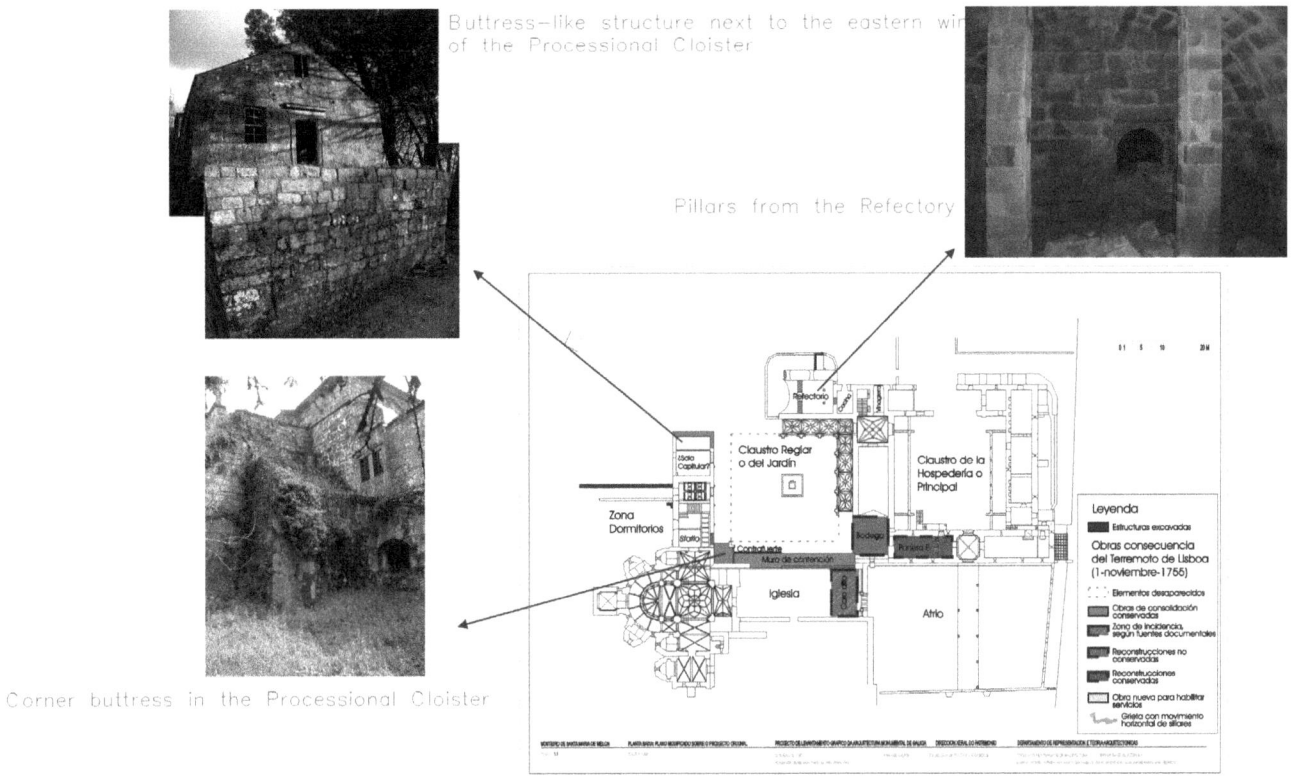

Figure 9. Structures used for reinforcement: pillars from the Refectory, corner buttress in the Processional Cloister, and buttress-like structure next to the eastern wing of the Processional Cloister.

One piece of data that had not appeared until that moment was the key to understanding the events that had been recorded until then. As mentioned previously, in the process of inspecting documentary evidence about the monastery it was found that there had been considerable damage after the selling off of church lands, as a result of the destruction of the naves by a lightning bolt and storm damage (Cameselle Bastos 1990). It also appears that the Processional Cloister was destroyed at this time, as if it were the result of a domino effect after the naves collapsed. However, there were a number of factors that did not appear to be in line with this hypothesis.

The whole enclosing wall of the southern nave was conserved along its whole length, although not in its height. This wall was the inner section in Mediaeval times, when the temple was built, although the outer layer was extremely affected, and the conserved area corresponding to the first and second stage, approximately, of the naves of the church, had an exterior layer from the modern period. Also, where the buttress was situated, the southern enclosing wall was conserved at full height both on the interior and exterior, and was the only area that had not been affected by the lightning bolt, conserving the first section of the naves. The question was: if the lightning and the storm had brought about the downfall of the naves and part of the Processional Cloister, how could we keep upright the wall that supported the vaults of both the southern nave of the church and the northern wing of the Processional Cloister, which were also in a very fragile condition as their outer layer had been removed to build another wall in modern times when the Cloister was built? But furthermore, if the angled buttress indicated did not previously exist, how had the first section of the naves been conserved, together with all of the southern enclosing wall, only in that area?

All of these factors would appear to indicate that the naves and cloister did not collapse at the same time. The first was obviously the result of the lightning bolt and the storm on the structure of the monastery, although the second must have been beforehand, as the presence of the buttress would have contributed to the first section of the naves remaining upright as well as the southern wall in the area, also making it possible to document the modifications made to the outer layer of the external northern wall that closed the cloister in modern times. Other questions then appeared, such as why was the inner layer of this Mediaeval wall conserved and not the outer layer, that was repaired with solid blocks of stone and was joined to a low containing wall? It is thought that this repair work was the result of an emergency that occurred before the naves collapsed, that made it possible to maintain the inner layer of the wall but not all of its height. More and more questions arose, until it was concluded, based on the number of buttress-like structures which appeared to date from the mid-eighteenth century, that emergency repair work on cracks in the building had been carried out as a result of horizontal movement within the building, and the possibility that the monastery had been affected in the mid-eighteenth century by an earthquake of considerable importance.

In effect, on the morning of 1 November 1755 there was a considerable seismic movement, today known as the Lisbon Earthquake. Some studies carried out recently have detailed the effects of the earthquake in Spain (Martínez Solares 2001), but although they indicate that some buildings were affected in the province of Ourense, none refer to the Monastery of Melón. Once again, in the final stages of documentary research, it was confirmed that a document had appeared, a reply by the legal authorities in Melón to a query from the King, Fernando VI, to ascertain the damage that the earthquake had caused in the country.

This was an inflection point for the monastery in Ourense, marking the beginning of the end, at the same time as it obliged some of its traditional spaces to be transformed in order to guarantee maintaining certain sources of income, or a whole series of emergency construction projects to consolidate the building undertaken by Cistercian monks to prevent the total collapse of the building, something that was impossible due to the political and social circumstances of the nineteenth century that affected the monastery. This undoubtedly explains why, despite being very much at the forefront of the intentions of the monks, this never actually fully took place.

References

AA.VV. 1974. Voz "Melón". *Gran Enciclopedia Gallega*. Vol. XX: pp. 252-256. A Coruña.

AA.VV. 2000. *San Martín Pinario*. Santiago de Compostela: Xunta de Galicia.

AA.VV. 2002. *Monasterios e conventos de Galicia*. Santiago de Compostela: Xunta de Galicia.

Avila y la Cueva, F. 1995. *Historia civil y eclesiástica de la Ciudad de Tuy y su Obispado*. Cuatro volúmenes. Edición facsímil. Santiago de Compostela: Consello da Cultura Galega.

Basallo Álvarez, Mª 1992. El Cister de las tierras centrales de Orense de la Desamortización de Mendizábal: Monasterio de Montederramo y Xunqueira de Espadañado. In VV.AA. *Actas del Congreso Internacional sobre San Bernardo e o Cister en Galicia e Portugal*. Vol. 1 (17-20 October 1991, Ourense – Oseira). Santiago de Compostela: Xunta de Galicia.

Bonet Correa, A. 1966. *La arquitectura en Galicia durante el siglo XVII*. Madrid.

Bugallo Álvarez, A. 1968. *El derecho patrimonial a través de los diplomas del Monasterio de Santa María de Melón, desde su fundación hasta 1282*. Universidad Pontificia de Comillas.

Burgo López, Mª. C. 1992. El señorío monástico gallego en la Edad Moderna. *Obradoiro da Historia Moderna*, 1: pp. 99-121

Cameselle Bastos, D. 1990. Melón: últimos días de una iglesia monacal. *Porta da Aira*, 3: 227-34.

Cardeso Liñares, J. 1995. *Santuarios marianos de Galicia*. Santiago de Compostela.

Carro García, J. 1993. *Monasterios del Císter en Galicia*. Santiago de Compostela.

Casado Nieto, M. R. 1989. Documentos para la historia del arte de Ourense: Monasterio de San Clodio y Puente Mayor de Ourense. *Porta da Aira*, 2.

Castillo, A. del 1980. La arquitectura en Galicia. *Geografía General del Reino de Galicia*. T. II. A Coruña.

Castillo, A. del 1989 *Inventario de la riqueza monumental y artística de Galicia*. Santiago de Compostela.

Cendón Fernández, M. 2000. El monasterio de Oia. *Monasticón cisterciense gallego*, T. I: pp. 198-223. León.

Cid Rombao, A. 1972. *Crónica y guía del Monasterio de Oseira*. Ourense.

Cid Rombao, A. 1974. *Crónica y guía del Monasterio de Montederramo*. Ourense.

Couceiro Freijomil, A. Monumentos de la Provincia de Orense. *Boletín de la Comisión Provincial de Monumentos*, T. XI: pp. 226-7.

Couselo Bouzas, J. 1932. *Galicia artística en el primer tercio del siglo XVIII y XIX*. Santiago de Compostela.

Chamoso Lamas, M. 1947. El Monasterio de Montederramo. *Archivo Español de Arte*, T. LXXVIII.

Chamoso Lamas, M. 1951. El puente y el lugar de San Clodio. *Cuadernos de Estudios Gallegos*, T. XXXV: pp. 53-61

Chueca Goitia, F. 1953. Arquitectura del siglo XVI. *Ars Hispaniae*, Vol. XI. Madrid: Plus-Ultra.

Domínguez Castro, L. 1992. Los cenobios cistercienses do Ribeiro na desamortización de Mendizábal. Análise dos seus bens e dos seus compradores. In VV.AA. *Actas del Congreso Internacional sobre San Bernardo e o Cister en Galicia e Portugal*. Vol. 1 (17-20 October 1991, Ourense – Oseira). Santiago de Compostela: Xunta de Galicia.

Dubois, M.G. 1992. Liturgia cisterciense. *Cistercium*, XLIV: pp. 241-59.

Duby, G. 1982. *San Bernardo y el arte cisterciense. El nacimiento del gótico*. Madrid.

Duro Peña, E y Platero Paz, J. 1990. *San Esteban de Ribas de Sil*. León: Caixa Ourense.

Eijan, S. 1920. *Historia de Rivadavia y de sus alrededores*. Madrid.

Fernández, M. 1967. Monasterio de monjes cistercienses en Galicia. *Yermo*. Madrid.

Fernández Cortizo, C. 2000. La reforma de las Órdenes de San Benito y el Císter en tiempos de Carlos V. In Eiras Roel, A. (Coord.). *El Reino de Galicia en la época del emperador Carlos V*. Santiago de Compostela: Xunta de Galicia, Dirección Xeral de Patrimonio Cultural. Pp.: 847-77.

Fernández Gago-Varela, C. 1979. Restauraciones en el Monasterio de Oseira, Cea (Ourense). *Abrente*, 11: pp. 171-82

Fernández Ramos, M. 1973. *Guía breve del Real Monasterio de Armenteira*. Pontevedra.

Fernández-Valdés Costas, M. 1995. El terremoto de Lisboa. Su repercusión en la Antigua Provincia de Tuy. *Cuadernos de Estudios Gallegos*, 10. pp. 303-11.

Ferro Couselo, J. 1971. Las obras en el convento e iglesia de Montederramo en los siglos XVI y XVII. *Boletín auriense*, 1: pp. 145-86.

Florez, E. *España Sagrada*. T. XIX: 1765-89. Madrid.

Folgar de la Calle, Mª.C. 1998. La arquitectura de los monasterios cistercienses de Galicia desde el Barroco a la Desamortización. En Valle Pérez, X. C. (Coord.). *Arte del Císter en Galicia y Portugal*. Catálogo. A Coruña: Fundación Pedro Barrié de la Maza. Pp. 280-327.

Gallego Fernández, O. 1992. Barcas y barcajes de los monasterios cistercienses de la Provincia de Ourense. En VV.AA. *Actas del Congreso Internacional sobre San Bernardo e o Cister en Galicia e Portugal*. Vol. 1 (17-20 October 1991, Ourense – Oseira). Santiago de Compostela: Xunta de Galicia. Pp. 337-68.

García Iglesias, J.M. 1990. *Galicia en tiempos del barroco*. A Coruña.

García Iglesias, J.M. 1993. El Barroco (I). La época. Los patrocinadores. Arquitectos del S. XVII (I). *Galicia Arte*. T. XIII. A Coruña.

García Martínez, P y Sánchez, P. (fot.) 1993. Santa María de Melón. In García Martínez, P and Sánchez, P. (phot.). *Monasterios de España*. Madrid: Ediciones Rueda. Pp. 48-51.

García Oro. J. 1966. La reforma de los monasterios gallegos en tiempos de los Reyes Católicos. *Cuadernos de Estudios Gallegos*, XXI: pp. 41-58.

González García, M. A. 1997. La reforma de las abadías orensanas del Císter, siglos XVI y XVII. *Estudios del Seminario Fontan Sarmiento*, nº. 18: pp. 8-22.

González López, P. 1989. La actividad artística de los monasterios cistercienses gallegos entre 1498 y 1836. *Cuadernos de Estudios Gallegos*, XXXVIII: pp. 213-33.

González López, P. 1989-1990. La labor artística cisterciense gallega desde los fondos documentales del Archivo del Reino de Galicia. *Brigantium*, nº. 6: pp. 151-73.

Hervella Vázquez, J. 1990. El arte en Oseira en el Siglo XVII. *Porta da Aira*, nº. 3: pp. 275-80.

Juan, H. 1960. Orígenes del Monasterio cisterciense de Santa María de Melón. *Cistercium*, XII: pp. 15-24.

Leiros Fernández, E. 1951. Algunos privilegios pontificios al Monasterio de Melón. *Museo de Pontevedra*, T: VI: pp. 54-60.

Leiros Fernández, E. 1951. *Catalogo de pergaminos monacales del Archivo de la Catedral de Ourense*. Santiago de Compostela.

Limia Gardón, F.J. 1988. Oseira en los últimos siglos. La época moderna. In *El Monasterio de Oseira, 50 años de la restauración*, Leon: pp. 61-81.

Limia Gardón, F.J. 1990. Un ejemplo arquitectónico en los orígenes del barroco gallego: la fachada de la iglesia monasterial de Oseira. *Porta da Aira*, nº. 3: pp. 39-74

Limia Gardón, F.J. 1990. Varia artística de la provincia de Ourense en el siglo XVII. *Boletín Auriense*, X: pp. 227-44.

López Ferreiro, J. 1895. *Compendio de la historia de San Clodio del Ribeiro*. Santiago de Compostela.

López Sangil, J.L. 2000. Monfero. En Yañez Neira, Fray Mª Damián (Coord.). *Monasticon cisterciense gallego*. T. II. Vigo: Caixavigo e Ourense. Pp. 97-149.

Losada Meléndez, Mª. J. 1992. *La colección diplomática del Monasterio cisterciense de Melón (pergaminos de la Catedral de Ourense). Siglo XIV*. (Unpublished Graduate Thesis). University of Santiago.

Losada Meléndez, Mª. J. and Soto Lamas, Mª. T. 1993. La documentación del Monasterio de Santa María de Melón en el Archivo de la Catedral de Ourense (ss. XII – XV). Boletín de Estudios del Seminario "Fontan Sarmiento" de hagiografía, toponimia y onomástica de Galicia. Year 15, nº. 14: pp. 67-70.

Losada Meléndez, Mª. J. and Soto Lamas, Mª. T. 1995. El conflicto entre el Monasterio de Melón y el Concejo de Monterrey por Villamayor de Xirona en el siglo XIII. In Jesús de Juana, Xavier Castro (director). *VIII Xornadas de Historia de Galicia* (Ourense 1995). Ourense: Servicio de Publicacións da Deputación. Pp. 37-46.

Losada Meléndez, Mª. J. and Soto Lamas, Mª. T. 1999. La formación del espacio señorial en el monasterio de Melón, siglos XII y XIII. In VV.AA. *Actas del II Congreso Internacional sobre el Cister en Galicia y Portugal*. Vol. 1 (1998, Ourense). Pp. 531-48.

Losada Meléndez, Mª. J., González García, M. A. and Soto Lamas, Mª. T. 2000. Santa María de Melón. En Yañez Neira, Fray Mª Damián (Coord.). *Monasticon cisterciense gallego*. T. II. Vigo: Caixavigo e Ourense. Pp. 137-51.

Madoz, P. 1849. *Diccionario geográfico estadístico histórico de España*. Madrid.

Manrique, A. 1643-1659. *Annales Cistercienses*. 4 vol. Lugduni.

Martín, E. 1953. *Los bernardos españoles*. Palencia.

Martínez Coello, A. 2000. Montederramo. In Yañez Neira, Fray Mª Damián (Coord.). *Monasticon cisterciense gallego*. T. I. Vigo: Caixavigo e Ourense. Pp. 111-35.

Martínez Solares, J.M. 2001. *Los efectos en España del Terremoto de Lisboa (1 de noviembre de 1755)*. Monografía, nº. 19. Madrid: Ministerio de Fomento.

Olivera Serrano, C. 1995. *La actividad sísmica en el Reino de Granada (1487-1531). Estudio-Histórico y documentos*. Madrid.

Pallares Méndez, Mº. C. 1978. Los Cotos como marco de los derechos feudales en Galicia durante la Edad Media (1100-1500). *Liceo Franciscano*, 2nd period, year 31, n. 91-93 (Jan. –Dec. 1998): pp. 201-25. Santiago de Compostela.

Peralta, Fray T. de 1998. *Fundación, Antigüedad y progresos del Monasterio de Osera*. Madrid, 1677. Edición Facsímil. Santiago de Compostela: Xunta de Galicia.

Pérez, F.J. 1996. O *Mosteiro de Melón no século XV*. Ourense.

Pérez Constanti, P. 1930. *Diccionario de artistas que florecieron en Galicia en los siglos XVI y XVII*. Santiago de Compostela.

Pérez Constanti, P. 1993. *Notas viejas galicianas*. Santiago de Compostela: Xunta de Galicia.

Portela Silva, E. 1981. *La colonización cisterciense en Galicia (1142-1250)*. Santiago de Compostela.

Portela Silva, E. 1996. *La región del obispado de Tuy en los siglos XII al XV*. Santiago de Compostela.

Portela Silva, E.; Pallares, Mª. C. and Barral Rivadulla, Mª. D. 2000. Sobrado dos Monxes. In Yañez Neira, Fray Mª Damián (Coord.). *Monasticon cisterciense gallego*. T. II. Vigo: Caixavigo e Ourense. Pp. 9-57

Rionegro Fariña, I. 1998. *La economía monástica gallega a finales del Antiguo Régimen: el caso ourensano*. Ourense: Caixa Ourense.

Sá Bravo, H. 1972. *El monacato en Galicia*. La Coruña: Librigal.

Sá Bravo, H. 1983. *Boticas monacales y medicina naturista en Galicia*. Madrid: Everest.

Sá Bravo, H. 1983. *Monasterios de Galicia*. Madrid: Everest.

Sánchez Belda, L. 1953. *Documentos reales de la Edad Media referentes a Galicia. Catálogo de los conservados en el Archivo Histórico Nacional*. Madrid: Ministerio de Educación.

Soto Lamas, Mª. T. 1992. *La colección diplomática del Monasterio cisterciense de Melón (pergaminos de la Catedral de Ourense). Siglos XII y XIII*. (unpublished Graduate Thesis). University of Santiago.

Tiburg, W. 1964. San Bernardo y la propagación de la Orden Cisterciense en España. *Cistercium*, T. XVI: pp. 79-88.

Torres Balbás, L. 1954. *Monasterios cistercienses de Galicia*. Santiago de Compostela.

Valle Pérez, J. C. 1981. *Las fundaciones de Clairvaux en la Galicia medieval. Filiación directa: el siglo XII*. Santiago de Compostela.

Valle Pérez, J. C. 1982. *La arquitectura cisterciense en Galicia*. Santiago de Compostela: Fundación Pedro Barrié de la Maza.

Valle Pérez, J. C. 1986. La Capilla de San Andrés, en el Monasterio de Oseira y las capillas funerarias en la arquitectura cisterciense en Galicia. *Boletín Auriense*.

Valle Pérez, J. C. 1998. La implantación de la Orden del Císter y su reflejo munumental en la Edad Media. En Valle Pérez, X. C. (Coord.). *Arte del Císter en Galicia y Portugal*. Catalogue. A Coruña: Fundación Pedro Barrié de la Maza. Pp. 2-41.

Valle Pérez, J. C. 1998. Entre la innovación y el recuerdo, notas sobre la implantación de la Orden del Císter en Galicia y Portugal. En VV.AA. *Actas del II Congreso Internacional sobre el Cister en Galicia y Portugal*. Vol. 1 (1998, Ourense). Pp. 1053-67.

Villamil y Castro, J. 1904. *Iglesias gallegas*. Madrid.

Vila Jato, Mª. D. 1998. La arquitectura de los monasterios cistercienses en Galicia durante el Renacimiento. En Valle Pérez, X. C. (Coord.). *Arte del Císter en Galicia y Portugal*. Catálogo. A Coruña: Fundación Pedro Barrié de la Maza. Pp. 184-229

Vila Jato, Mª. D. 1993. *O renacemento. A arte en Compostela*. A Coruña

Vila Jato, Mª. D. 1993. Galicia en la época del Renacimiento. *Galicia Arte*. Vol. XII. A Coruña: Hércules.

Yánez Neira, F. D. 1997. *Continuación de la Historia del Padre Peralta*. Santiago de Compostela: Xunta de Galicia, Dirección Xeral de Patrimonio Cultural.

Yánez Neira, F. D. 1997. El Císter en Galicia. In 'Galicia románica y gótica'. Exhibition in Ourense. 27 June - October 1997. Santiago de Compostela. Consellería de Cultura e Comunicación Social. Pp. 202-09.

Yánez Neira. D. and González García, M. A. 1996. *El Monasterio de Oseira*. Ourense: Caixa Ourense.

Yepes, Fray A. De 1959. *Crónica general de la Orden de San Benito*. (1609-1621). Madrid.

9

Deep-mapping the Gumuz house

Alfredo González Ruibal

Universidad Complutense de Madrid

Xurxo M. Ayán Vila

Spanish High Council for Scientific Research

Álvaro Falquina Aparicio

Universidad Complutense de Madrid

Abstract

This paper embraces the results of an ethnoarchaeological research developed by *Spanish Archaeological Mission* with Gumuz populations in Mettekel (north of Blue Nile, West Ethiopia) during March 2006. Gumuz is an ethnical Nilo-Saharian group which presents strong cultural and linguistic resemblances with another communities of the border between Sudan and Ethiopia, as *Kuama* or *Uduk* groups. From the point of view of the *Archaeology of domestic space*, we made archaeological fieldwork in three Gumuz settlements (Bowla-Dibas'i, Manjäri and Maataba). We designed with GPS a complete planimetry of every hamlet, recording the UTM situation of domestic structures as palisades, compounds, houses, farmyards, granaries, external activity areas, ash zones, graves, etc... This etnhoarchaeological record was completed with the inventory of the kinship relations among the different compounds of household entities. In the same way we registered the clan of every woman who lives in every settlement (Gumuz is a exogamic culture). Too we drawed maps (1/50 scale) of selectioned houses and, finally, we ultimated complete inventories of material culture inside 30 houses. This research let us to know the cultural pattern of domestic space built by Gumuz communities and, from a general point of view, to think about the relations among home, space, material culture, ethnicity and construction of social reality in a multicultural complex context

Introduction

Archaeologists and anthropologists tend to study houses with disregard to their often chaotic materiality. The usual ethnographic procedure consists in imposing order on domestic space, bringing forward meaning and structure, in order to read society through space. In so doing, however, ethnography conceals the messy reality of artefacts, people, animals and dirt that compose any traditional home. This sanitizing and idealistic approach is quite surprising given the sheer intimacy of ethnographic research towards the subject of study – an intimacy that is generally obvious in the way particular situations, institutions and persons are deeply interwoven in narratives of nuanced detail and psychological depth.

Our study of the domesticity of the Gumuz compounds in western Ethiopia tries to convey the material richness of homes, the strong relationship between people, places, things and animals, that shape the experience of the house, and the chaotic, and simultaneously ordered, nature of domestic space. At the same time, we perceive the materiality of homes as historically constituted. It is not only social norms that permeate the structure of the house, but also long-term historical events that have action in the present. Rather than viewing social and historical features as conditioning domestic space in an abstract way, we try to prove how they are intertwinned in the very materiality of houses – indoors and outdoors, in structural elements as well as in artefacts – and therefore affect the daily life of the people that inhabit those spaces.

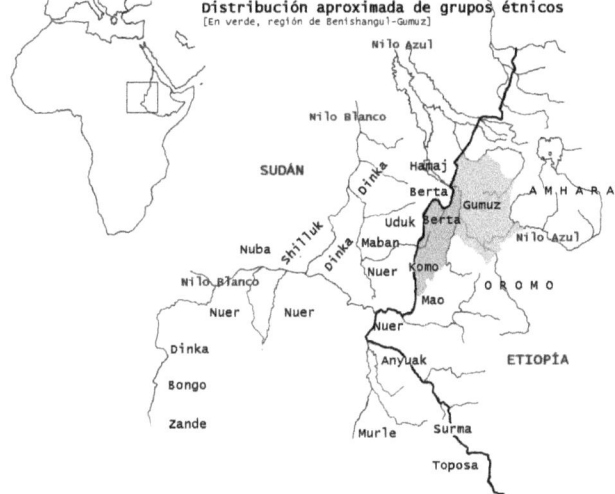

Figure 1. Geographical distribution of ethnical groups in the study area.

In our research, we use an archaeological approach that combines detailed drawings of structures and artifacts, GPS mapping, micro-spatial distribution plans, syntactic analysis of space, ethnographic interviews and historical research with the aim of exploring the materiality of Gumuz homes and Gumuz culture in general.

Our fieldwork is a long-term (ethno)archaeological project in Benishangul-Gumuz, funded by the Dirección General de Bellas Artes (Spain) and started in 2001, whose aim is studying the complex relations between social identity, ethnicity, space and material culture among the Nilo-Saharan communities of the Ethio-Sudanese borderland.

Figure 2. Gumuz boys of Bowla Dibas'i settlement with *mes'a* behind them.

Aims of the project

The aims of the project were the following:
1. To increase our knowledge of the material culture of the gumuz North of the Blue Nile in order to complete recorded information about Nilo-Saharan material culture in the Ethiopian West (cf. González Ruibal and Fernández Martínez 2003; 2007; González Ruibal 2005).
2. To study interethnic relations between gumuz and highland communities (amhara, agaw), through production, use and consumption of material culture, with a specific focus on pottery, calabashes, baskets and agricultural tools.
3. To analyse gumuz domestic spatial organisation focusing on two main aspects:
    - Understanding space production within this community and its relations with other Nile-Saharan peoples, especially the bertha, known to us through previous campaigns (González Ruibal 2006b).
    - Observing the relations between spatial organisation and such aspects as ethnicity, cultural contact and historical circumstances (invasions from the highlands, slavery) as well as its potential changes in contexts of higher inter-ethnic tension.

Our study of living communities at Benishangul-Gumuz is generally conceived as a contribution to cultural and historical research on the region and hence as a form of Archaeology of the present.

Methodology

Our first step was to select several hamlets to carry out the fieldwork. In doing so we were guided both by our previous experience and Wolde-Selassie Abutte's work (2004). We intended to compare different contexts of cultural interaction between gumuz and highland communities. Our first choice was Bowla-Dibas'i (Gublak) in the Mambuk wereda, given its distance (some 100 km.) from the Abyssinian high plain and the fact that this area has not seen agaw or amhara settlement in historic times or the recent past. Our intention was thus to study a gumuz community as far away as possible from outside influences.

Figure 3. An example of gumuz *domestic mode of production*.

Once our work in this community was completed (a task for which we scheduled five days) we intended to study another two or three settlements (depending on time) closer to the high plain. We chose Manjäri, Wondbil and Maataba based on our previous experience at Manjari, where we had carried out ethnoarchaeological work in June 2005, and our knowledge of unequal interethnic relationships in each settlement. According to Wolde-Selassie (2004) a gradual increase in interethnic tension can be perceived between Wondbil and Maataba. Tension between the amhara and the gumuz has eased ostensibly in Wondil and relations are harmonic while in Maataba the period following the communist government era (especially 1992-1995) saw intense interethnic conflict. This caused a high number of deaths among both the gumuz and the amhara who were displaced to the region. Due to administrative reasons, work in Wondbil (now part of the Amhara region) was discarded while logistic reasons and timing caused research in Maataba to restrict to two days.

The size of Manjäri (near to 700 inhabitants) suggested that our efforts should concentrate on this hamlet given that Maataba is made up of very small separated hamlets (1 to 3 km. away from one another). This fact further complicated the type of spatial analysis we intended to carry out.

The work process at the three hamlets included the following aspects:
- High definition detailed GPS mapping of the structures in each hamlet (dwellings, granaries, farmyards, fences, activity areas, ash-pits, graves, etc.).
- Sketches of these habitation structures and complexes were made to allow an analysis of the GPS-generated map.
- Once the sketches were finished, we drew up kinship diagrams referring to all habitation structures in each hamlet. These diagrams reflected intra-domestic and

extra-domestic relationships. The clan to which each of the women in the settlement was related to was also recorded given gumuz culture's exogamic character.

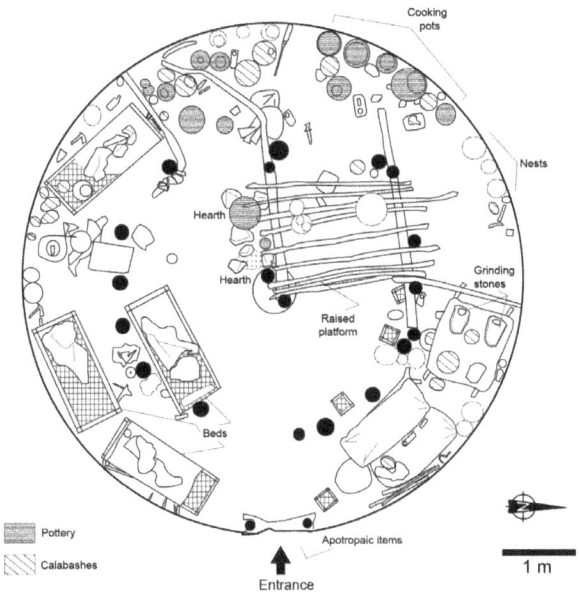

Figure 4. Archaeological plan of a gumuz dwelling.

- Detailed 1:50 scale maps were drawn for several gumuz and agaw dwellings at Bowla-Dibas'i and Manjäri.
- A complete *corpus* of material culture was collected including pottery, basketry, metallurgy, carpentry, home-building, etc. All indigenous terms for each artefact in the gumuz material world were recorded. Five female potters, three male blacksmiths and one male basket-weaver were interviewed. This work was carried out by Geremew Feyissa and Alfredo González Ruibal. Indigenous terms were also recorded by Álvaro Falquina Aparicio.
- Detailed inventories were made of all existing artefacts in several gumuz and agaw dwellings in order to account for variations derived from interethnic contact. Inventories were made for a total of 30 dwellings: 11 at Bowla-Dibas'i and 19 at Manjäri. As part of these inventories, some 300 ceramic vessels were drawn from both gumuz and agaw dwellings in order to study interethnic relations through ceramic consumption and variability.
- Ethnographic information was collected to contribute to the interpretation of material data as well as marriage, funerary rituals, myths of origin, historical data, religious beliefs, etc.

Once we have processed the information from this campaign, a syntactic spatial analysis method will be applied (Hillier and Hanson 1984) to GPS generated maps. We shall incorporate kinship diagrams and furniture data to spatial information to draw conclusions about gumuz domestic space organisation. At a more general level, relations between space, material culture and ethnicity will be analysed in complex multicultural contexts.

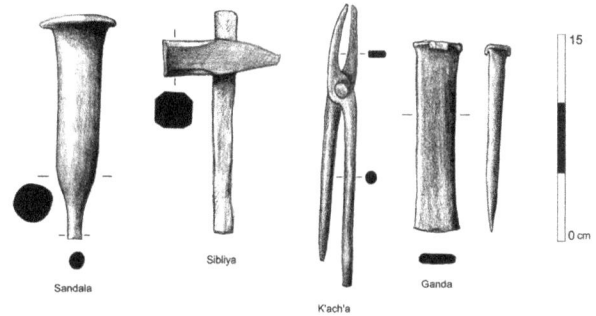

Figure 5. Ironsmith tools (from Manjäri sttlement).

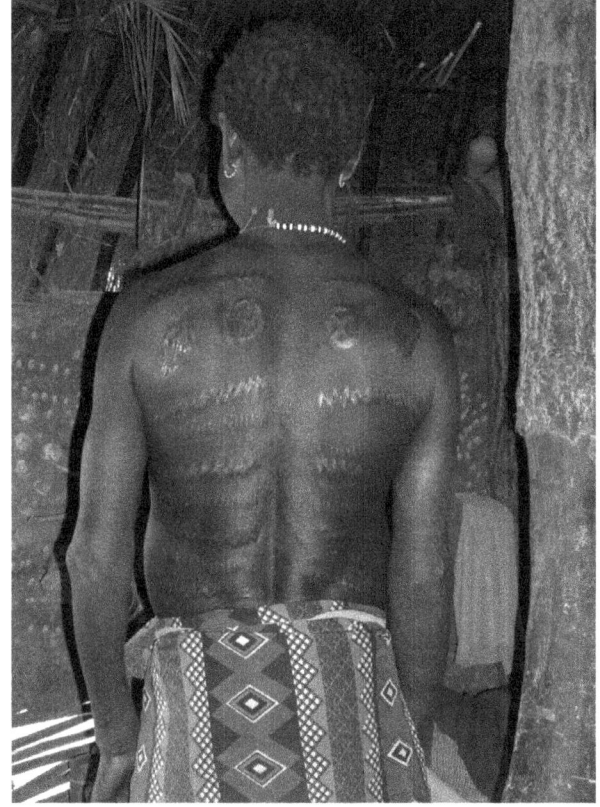

Figure 6. Woman with ritual scarifications in her back (Bowla Dibas'i settlement).

The Gumuz of western Ethiopia

The Gumuz are a Nilo-Saharan speaking community that live in the lowlands of western Ethiopia. Originally, they occupied a much larger area, but they were progressively expelled from the Highlands to the lowland river valleys by their more powerful neighbors, the Amhara, Agaw and Oromo, who used to enslave them and occupy their lands. Today, the Gumuz inhabit the banks of the Blue Nile, the Didessa and the Gilgel rivers. The majority of the population, around 100,000 people in all, lives in the zone of Metekel, which occupies 26.500 sq. km north of the Blue Nile.

Figure 7. Traditional gumuz granary in Bowla Dibas'i settlement.

Figure 8. Agaw women of Manjäri settlement.

The Gumuz traditionally live in small villages, inhabited by less than 200 people. Today, with the increasing sedentarization, the arrival of immigrants from the Highlands and a steady demographic growth, some villages attain as many as 700 individuals. Although the villages are more stable now than they used to be, the swidden agriculture practiced by the Gumuz leads to the displacement of settlements from time to time, especially in those areas where the soil is less fertile.

The Gumuz live in fenced compounds, which have a number of structures, including a main house, one or more youngsters' houses, goat pens and granaries. Inside the compound resides an extended family: a man with his wife or wifes live in the main house and a secondary house is occupied by elder sons or by a young married son and his wife. Other close relatives live in nearby compounds. The main house (*mes'a*) is a round bamboo structure with conical thatched roof, of around 8 meters in diameter.

How will we describe, as archaeologists, the intersection between space, people and technology that makes a Gumuz village?

Is *thick description* thick enough?

In his *The interpretation of cultures*, Clifford Geertz criticized prevailing concepts of culture of his time, that held that "culture is located in the minds and hearts of men" (Goodenough, quoted in Geertz 1973: 11). While he counter-attacked these extremely idealist and formal positions, he replaced them with symbols and the social, proposing a semiotic anthropology. Cultural analysis, he says, is "guessing at meanings, and drawing explanatory conclusions from the better guesses" (Geertz 1973: 20). The gist of a semiotic approach to culture would be "gaining access to the conceptual world in which our subjects live so that we can, in some extended sense of the term, converse with them" (Geertz 1973: 24). Geertz' thick description has been widely admired by postmodern archaeologists (Hodder 1986), who aspire to disentangle similar nets of social meanings through material culture and discover the cultural logic behind artefacts. Things are the way to get to meaning for want of anything better – living informants. What archaeologists do is to recover in an indirect way particles of meaning by means of different sorts of material evidence in context and in relation to each other (pottery, metal-

As many other Ethiopian societies, the Gumuz still cling to premodern customs. Most of them practice a traditional religion, characterized by a profussion of deities (*mus'a*), and they visit ritual specialists (*gafea*), who can cure several kinds of diseases. The social organization is egalitarian among males: male elders take decisions in a collective way. Although the Ethiopian state appoints local political representative, they have very little power within the community. Marriage customs also emphasize egalitarian values among males: the prevailing system is sister-exchange marriage (*angiya*), which means that any man who wants to get married has to provide a female relative for the family from which she is obtaining a wife. Technology can be labelled as a "domestic mode of production" (sensu Sahlins). This means that all adult members of the community are capable, or in a position to be capable, of producing the artefacts and structures needed for the social and biological reproduction of the community. Pottery, in particular, is a very widespread knowledge amidst women, even if only a few of them in each community are really proficient and can make all the types of pottery used in any home. All Gumuz are organized in clans and each clan has a delimited territory. Feuds between clans and families are frequent, as are the conflict resolution ceremonies (*mangima*) that put an end to them. Marriage, which is always exogamous, serves as an strategy to create alliances with other clans.

lurgy, domestic architecture, tombs, landscape). In so doing, they try to produce a thick description of a past society, which is admittedly less complete than that achieved by an ethnographer who has access to a living culture. This is a too idealistic, in a Platonic way, and logocentric approach. Logocentrism does not end there, but also affects the way in which the past is mediated. What does the ethnographer do? – asks Geertz (1973: 19), and the answer is "he writes". Many anthropologists, especially postmodern ones have followed this statement literally, considering ethnography a literary engagement. Archaeologists have followed the trend too, by stressing the need of writing stories about the past (Praetzellis 1998; Edmonds 1999; Joyce 2002). However, Geertz himself is more cautious: in a footnote he qualifies the idea of writing, saying that what the anthropologist actually does is "inscribing", a practice that includes diagrams, photographs, drawings. "Self-consciousness about modes of representation (not to speak of experiments with them) has been very lacking in anthropology", he bemoans. Experiments with modes of representation in anthropology are not plentiful in the discipline (although they have increased substantially from the time he wrote that), and they tend to focus narrowly on the way anthropologists write (e.g. Clifford 1997; Taussig 2004).

Figure 9. Grave and compound in Bowla Dibas'i settlement.

Recently, archaeologists have criticized idealist stances and logocentric statements: Bjornar Olsen (2003) claims that there is more to understanding than meaning, and Michael Shanks proposes other ways of mediating the past that go beyond narrative in the usual sense. In general, there is a stronger sensibility among archaeologists and some anthropologists, towards materiality, a term that is becoming a new buzz-word in archaeology and related studies. By taking into account materiality and the non-verbal in any given culture, we should not give up our attempts to recover meaning. The retrieval of meanings, however, seems to be better articulated through the theory of practice than semiotics.

Our work in Gumuz villages tries to emphasize the materiality of the domestic world in which people live, but without leaving aside the meanings that are played out in daily practice. For so doing, we consider that the way in which we translate the material world is extremely important: we try to produce a thick description that is really thick, in that it takes into account not only meanings as expressed in social action, but also things. We need first of all a thick material description of life, which is attained, in our case, by the combination of several media: photographs and drawings of artefacts (in the making, in use and abandoned), plans of houses and compounds with the distribution of artefacts in them; maps of activity areas and areas of debris and waste; and very detailed maps of whole villages that are made both with a professional GPS and with hand-made interpretive sketches. These maps do not only include structures (houses, pens, fences, tombs), but also holes, dumps, pits, ash heaps, trails, gutters, poles and trees. The data are then crossed with information about daily activities and kinship.

Figure 10. Women cooking inside a gumuz dwelling.

We also take photographs of minute material details that are usually overlooked, but that are key to convey the textures of daily life: the ruggedness of a ravine, the dusty surface in front of a house, or the mismash of sherds, bones, lumps and parched grass that extends between compounds. This data are later crossed with oral information regarding the names given to particular areas in the compound and the activities conducted in different places. We have thus discovered that different activity areas do not only have different names, but also very different material textures – a fact that is rarely considered by anthropologists. The image that emerges from our description may appear as the opposite of what Geertz (1973: 16) postulates: instead of "reducing puzzlement", we convey the chaotic nature of life in a village. Not that abstraction is not necessary, but the problem in many ethnographic accounts is that anthropological abstraction tends to result in a too ideal image of a certain society: complex cosmologies, subtle kinship systems, sophisticated institutions could have very different backgrounds. The problem is when one considers the material world in which people live as that: the scenario of social dramas, instead of something active.

The aim of the kind of thick description that is proposed here is not only to give a more accurate view of how life is actually lived by the Gumuz, but also to take into account other actors that are rarely allowed in ethnographies, except as reflections of social activities or as their backdrop: the ash dump, the beer pot, the wall of a house.

Figure 11. Archaeological remains of a gumuz hut (Manjäri settlement).

Some preliminary results

Bowla Dibas'i settlement

This settlement is located some 100 km away from Gilgel Beles. For this reason we decided to stay in it while carrying out our research.

For a better understanding of relationships between the gumuz and highlanders in historical context we interviewed several old members of the community. These fruitful interviews produced information related to slavery in the early twentieth century. The informant Duri Demeka (interview in the annex) spoke of Zäläk'ä Liku, known to us through other sources as an agaw boss appointed *Fitawrari* by Gojjam's regent Ras Haylu, around 1905-1910 (Abdussamad Ahmad 1984: 238). Information on slavery similarly completes that collected by other historians (Abdussamad Ahmad 1999). We were also told about the gumuz collaborationist attitude towards Italians, to be understood in the context of their conflictive relations with the Amhara/Agaw. Italian officers had highlighted the unexpected collaboration of the "negroidi del bassopiano" (low-plain negroids) (Lauro 1949: 135) in their struggle against Abyssianian patriots. The entrance of Haile Selassie's column in Ethiopia (Rennell of Rodd 1948: 5) made a lasting impression upon gumuz collective memory as can be perceived through interviews made here and last year at Manjäri and Maataba K'uter 2.

The whole settlement was intensively mapped and inventories were made of 11 huts. One of these huts was sketched at a 1:50 scale featuring all movable artefacts. A preliminary model for a gumuz habitation complex was defined in terms of its material (number of structures, surface, limits, etc.) and kinship aspects.

In terms of movable artefacts, some 60 ceramic vessels were documented and drawn. A ceramic typology was designed and local names for all material culture were recorded. Four female potters were interviewed from three of the four neighbourhoods into which the village is divided, as well as one male blacksmith. The following are some preliminary conclusions:

-Habitation complexes are grouped according to kinship: within each neighbourhood, close habitation complexes usually share a common real ancestor, generally a paternal grandfather.

-Habitation complexes appear more diffusely delimitated than in other settlements visited. This can be due to smooth intra-community relations and very limited extra-community relations.

-There is a spectacularly high variability in ceramic production, especially in terms of shapes and colours, which can be in relation to gumuz society's exogamy. Women learn to make pottery in the final stages of their childhood. When they move to their husband's settlement, they maintain the style they learnt as children. Diversity in ceramic styles is parallel to the number of different clans from which women come.

-Artefact names do not coincide with those of the scarp, where Manjari and Maataba stand but do coincide with those recorded at Jarenja (Gubba) last year and at Berkasa (Sirba Abbay) in 2002. Thus, more intense communication seems to exist with gumuz inhabiting West and South lands than with those in the East, although distances are similar (and physical communication is presently easier).

-Both ceramic production and metallurgy respond to what Sahlins (1972:121) dubbed the Domestic Mode of Production, which does not mean the same as "familial production". According to this author, in this way "families are equipped to govern production through the availability of necessary tools and techniques; they generally have access to current and specific resources. This mastery corresponds to a certain simplicity of resources; it could be said, with a certain democracy of technology". Such technologic democracy can be perceived in the fact that practically all gumuz women can supply themselves with pottery, in that both potters and blacksmiths lack a privileged status (quite on the contrary) in the community and in spatial distribution of activities in the settlement.

Maataba

Several reasons dissuaded us from carrying out an intense research at this settlement. However, detailed cartographic records were made of two habitation complexes and several elders were interviewed. From the point of view of spatial organisation the advantage at Maataba lies in the existence of neatly defined neighbourhoods whose members are clearly related. On the other hand Maataba presents a model considerably different to that envisaged by Dibas'a and Manjäri, where different neighbourhoods are much closer together to the point that they become difficult to distinguish.

Collecting data on interethnic relations wasn't a simple task. This is particularly true of information concerning relations with the amhara, a fact that can be seen as a symptom of an ongoing conflict. As we could witness in the areas of the market and the electric mill, relationships are positive at least with the agaw. The most interesting information collected was that related to myths of origin, reflecting new variations and nuances. Information on the house "spirit" or divinity and associated rituals particularly cast light upon symbolic aspects of domestic spatial organisation.

Figure 12. GPS mapping of Bowla Dibas'i settlement.

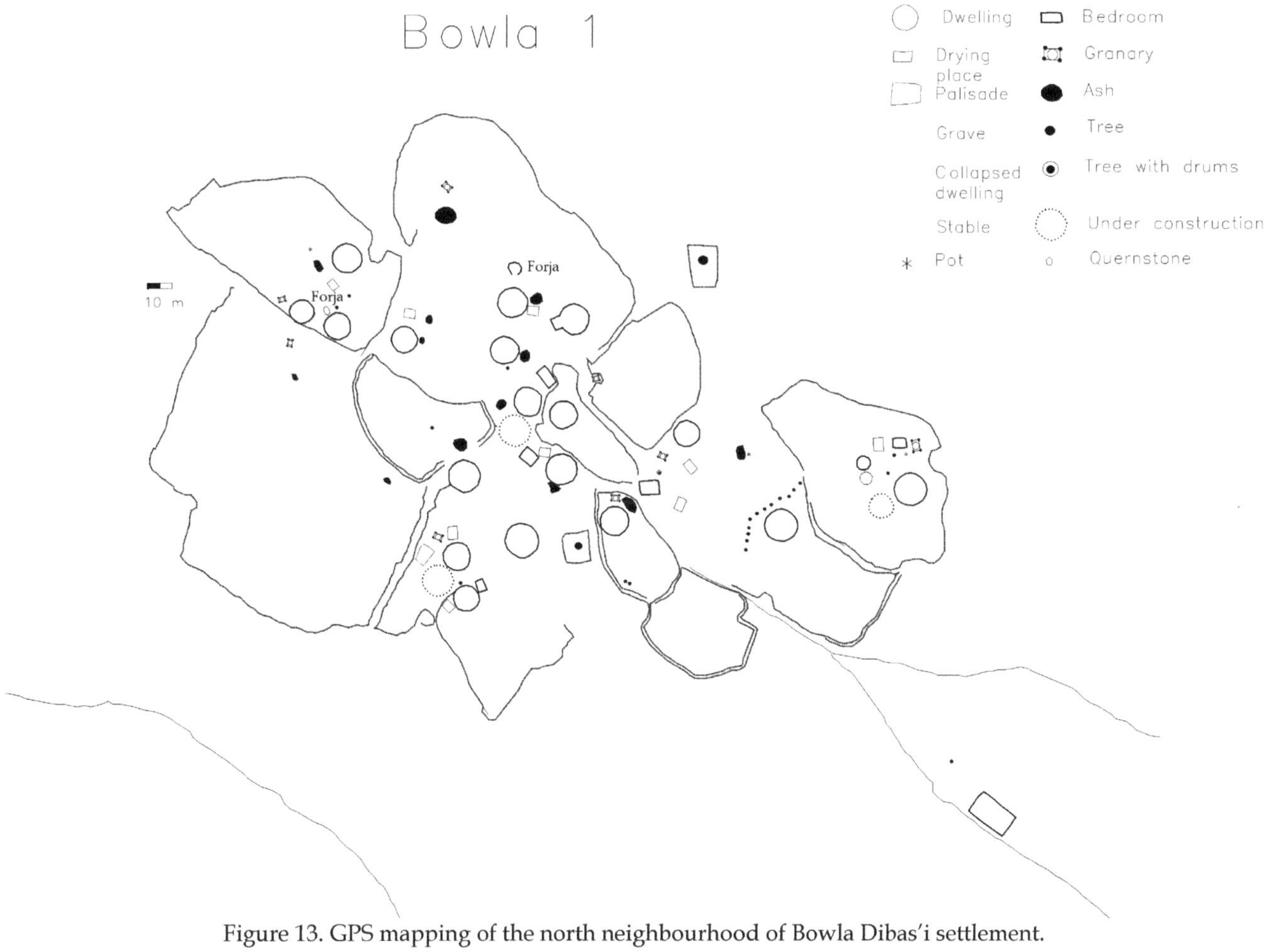

Figure 13. GPS mapping of the north neighbourhood of Bowla Dibas'i settlement.

Figure 14. Entrance to the Matoha hamlet in Maataba settlement.

Manjäri

This settlement is the most interesting and at the same time the most complex of those studied, since it hosts a multiethnic and fragmented community: its inhabitants are gumuz, kumfel agaw and high-plain agaw. There is great rivalry among different gumuz sectors, especially between inhabitants of both riversides and different families. The kumfel agaw and the high plain agaw (Ch'ara agaw) do not foster relations with each other (Gamst 1969; Sewageñ Shiferaw 1998). The latter accuse the former of not having been supportive when they first settled in the area while the kumfel feel looked down upon by the highplain agaw. Tensions among the gumuz usually build up to violent conflicts resulting in death of one or more persons. To this one must add this community's state of social disruption due to several factors including repeated displacement after hostilities with the amhara (since the latter settled in the area in the 1980s); closeness to semi-urban centres in the area; land property and wealth source changes and alcohol, as much a symptom as a cause of stress. This has generated a highly unstable situation considerably uncomfortable to our group: the gumuz at Manjäri are more aggressive and distrustful than those at Dibas'a, in turn much more so than those South of the Blue Nile who we had chance to study in 2002 at Berkasa.

The following preliminary conclusions can be drawn from our fieldwork:

-Space is organised in a much more delimitated fashion here than in Bowla Dibas'i. Manjari offers a labyrinth-like picture with well defined and controlled walking routes. Habitation complexes are enclosed with fences making visibility and access- leading to funnel-shaped entrances – difficult.

-Manjäri is a much larger settlement in both population and surface than the average gumuz hamlets. This, alongside its multiethnicity, generates a series of social problems probably negotiated in spatial terms. Syntactic analyses to be carried out by Xurxo Ayán and Álvaro Falquina will probably help to clarify this aspect.

Figure 15. GPS mapping of Matoha hamlet (GPS).

-Intra-ethnic relations (between gumuz and between agaw) are surprisingly more complex than interethnic relations: this explains the fact that gumuz and agaw can be found living together, while spatial proximity of Ch'ara agaw and Kumfel agaw is comparatively rare. Also against what common sense would suggest, technologically more complex groups (as the agaw) tend to use the material culture of the simpler (gumuz) rather than viceversa. Thus, agaw huts featured hoes, sickles, bows, arrows, baskets and large ceramic vessels produced by gumuz (up to half a dozen per dwelling) while highland pottery is scarcer among the gumuz (normally one or two vessels to prepare porridge). Occurrence of other artefacts is not systematic (baskets, plough, etc.).

Figure 17. Gumuz (left) and Agaw (right) neighbours of Manjäri settlement.

-Differences in spatial organisation between gumuz and agaw are however very marked, especially in terms of the internal structure of dwellings. Agaw dwellings present a compartmentalized and monumental internal space. Thes complexes typically feature a higher number of adjective struc-

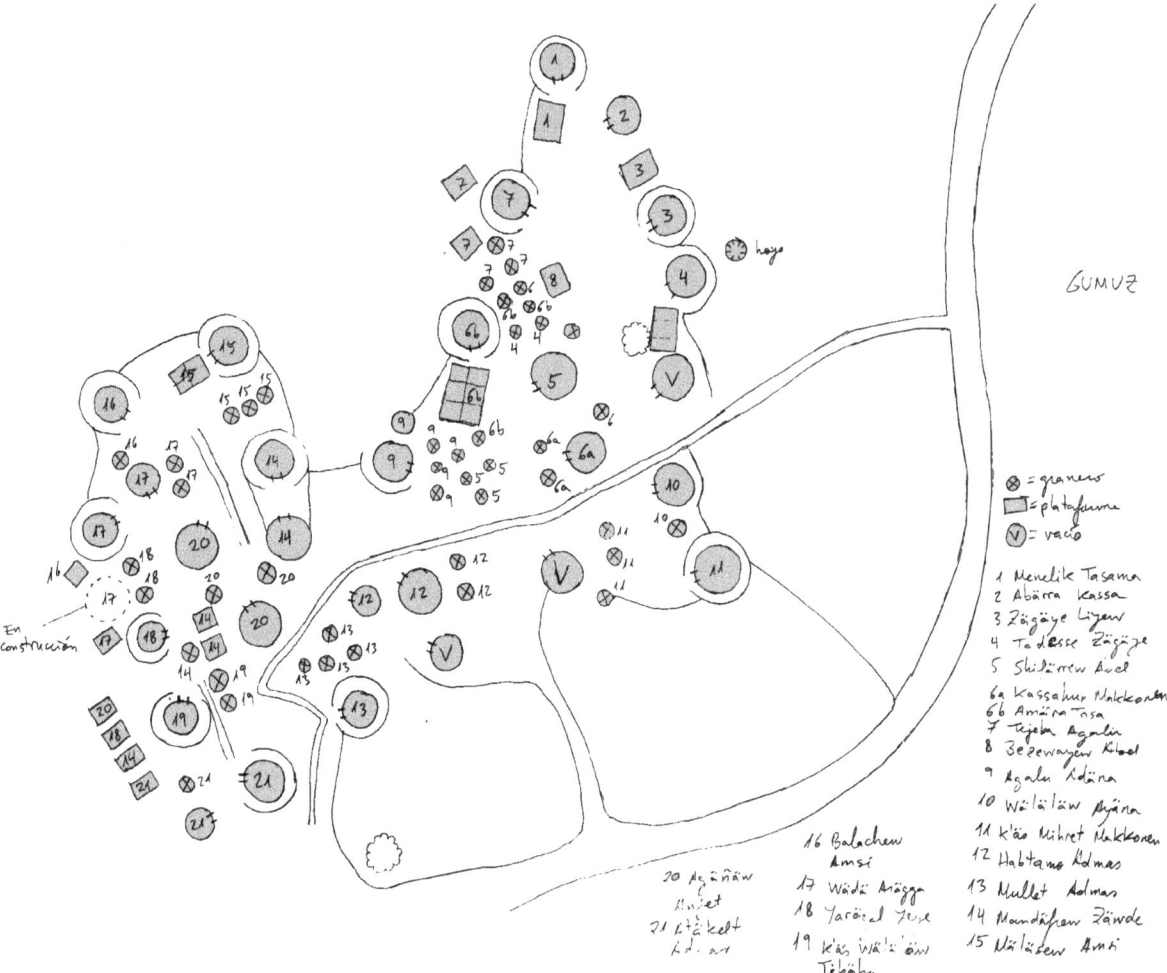

Figure 16. Sketch of agaw compounds in Manjäri settlement. First step to study the kinship relations inside the settlement.

tures per square meter. This can be examined in view of their practising a more intensive form of agriculture (see González-Ruibal and Fernández Martínez 2003 for a comparison of bertha and amhara spatial organisation).

-Gumuz dwellings are simpler and smaller than in the Bowla-Dibas'i area and always contain a smaller number of objects (near to half) than those in other settlements. This is rather striking given that their economic situation here should be comparatively better. Gumuz in Bowla-Dibas'i receive a rent from their agaw and amhara neighbours forced to hire gumuz land.

Decorations on gumuz granaries are a prominent element of this settlement in abundance and variety. These decorations in gumuz hamlets South of the Nile and the Gubba region present are much less varied. The presence of masculine motives (penises, testicles and whole male bodies) is one of the most interesting aspects which could be somehow connected to social stress.

Material culture and trauma: the inscription of the past in Gumuz houses.

The history of slavery to which the Gumuz have been subjected is interwoven in the structure of the houses in which they live. It is incorporated into the domesticity of the Gumuz culture. By being part of the fabric of their homes, trauma is continuously played out in daily life: it is a past no longer past. Two basic material elements can be related to this everlasting history of oppression: the fence and the double door. Fences are a remarkable element in Gumuz compounds and villages. They are everywhere: they determine and restrict perambulation, visibility and interaction between people – between foreigners and locals, and between neighbors. Entering a Gumuz village is a similar experience to that of accessing a labyrinth, with closed alleys, narrow passages, funnel-shaped entrances and exits, countless junctions and unexpected open spaces. Due to this fragmented layout, it is difficult to get a whole view of a settlement.

The explanation of such a complex plan, which is not found among other Nilo-Saharan communities in the area and not even in the Gumuz villages that inhabit the areas located in the secluded Blue Nile valley, has a historical explanation: the annual invasion of their lands by slave traders since at least the Middle Ages. The complex plan of the Gumuz village made both escape and defence easier, by confusing the enemy. The same happens with the house itself. Traditionally, Gumuz main houses are endowed with two doors, one in the front and one in the back. According to our informants in different villages, the back door was used to flee from the slave raiders when they were approaching and at least an old man from Dibas'i remembered to have used the door in this way as a child.

The point that we want to make here is not a functionalist one – that the Gumuz developed a particular kind of domestic architecture and settlement to defend themselves against raids. There are many examples of defensive settlement layouts all over sub-Saharan Africa – the Dogon of Mali being the most famous example.

The point that we want to stress here is that the past, through the materiality of homes, has an effect in the present daily experiences of the Gumuz. Furthermore, the intention of our research is to explore how in a Gumuz village time, people and things are simultaneously constituted. It is not possible to tear off the materiality of homes, from their meanings, from the Gumuz as a historically-situated people. Gumuz identity, marked by a millennia-old resistance against encroachment from aliens, slave raids and persecution, is not only played out, reflected or negotiated in social institutions alone or oral memory. Gumuz identity is inseparable from their houses: they are built together. And houses themselves are a collective made of bamboo, elephant grass, mud, ancestors, beer pots, house gods (*Mus'a Mes'a*), people, and historical trauma.

In conclusion, if we want to understand the materiality of homes better, we need other ways of translating that materiality: new, denser ways of describing homes, and we need to understand houses as part of a wider collective that includes people, things, animals, matter, and history.

Figure 19. Typical back door. Settlement of Manjäri.

Figure 20. Houses themselves are a collective made of bamboo, elephant grass, mud, ancestors, beer pots, house gods (*Mus'a Mes'a*), people, and historical trauma.

Figure 18. Typical fence. Settlement of Manjäri.

References

Abdussamad Ahmad. 1988. Hunting in Gojjam: the case of Matakal (1901-1932). In Tadesse Beyene (ed.): *Proceedings of the Eighth International Conference of Ethiopian Studies. University of Addis Ababa, 1984*. Addis Ababa: University of Addis Ababa, 237-44.

Abdussamad Ahmad 1999. Trading in slaves in Bela-Shangul and Gumuz, Ethiopia: border enclaves in history, 1897-1938. *Journal of African History* 40(3): 433-446.

Clifford, J. 1997. *Routes. Travel and Translation in the Late Twentieth century*. Harvard: Harvard University Press.

Edmonds, M. 1999. *Ancestral geographies of the Neolitihic: landscape, monuments and memory*. London, ne York: Routledge.

Gamst, F. 1969. *The Qemant. A pagan-hebraic peasantry of Ethiopia*. Nueva York: Holt, Reinhart and Winston.

Geertz, C. 1973. *The interpretation of cultures: selected essays*. Basic Books.

González Ruibal, A. 2005. Etnoarqueología de la cerámica en el oeste de Etiopía. *Trabajos de Prehistoria* 62(2): 64-93.

González Ruibal, A. 2006a. The Dream of Reason. An archaeology of the failures of modernity in Ethiopia. *Journal of Social Archaeology* 6(2).

González Ruibal, A. 2006b. Order in a disordered world: The Bertha house (Ethiopia). *Anthropos* 101(2): 379-402.

González Ruibal, A. and Fernández Martínez, V.M. 2003. House ethnoarchaeology in Ethiopia. Elements for the analysis of domestic space in Benishangul (W. Ethiopia). In X Ayán, P. Mañana y R. Blanco (eds.): *Archaeotecture: Archaeology of Architecture*. Oxford: British Archaeological Reports / International Series 1175, 83-97.

González Ruibal, A. and V.M. Fernández Martínez 2007. Exhibiting cultures of contact: A museum for Benishangul-Gumuz (Ethiopia). *Stanford Journal of Archaeology* 5: 61-90.

Hillier, B. and Hanson, J. 1984. *The social logic of space*. Cambridge; New York: Cambridge University Press.

Hodder, I. 1986. *Reading the past. Current approaches to interpretation in Archaeology*. Cambridge: Cambridge University Press.

James, W. 1975. Sister exchange marriage. *Scientific American* 233(6): 84-94.

James, W. 1979. *'Kwanim Pa. The making of the Uduk people*. Oxford: Clarendon.

James, W. 1986. Lifelines: exchange marriage among the Gumuz. In *The southern marches of Imperial Ethiopia. Essays in history and social anthropology*, edited by D.L. Donham and W. James. Cambridge: Cambridge University Press: 119-147.

Jedrej, M.C. 1995. *Ingessana: the religious institutions of a people of the Sudan-Ethiopia borderland*. Leiden: E.J. Brill.

Joyce, R. S. 2002. *The languages of archaeology: dialogue, narrative and writing*. Oxford, Malden (MA): Blackwell.

Lauro, R. di 1949. *Come abbiamo difeso l'impero*. Roma: L'Arnia.

Olsen, B. 2003. Material culture after text: re-membering the things. *Norwegian Archaeological Review*, 36(2): 87-104.

Praetzellis, A. 1998. Introduction: Why every archaeologist should tell stories once in a while? *Historical Archaeology*, 32: 86-93.

Rennell of Rodd, F. 1948. *British military administration of occupied territories in Africa during the years 1941-1947*. London: H.M. Stationary Office.

Sahlins, M. 1972. *Las sociedades tribales*. Barcelona: Labor.

Sewageñ Shiferaw (1998): *The Qemants of Matakal*. BA dissertation in History. Department of History, Kotebe College of Teacher Education, Addis Abeba. Manuscrito inédito.

Taussig, M. 2004. *My Cocaine Museum*. Chicago. University of Chicago Press.

Triulzi, A. 1981. *Salt, gold and legitimacy. Prelude to the history of a no-man's land. Bela Shangul 1800-1898*. Nápoles: Istituto di Studi Orientali.

Unseth, P. 1985. Gumuz: a dialect survey report. *Journal of Ethiopian Studies* 18: 91-114.

Unseth, P. 1989. Selected aspects of Gumuz phonology. *Proceedings of the 8th International Conference on Ethiopian Studies*, Addis Ababa, 1984: 617-32.

Uzar, H. 1993. Studies in Gumuz: Sese phonology and TMA system. In M.L. Bender (ed.): *Topics in Nilo-Saharan linguistics*. Hamburg: Helmut Buske: 347-383.

Werbrouck, R. 1946. *La campagne des troupes coloniales belges en Abyssinie*. Courier d'Afrique : Léopoldville.

Wolde-Selassie Abutte 2004. *Gumuz and Highland resettlers. Differing strategies of livelihood and ethnic relations in Metekel, Northwestern Ethiopia*. Göttingen: Göttinger Studien zur Ethnologie.

Appendix 1

Inventory of House 1 (C. 1, structure 13), Bowla Dibas'i settlement

Left half

On floor

A blue plastic water bottle

An *indigá*

Some signs writen in amharic alphabet

A glass bottle

A deteriorated rucksack

Two horizontally stringed arrows in the straw cover

Some sorghum sacks piled against the wall

A bird-hunting arrow leaning against the sorghum sacks

Seven chairs

A saddle

A small wooden table (to serve coffee)

A wooden stool

A wood and string device to carry corncobs

A bottle of liquor (*areki*) closed with a corncob

A plastic jug to serve beer

Two iron sickles

Three pairs of shoes

A fishing net

Two *indigá*

A wicker basket used as a henhouse

A calabash for water

A fragmented ceramic pot

A metal pot for washing

A wooden platform with two navicular mills

A calabash

An umbrella

A metal bowl to drink water

A *kolinga*

A plastic bottle with mineral water of the trademark Topland
A porcelain small cup to drink coffee
A net and wooden device to hang corn from
Three hand millstones
A wooden mortar to grind toasted coffee
A calabash to collect sorghum
A *missikua* with non grinded sorghum
A metal coffee-pot
Two *kouga*
Three *enchiyisa*
A *jebena* to serve coffee
A plastic container with sorghum
A calabash with sorghum
A basket with sorghum
A plastic object with sorghum
A wooden stick to stir beer

Left half

Hanging

A wicker basket
A plastic jug for beer
A calabash for water
A *kolenga*
A plastic jug
Two wooden sticks to winnow
A sack with sorghum
A net with a calabash containing:
-Three crystal glasses
-Two *embarrá*
-A metal plate
-Two more calabashes

Right half

On the floor

A *kakeá* with sorghum
Two *meshikúa*
Two very large *messhikúa*
A large metal pot
Two *embarrá*
A large metal pot
Two plastic containers
A small shelf with:

A block of salt
A straw broom
An old bed with a mat, upon which there are:
Three blankets
A mosquito net
A rifle (*libinda*)
An *ontoa*

Hanging

A net containing:
Three *embarrá*
A metal container
Two plastic containers
Two cups of coffee
A plastic cup
Two plastic *gwana*
Three wicker baskets with two plastic jugs and a glass bottle

Separate room

A tobacco dryer on the wall
A bow and an arrow
A wooden bed
A pair of shoes
Seven cups of coffee
A crystal bottle to serve liquor (*areki*)
Two plastic containers
A large crystal bottle
A cap
A mosquito net
A net with two wicker baskets and a calabash

Hanging from post in the corner

A *bákea*
A plastic bottle for water
A plastic cup
A metal cup
A bag with clothes

Next to the door

A drawing saying Happy new Year

A pendant

An air-pump

A spear

Clothes hanging from the crossbeam and a Reebok rucksack

Space inside the room

A bed with a mat

A sack

A bag with clothes

A plastic demijohn

A plastic jug

A pair of sandals

An axe

A trunk with clothes

Two nets with two wicker baskets

On central platform

Two beehives

A sack containing corn

A very large wicker container

A bird-hunting arrow

Sorghum bundles

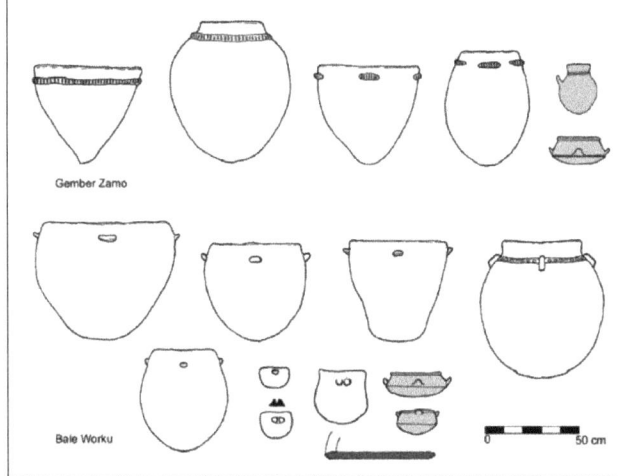

Figure 21. Inventory of pottery from two domestic units from Manjäri settllement.

Appendix 2

Interview with Duri Demeka (Bowla-Dibas'i).

Tuesday-Wednesday. March 7th- 8th 2006.

Translators: Gumuz: Gebru (Sinasha, from Gublak). Amharic: Dawit Tibebu.

Duri Demeka is an 80-85 year-old man. He has had three wives, but only one survives. These wives gave him three sons and six daughters. The three sons and four of his daughters have died. All the daughters have got married in Gilgel Beles, Gis'i (Jimta, Dangur), Gublak, Pudupta (both in Dangur).

He was born somewhere in the road to Mankush. When the war between the Ethiopians and the Italians broke out, he fled to Mandura and he lived there for fourteen years, until he settled definitely in Bowla Dibas'i [around 1945?]. He remembers very clearly the Italian period, although he was too young to be married by then [so he was less than 15 years old in 1936].

Although he says that he does not know much about ancient history, he knows that both Amharas and Gumuz were created the same at the same time: "Our grandfather [i.e. ancestor] is the same". Both Gumuz and Amhara lived together in peace around Bahar Dar. When the Amharas started to enslave the Gumuz, they had to flee to the lowlands. The Amharas did not want the Gumuz to have the opportunity to learn, and this explains the unequal relations between Highlanders and Gumuz. The same mother gave birth to an Amhara and a Gumuz. The Amhara took a horse and ride away. He learned many things outside and came back to the area to rule it. The Gumuz remained in the region and learned nothing. Agaw and Amhara are the same. The Gumuz come originally from Sudan. They came through Asosa and Kamashi and settled in different areas, however they were the first to settle in Metekel. No one lived in the region before. [This myth is somewhat contradictory with the previous one, which asserts that both Gumuz and Amhara were begot by the same mother and lived together around Bahar Dar].

When Duri was young, the people that did not pay the tax were obliged to sell his children as slaves. Those who refused were compelled to escape to Sudan, Metemma or Wenbera. The Gumuz were enslaved by Sinasha, Agaw and Amhara, although the Sinasha themselves were enslaved by the Amhara.

The Agaw chief in the area when he was young was Zäläk'ä Liku. He pursued the occupation of Metekel started by his father Liku. He collected taxes for the Amhara and took slaves among those who did not pay them. Zäläk'ä enslaved everybody: women and men, children and youngsters. The sheikh of Gubba, Banjaw, had also an alliance with the Amhara and provided them slaves and taxes exacted from the Gumuz. A Sinasha chief, Merka Gai, also enslaved Gumuz and Sinasha. Many Gumuz escaped to Sudan to avoid slavery. They went to Gondar and Metemma to circumvent Banjaw in Gubba. Others took the road to Addis Ababa, crossed the Nile and went to Asosa, from where they headed to Ad-Damazin in Sudan.

All this was before the Italians came. The Italians stopped the raids. However, those areas that were beyond the Italian control were still raided. Zäläk'ä Liku enslaved Gumuz in remote areas and said "Who's going to protect you now that you don't have the Italians to protect you?". For this reason, the Gumuz collaborated with the Italians. A Gumuz man called Lemma enrolled in the Italian army. After the war, he was considered a traitor, so he tried to escape to Asmara. However, he was caught on the way by patriot Agaws and killed.

Duri remembers people from his family being taken as slaves. Some returned, others were missed forever. His elder sisters were enslaved at that time [ca. 1930s]. They used the house's back door to escape from the slavers. His family saved itself by using the back door once.

The place where the slaves were sold was Egumb, in the way to Mankush. It is a village, not a market, but many people were sold at that place. The Agaw took people from everywhere and sold them there. The Agaw came to the villages with mules and guns. They killed people, looted and took slaves. They accused the Gumuz of collaborating with the Italians. However, after Haile Selassie came back, slavery stopped. In Haile Selassie's time, some people were educated outside the region. They were told not to creat conflicts, to work hard, cultivate, etc. This continues today.

The Gumuz used to hide in caves to escape from the Agaw, who used to come during the rainy season [this is probably an error: all writen accounts say that the raids took place in the dry season, which is more reasonable]. The Agaw ate lots of goats and chicken. They slept in the Gumuz' houses after expelling their owners. They forced the women to work for them. They stole oild seeds and obliged the women to grind them and prepare food.

When they came to the area, the Italians settled around Gublak temporarily. They lived in tents around the trees. They did not build any houses. He remembers planes flying around during the Italian occupation. Haile Selassie arrived to the area with many people and mules through the main road between Mankush and Chagni.

The Gumuz call the Bertha "Gujja". Their fathers and grandfathers told them that the Gujja lived in the Beles river up to Pawe. As a result of the conflict with the Amharas, they had to retreat to other areas. The Gujja still lived today in Bonga and Mezijja, near the Sudanese border. Before, they used to come to this area, and the Gumuz used to go to their places. They never enslaved the Gumuz and they had good relations. In ancient times, they lived together, even in the same villages.

They have not relations with the Mao and Komo, although he knows that they live around Asosa. They came here some time ago, but never inhabited the area. He knows that the Mao and Komo have relations between them, but does not know anything else. He says that when people moved to Sudan in the rainy season to cultivate, they saw them there (during the Italian occupation and before the Därg). Many Gumuz migrated to Sudan and settled there.

The Sinasha have their own genealogy, which is not related to the Gumuz. Gumuz and Sinasha never intermarry.

In ancient times, the Gumuz did not have guns or drums. They only had spears and they used to dance and sang with them. They had flutes and horns (from an animal called *wandabe*). Also, the ancestors (grandparents) did not use metal tools, only sharpened wood tools. They cultivated *kwancha* (sorghum). They have always cultivated and agriculture has always been the basis of their subsistence. Metallic tools came later, from Sudan. They had pots already in ancient times, but not of such good quality as today's. Before, potters went to termite mounds and used their fresh soil. After they learned how to make pots (*kula* and *nsea*), they learned how to cook leaves and other things. Later they learned the use of clay for making pots and they started to make big pots (*koga*), for preparing beer. They learned to make beds in Sudan, when people went there.

The preparation of beer. First it is necessary to mix sorghum floor with water in the *koga*. Then they leave it to ferment there. After that, they cook it a little bit in the *mishikwa*. Afterwards, they grind it in the quern stone and boil it in the *mishikwa*. The paste becomes very smooth then and it is introduced again in the *koga*, with water and sorghum sprouts for fermentation. After a day, they filter it with a *diŋa*, a traditional filter made with vegetal fibers. Although beer itself is local, the filter came from Sudan, with the ancestors of Banjaw [it is important to note that Banjaw Abu Shok and his father, Hamdan, claimed ancestry from the Sudanese Funj kingdom of Sinnar].

Interview with Amäna Shami (Bowla-Dibas'i), potter.

Wednesday. March 8th 2006.

Translators: Gumuz: Gebru (Sinasha, from Gublak). Amharic: Geremew Feyissa.

Amäna Shami is a potter (*eté gezezâ*) from the Dach'igra clan, which occupies the area to the east of Bowla-Dibas'i. She is the wife of Urku and the mother of seven children (six boys, one girl), among them Shibabo and Kornel, who have lent their houses for us to live.

She learned to make pottery when she was 12 years old by practicing, under her mother's surveillance (a potter herself). On the contrary, she only learned to make big pots after she had a revelation. A spirit appeared to her and taught her how to make *koga*. She says that the same thing occurred to other potters who are able to make big pots.

The clay for pots comes from the Beles river bank, where all the potters in the village go. It takes an hour and a half walking to reach the spot where fine clay is found. Sometimes Amäna goes with here potter friends, sometimes she goes alone. They dig the earth with a long iron stick. They carry the clay back to the village on the *ndigha* (carrying stick). Old pots are crushed and the grit is mixed with straw and clay to make the paste (*bes'es'a*) used for making pots. They never use mineral grit.

Figure 22. Amäna Shami potter working in front of her dwelling.

She can make four *nsekugha* (small pot for cooking sauce) or one *koga* (big pot for preparing beer) and a *mishikwa* (large plate for cooking porridge) per week. Once the pot has been modelled, it is left two days under the sun to dry up (four days during the rainy season). The place were the vessel stands during the process is a circular area of trodden earth, which is marked with a piece of grinding stone stuck in the ground. After the polishing, and before the firing, the whole vessel is polished with a piece of soapstone (*dukusa*) first and then with a black pebble. Next, the pot is fired in an open bonfire during 30 minutes. All pots are fired in front of the house: small pots closer than bigger pots. They are fired always in front of the house to prevent the fire from damaging the hut.

She sells the pots in the same village or in the market in Gublak. Potters make more pots during the dry season, than during the rainy season. During the dry season, she can produce around 30 *nsekugha* and 20-25 *koga*, whereas in the rainy season she makes 8-10 *koga*, 10 *mishikwa* and 10 *nsekugha*.

Interview with Destaw Birhane (Manjäri). A Metekel Agaw.

Saturday. March 18th 2006.

Translator: Dawit Tibebu (Amharic).

Destaw arrived to Manjare in 1990. He was born in Metekel (Kebele 02). His family was from Metekel. His grandmother was and Agaw, born in Metekel, who went to Achefer (Amhara region) to marry. She ate what the Gumuz ate and was used to the region. Destaw's grandfather was Amhara. Destaw considers himself an Agaw. In the Amhara region the land was poor and there was drought, so his grandmother convinced his son to go to Metekel, because she knew it was a fertile area, rich in wild animals, too. When his father arrived to Metekel, he was already 40 years old. His mother was a nun when she was young. Destaw is 40 years old now. "I look older because of the weather and the hard work. I live without comforts. People from my age look younger". He does not speak Gumuz, but many Gumuz speak Agaw. It is a kind of lingua franca in the region. His children, however, speak Gumuz and Amhara. His wife is Amhara and only speaks Amharic.

During the Derg time, since the Agaw had had relations with the Gumuz for a long time and the Gumuz spoke Agaw, the relations were good. The Agaw collected taxes in imperial times and they both knew each other very well. All business transactions were carried out in Agaw: selling guns, salt, etc. The Agaw came also to the region for hunting. When the Gumuz met the Agaw, the Gumuz said "Oh, you are my relatives", so they could hunt anything in the forest. The relation with the Amhara, on the contrary, was not good. The Amhara did not speak Gumuz nor knew their culture or vice versa. When an Amhara came to the area and tried to sell guns or communicate with the Gumuz, they were not able to get through. The Gumuz did not like the Amhara. When the resettlement began, the Gumuz killed many settlers from Wollo and other areas. The Gumuz started killing the resettlers in 1973 when the first drought in Wollo [1972-1973], when some people came here fleeing from the famine. The Gumuz speared them and the killing continued in Därg times. They consider killing as part of their culture: it means winning trophies.

After the downfall of the Därg the killing continued until 1997. With this new government's concession of full rights to the Gumuz, they are now respecting the law. The killing continues, but not so hard: it occurs especially in other areas. Besides, the military camp [near Almu] scares the Gumuz, and the Mender 32 and 34 have a lot of resettlers, so the Gumuz are afraid of them. In former times, they did not kill Agaw. After the resettlement, they made no distinctions and killed everybody. Before, if they heard somebody speaking Agaw, they did not kill that person. When the Gumuz kill an Amhara, the Amhara blame the Agaw and accuse them of giving information to the Gumuz. So the Amhara do not trust the Amhara and do not give them any information. Now the Gumuz do not distinguish between Amhara and Agaw. They attack the Agaw, even if they know they are Agaw. Thus, 6 Agaw were killed on the road to Chagni. In former times, women were proud of the men who killed other men, especially K'ai [Highlanders]. They took hands as trophies.

Until 1995 [or 1997?] the Gumuz killed anybody they disagreed with. If someone sells a donkey to a Gumuz and the donkey dies, the Gumuz would ask for their money back, thinking that the donkey was ill and that he has been cheated. If the money is not returned, he would kill the man who sold it to him. If someone borrows money from the Gumuz, if he does not pay in time, they will go to his house stealthily and kill him with spears or guns.

They are not a tolerant people, I never borrow [money] *from them.*

In former times, nobody knew about this land or wanted to use it. One could buy a large lot for a bottle of arek'i or 50 birr. But now the Gumuz know about agreements and they have their own separate land and make separate agreements with the Amhara. They ask seven quintals [per hectare] without doing anything and even ask the Amhara to cultivate the rest of the land [who has not been rented] for them. So now they are taken advantage. Seven quintals per hectare is too expensive. The man who rents the land has to pay also the tax to the government. A person may get 20 quintals per hectare. A man here has to till the fields twice and weed twice. He has to pay for workers to harvest. It is too expensive. Anybody who rents the land does that because it lacks any other means of survival. Any Gumuz can build a house in a Highlander's plot and claim the land. The Gumuz may threaten the *kebele* authorities so that they won't take any measure against them.

There are about 80 settler families in the Manjäri *kebele* [village administration]. They do not have their own land. They work for the Gumuz. When there is a meeting in the *kebele*, they elect only Gumuz. They do not know about rules and regulations. Nobody controls them. When there is a disagreement between Amhara and Gumuz, the *kebele* authorities do not intervene, but when the conflict is only between Gumuz, they arrive on time and solve the problem, because there are always things to eat and drink [in these meetings]. They do not respect the law and do not pay taxes, but the Amhara do.

They are not in direct conflict with the Gumuz. There are personal conflicts between K'ai and Gumuz. In those cases, the *kebele* does not want to solve the problem. The only real problem is between those Gumuz that live in the forest and the Agaw [that is, a long-term, structural conflict]. The Gumuz who inhabit the forest live in the area right to the road of Gilgel Beles to Chagni, in a remote area where only Agaw and Gumuz live. Whenever they disagree, they kill the Agaw. The Gumuz most of the time create problems related with adultery. A woman tells her husband with whom she has committed adultery, so if the elders do not negotiate, the husband can kill even his own brother or relative, and the killings [once started] go on.

We don't confront the Gumuz, even when they want us to. We cultivate their land and don't want conflict. Even if we believe we are the losers, we accept that. If we try the Gumuz to be punished in a trial, they will revenge, so we resign ourselves and continue with our lives.

The government is trying to teach the people to be tolerant, cultivate their land, buy an ox instead of a gun and work as the other people. This area is very fertile. Many people come from other *weredas* [municipalities] to cultivate. But the *kebele* do not try to prepare any office documents or stamps for the staff of the administration. They just sit and drink alcohol. People are afraid of striking back. If somebody kills a Gumuz, they will kill everybody as a revenge.

Destaw took part in a *mangëma* [ritual of conflict resolution] in Gilgel Beles, when a husband killed an adulterer. He also killed the adulterer's father and wounded a relative. The killer himself was killed by the adulterer's relatives. The people with guns are not militia. They have just bought the guns themselves. The K'ai, however, are not allowed to arm themselves. If they try, the Gumuz would inform the government and the government would disarm them.

We don't have even a knife when we walk about, but nobody asks them when the Gumuz go around with their guns. The local authorities say in meetings that they are militia, but they are not. They move from village to village with their guns. This is their culture, they do not move without a knife, gun or bow. Even if they go to the toilet or when they are taking coffee, they carry a gun. When a baby is born, the relatives try to get a gun for him. When there is a quarrel, they shoot each other.

Destaw does not have land of his own.

I built this house after I got a permit from the government. I payed 70 birr as a tax. The Gumuz now demand this land and have built three houses here on my land. I have asked the administration to solve the problem and have my land back. But there is no solution at all yet. I have been warned to demolish my house and move, but I have no alternative, I have lots of children. I have to stay here and cultivate. That's why I'm renting others' land. There were Gumuz houses nearby when I arrived, but not here, so the government gave me this land. I'm the only one who got a letter from the government allowing to settle here. I came to this area to cultivate the land, grow rich, teach my children.

He has to pay 40 birr a year for the land. He is disappointed. The situations is too hard. There is no future. He also has to pay the Gumuz – to the particular family that owns the land that he cultivates.

Andergé [A Gumuz elder, who is his neighbor] lived here already. I have good friends here and I also belong to associations. We eat and drink together. Because I have been living here for eight years I know who's trusty, who's aggressive, who's tolerant. So I borrow money from them and they borrow money from me. This is why I moved to this area, because I have Gumuz friends. I can't move to any area without trusty people, who can support me in case of conflict.

A list of friends: Anderge Tanka was a good friend and trusty, now he is older and he is less trusty; Mammur Tanka Anderge's older brother; Gunda Damte, his best friend, still trusty, young; Gide Red, the *kebele*'s secretary; Wěndim Mango; Bazabih Kore. Mammur Tanka and Andergé Tanka were very trusty, that's why he came to the area. They are now old and no longer trusty. They even tell things against him. Before, they threatened violators of Destaw's property.

I have a lot of close friends in Mandura, Dek [Maataba], and Mambuk also. I trust this people. In bad times, they gave me information and refuge. Not only for me, but also for my relatives and my family.

His relatives came to this area after him: Welelew Jenbere, Subalew Abebe and Dessaleñ Worku. They are all his cousins. They came to this area after he settled. The Gumuz do not allow other people to settle, except as *k'enja* (laborers) for them. When people ask why Destaw's relatives were allow to settle, they say "we are working for the Gumuz". The Gumuz themselves say "they are our *k'enja*". After that, they brought their families little by little.

Appendix 3
Life-cycle of gumuz house

Archaeotecture: Second Floor

www.ingramcontent.com/pod-product-compliance
Lightning Source LLC
Chambersburg PA
CBHW061548010526
44115CB00023B/2981